The Returned

David Thomson

The Returned

They left to wage jihad, now they're back

Translated by Gregory Flanders

polity

First published in French as *Les Revenants. Ils étaient partis faire le jihad, ils sont de retour en France*, © Éditions du Seuil, 2016

This English edition © Polity Press, 2018

Polity Press
65 Bridge Street
Cambridge CB2 1UR, UK

Polity Press
101 Station Landing
Suite 300
Medford, MA 02155, USA

ISBN-13: 978-1-5095-2690-1
ISBN-13: 978-1-5095-2691-8 (pb)

A catalogue record for this book is available from the British Library.

Library of Congress Cataloging-in-Publication Data

Names: Thomson, David (Journalist), author.
Title: The returned : they left to wage jihad, now they're back / David Thomson.
Other titles: Revenants. English
Description: Cambridge, UK ; Medford, MA : Polity Press, 2018. | Includes bibliographical references and index.
Identifiers: LCCN 2017054308 (print) | LCCN 2018004836 (ebook) | ISBN 9781509526949 (Epub) | ISBN 9781509526901 | ISBN 9781509526901(hardback) | ISBN 9781509526918 (pbk.)
Subjects: LCSH: Terrorists--France--Biography. | Terrorists--Recruiting--France. | Islamic fundamentalism--France. | Jihad--Political aspects--Syria.
Classification: LCC HV6433.F7 (ebook) | LCC HV6433.F7 T4813 2018 (print) | DDC 956.9104/230928970944--dc23
LC record available at https://lccn.loc.gov/2017054308

Typeset in 10.75 on 14 pt Janson Text by
Servis Filmsetting Ltd, Stockport, Cheshire
Printed and bound in the UK by
CPI Group (UK) Ltd, Croydon, CR0 4YY

The publisher has used its best endeavours to ensure that the URLs for external websites referred to in this book are correct and active at the time of going to press. However, the publisher has no responsibility for the websites and can make no guarantee that a site will remain live or that the content is or will remain appropriate.

Every effort has been made to trace all copyright holders, but if any have been inadvertently overlooked, the publisher will be pleased to include any necessary credits in any subsequent reprint or edition.

For further information on Polity, visit our website:
politybooks.com

Contents

The Protagonists

Abu Bakr al-Baghdadi
Caliph of the Islamic State
In his mid-forties, Abu Bakr al-Baghdadi, unknown to the general public before 2014, became the emir of the Islamic State in 2010 after the death of his predecessor, Abu Omar al-Baghdadi. Since the proclamation of the caliphate on 29 June 2014, he has adopted the Caliph name of 'Ibrahim'. A former detainee in the American prisons in Iraq, he was, before the invasion of 2003, an imam in Fallujah. He holds a doctorate in Islamic Sciences from the University of Baghdad. He belongs to the tribe of the Bou Badri of Samara, which claims to descend from the Prophet.

Abu Maryam
The jihadist who joined the IS with Bilel
Kevin (his real name) is a 25-year-old convert from the Mirail neighbourhood in Toulouse, known in France for being a drug addict, juvenile delinquent and burglar. In 2013, he went to Syria and joined Harakat Sham al-Islam, a combat unit made up of Moroccan jihadists, where he met Bilel. After integrating into the Islamic State, Abu Maryam

became famous in his home country for burning his passport in a video in which he threatened the people of France while holding a sword and a Kalashnikov. He was killed in a suicide attack when he drove a truck loaded with explosives into an Iraqi army base.

Abu Mujahid

20 years old, still in Syria

His dream is to die under the Islamic State flag and fight against France in order to reach paradise. A soldier and imam for the IS in Mosul, his life before the jihad was anything but religious. Born in France to Maghrebian parents, he was a high school student, rapper and dope dealer in his neighbourhood in Seine-Saint-Denis, the French dépar-tement that has sent the most jihadists to Syria. Within the IS, Abu Mujahid moved from rap lyrics to nashids, and now broadcasts videos on the internet to incite other young people to carry out attacks against civilians in France.

Bilel

27 years old, returned from the Islamic State

After crossing the Syrian border, Bilel (his first name has been changed) became the first Frenchman to be prosecuted on Turkish soil for terror-ism. Holding a high school diploma, Bilel lived on welfare and worked a series of temping jobs. He says that he embraced jihadist ideology after a brief spell with Quietist Salafism. He went to Syria in the spring of 2014. Bilel first took up with a combat unit close to Al Qaeda before joining the Islamic State, where, he said, he never took part in fighting. It was the attacks of 13 November in Paris, he says, that made him decide to return to France.

Faisal

Yassin's father

This short-bearded, slender and discreet man in his fifties, the father of Yassin, is a private doctor and has lived in France for nearly thirty years. He was born in Algeria. He is a practising Muslim and French citizen, and is also the father of three daughters. Every summer he spends a relaxing holiday with his large family in hotels outside of France: Dubai, Turkey, etc. His children were born and raised in France in a relatively well-off environment, brought up according to a liberal Muslim tradition and encouraged to succeed in their studies.

Former French soldiers in the IS

Born in France, these former French soldiers are both under the age of 30 and have joined the Islamic State. The first admits to having enlisted in the French army before his conversion to Islam simply out of a desire to kill. The second finished school and then became a French paratrooper, taking part in several military operations outside of France. He joined the French armed forces in order to receive a solid military training and then join a jihadist group to fight for the enemy. Both put their French military expertise to use in the caliphate's army.

Ibrahim Benchekroun
Founder of the Harakat Sham al-Islam Brigade

Harakat Sham al-Islam is a jihadist brigade with close ties to Al Qaeda and made up mainly of Moroccan fighters. The group was founded in 2013 by former jihadists in Afghanistan, including Ibrahim Benchekroun. A former detainee in the US prisons in Bagram in Afghanistan, and then in Guantanamo, he was released in 2004 and then re-incarcerated in Morocco for terrorism. He then left for Syria in 2012, where he trained and led the Harakat Sham al-Islam group. Before his fortieth birthday, Benchekroun was said to have been killed in combat in Syria in 2014 during the Battle of Kassab against the Syrian regime in the coastal region of Latakia. The brigade, classified as a terrorist group by the United States, lost much of its influence after the death of its founding emir. It partially merged with other pro-Al Qaeda jihadi groups, while other members preferred to join its rival, the Islamic State.

Kevin
21 years old, returned from the Islamic State

Raised a Catholic, this Breton converted to Islam at the age of 14, embraced jihadism at 17 and ended up a few years later in the Islamic

State. His name was placed on the UN Security Council's list of sought-after international terrorists. Kevin is far from being a high-ranking figure within the organization, but he drew attention to himself on the internet by recruiting several French women to join the IS, in order to marry them. After four years in Syria, worried about the organization's military retreats, he now claims to have rejected its vision of Islam and has decided to return to France with his four wives and their six children.

Nabia
22 years old, Bilel's wife
Nabia (her first name has been modified) is a young French woman of Algerian origin. She got to know Bilel through Facebook and left France to join the Islamic State in the company of her two daughters. Upon her arrival, she was sent to one of the women's homes in Raqqa. Bilel and Nabia married in Raqqa and she gave birth to a boy. After leaving the IS, Nabia and her three children were expelled from Turkey to France.

Nadia
Yassin's mother
Nadia, around 50, is the head of the family. She works as a private physician like her husband, and was also born in Algeria. She is a French citizen. This warm, energetic and determined woman is a practising Muslim, who does not wear the veil. Mother of four children, she says that she is ready to do anything to save her son Yassin and has no regrets about her decisions.

Quentin
17 years old, in prison in France
Quentin represents a French Riviera version of jihad recruitment. He might have remained just another lady's man on the Promenade des Anglais had he not crossed paths with Omar Omsen. For several years, this former armed robber had taken up jihadist preaching in the working-class neighbourhood where Quentin grew up. At the age of 16, Quentin left behind his parents and his vocational diploma to join Omar

Omsen in Syria with his older brother and a neighbourhood friend. Once in Syria, however, he discovered a reality that was far removed from what he was expecting, and returned to France seven months later, without his brother, with the intention of reintegrating himself into society. He wound up in prison instead.

Yassin
23 years old, returned from the Islamic State

Yassin – whose first name has been modified and whose place of residence in France has not been specified for security reasons – arrived in Syria in September 2014. He was wounded three weeks later. Now he has returned to France at the age of 23. Before leaving for Syria, Yassin, who had never had any problems with the law, graduated from high school with good notes.

Zubeir
20 years old, returned from Syria

Born in France, Zubeir grew up in a rather quiet public housing district in Seine-Saint-Denis. This discreet, solitary, intelligent and humorous child was brought up in a conservative Muslim family by parents from the Maghreb, both of whom work in France. When he left for Syria, Zubeir was a normal high school student, leading a somewhat monotonous life. A lover of manga, rap and video games, he never fell into crime. He admits, however, to having a penchant for political radicalism. Zubeir, who voluntarily returned to France, disgusted by the year he spent with Al Qaeda and the Islamic State in Iraq and the Levant (the current ISIL), now goes so far as to reject his religion completely, after spending one year in prison. Today, he is the first French returnee from Syria to agree to collaborate with the authorities and talk about his experience in order to fight against jihadist indoctrination.

Introduction

Covering the jihadist movement today is thrilling but exhausting work. Often thankless, it can be dangerous too. In practical terms, it means practising a 'journalism of anxiety', one that predicts and announces nothing but bad news. 'David Thomson, or the kind of person you want to invite to parties, because he puts everybody in a good mood', a colleague tweeted one day, in jest. I first encountered jihadist ideology by chance in Tunis in late 2011, when I spotted a roadside stand adorned with black flags. I stopped, talked. The uninhibited radicalism of this discourse after the revolution gave me pause. I was struck by its growing popularity with Tunisian youth, who were becoming increasingly violent. Since then, I've devoted a large part of my life to trying to understand this current of Islam – not entirely successfully.

This kind of journalism teaches you humility too. It's a schizophrenic juggling act. I've discovered complexity where the explanation seemed obvious. I've often been forced to think against the grain of my own prejudices. To accept mystery beyond understanding. To keep the right distance, maintain a journalist's neutrality. I've never been more than a mere observer. Even when conducting interviews with an old source who, at the same time, was holding hostage in Syria reporters I had worked with, before their execution. Of James Foley, my last memory is not of a man in an orange jumpsuit in an Islamic State execution video – rather, of a colleague I saw risk his life in Libya during the battle of Syrte to save a friend, under Kadhafist fire, whose body had just been torn to pieces by an RPG. My last memory of Steven Sotloof is that of a talented reporter who, during an evening vigil, generously helped me finish off a bottle of cognac after the fall of Tripoli. My last memory of Ghislaine Dupont, murdered together with Claude Verlon on another continent by AQIM [Al Qaeda in the Islamic Maghreb], is that of a courageous, demanding and passionate colleague, the terror of African despots, who edited my first articles at Radio France Internationale.

Covering contemporary jihadism also means talking with another source I've worked with for a long time, whose joking demeanour belies his role as an executioner inside the Islamic State – and the fact that he wouldn't hesitate to threaten or even kill me if necessary. Five years of daily conversations, of impossible trust and relentless suspicion, between enemy camps. Where every interviewee, at any of our meetings, can decide to kill me. An immersion in death, with young men and women barely 20 years old, whose goal in life is to kill and be killed. It also means hearing regularly that a contact you've known for years has just been killed in combat, by a drone, or in a terrorist attack. Or finding out through a notification on my iPhone that another has just been arrested in a 'sweeping anti-terrorism operation'.

These are some of the most difficult milieus to gain access to. That's why journalists are almost always forced to work at one remove, via secondary sources, through the police or judicial system: police custody reports, indictments, wiretaps, etc. Knowing that such an approach was indispensable yet biased, I decided from the outset not to use that kind of information, but to work only with primary sources, i.e. the jihadists themselves.

Almost all of the sources here have been anonymized so as

to let them speak freely. The only material I've used is from my own articles and from interviews I've been conducting since 2011 with around 100 different jihadists – first with Tunisians, then with French, Belgian and even Swiss nationals. I've kept track of most of these jihadists for five years – some right up to their deaths. This has meant having to convince people who hate you three times over (as a French citizen, a Christian and a journalist) to spend a lot of time with you. This was made possible by my work as a regional correspondent in Tunis for Radio France Internationale for three years following the revolution.

It was in Tunis, in 2012, that I first established relations with jihadists. At that time, I knew nothing of their mental universe. I was filming a Salafist party meeting where sharia and Islamic jurisprudence on women's rights were being discussed. At the end of the meeting, two young men with long beards and shaved moustaches approached me. One of them stood in front of me and waved a finger to say 'No'. I thought he wanted to forbid me from filming. But it was something else. 'These people aren't real Salafis', he said to me in French; 'We are the real Salafis. We are jihadist Salafis.' I didn't know it then, but these two young men, both under 30, were already very influential within the Tunisian jihadist movement.

Before the revolution, they had been imprisoned for their relations with a group linked to the Algerian GSPC [Al Qaeda in the Islamic Maghreb], who had attacked the Tunisian army under Ben Ali near the village of Soliman. After the revolution, they were granted amnesty. One currently holds an important position within the Islamic State. They agreed to let me follow them for several months, but only on the condition that I wouldn't record, film or write anything down. Over the course of several months, they introduced me to the recently formed jihadist movement Ansar al-Sharia, which was taking advantage of the post-revolutionary instability to quickly become a mass movement preaching jihadism.

I followed them when they brought money to the families of

the first 'martyrs' killed in Syria. And when they stepped in for the failing government, providing milk packs, blankets, copies of the Koran and niqabs to people left to fend for themselves in the mountains near the Algerian border. I followed them as their officers, some of whom would become muftis in the Islamic State, tirelessly preached jihad, every day, in the suburbs of Tunis. And again, when they attacked the American embassy in Tunis. And when, after fighting with the state security forces, they buried their first dead.

It was because of this same movement that Tunisia was affected by the jihadist phenomenon more than any other country in the world. Almost 6,000 young Tunisians have left to take part in jihad since 2012, out of a population of 11 million. The same Tunisian youths who, throughout 2011, had tried to reach Europe illegally via Lampedusa, now began to flock to Syria the following year. Disappointed by the revolution, their hopes switched from the ideal of a land of plenty to that of a heavenly paradise. From economic to jihadist emigration.

I produced my first report on Tunisians leaving to fight in Syria in the spring of 2011. It featured a charismatic young man with a long beard and piercing green eyes. His name was still unfamiliar to me, but he quickly became an important figure in international jihad. The following year he was part of the commando team that assassinated the Tunisian opposition leader Chokri Belaid and the politician from Sidi Bouzid, Mohamed Brahmi.

His brother had been in Iraq since 2003 and was already an important member of the jihadist movement. After a brief spell in prison for participating in the attack on the US consulate in Benghazi in Libya, he joined his brother in 2014, and became the emir of the borders of the Islamic State. The United States put a $3 million reward on the head of his brother, who was the emir of suicide operations. Both ended up being 'droned'.

In Tunisia, after a few months, the emir of Ansar al-Sharia, Abu Ayadh, agreed to let me film his supporters. He was a veteran of the jihadi movement in Afghanistan, and formerly one of Bin

Laden's lieutenants in Europe. He had been the leader of the Tunisian Combat Group (TCG) under Al Qaeda, responsible for the assassination of Ahmad Massoud on 9 September 2001. He too had been granted amnesty after the Tunisian revolution. I followed Ansar al-Sharia for a year making a documentary about the group, which was later broadcast on the French–German cultural television channel, Arte.

At that time, I was publishing my work every day on social networks, especially on Twitter. From France and Belgium, jihadists following the turmoil in Tunisia would subscribe to my feed to stay informed. That's how we began to communicate, freely. Some of them came to Tunisia to attend classes in the mosques of Ansar al-Sharia, before leaving for Libya, then on to Syria. This was the context in which our meetings took place. Among these French citizens, some went on to have significant 'careers' in the Islamic State. This allowed me to make my first contacts with dozens of jihadists from France, and with a few from Belgium. These relations were forged before their departures for Syria, and maintained during their stay – in some cases right up to their deaths or their return to France.

The jihadists try to give the impression that they represent a nebulous and sprawling organization. But it is actually a small world, where almost everyone knows everyone else and everything gets done on the basis of personal recommendation. One contact leads to the next. My first book came out in March 2014 and contained interviews I had conducted for over a year with twenty of these jihadists, all of whom were by that stage totally dedicated to their project. This second book, stemming from my work with the news website Les Jours, is the result of two years of interviews conducted with jihadists between 2014 and 2016, at their homes in France, in prison, in Syria and in Iraq by telephone, and with twenty or so others who came back disappointed, without necessarily having repented of jihad. A few are now free; many are in prison. Most are men, but there are a few women too.

This book tells their story, and tries to deconstruct the social, religious, political, familial and psychological mechanisms that pushed them over the edge. It also portrays their disappointments and the threat they continue to represent in France – an unprecedented threat that the state authorities, literally overwhelmed by the flood, have yet to learn how to manage.

Reporting on this reality, I have seen people come back to France to commit the most murderous attacks in its history, people I have known and kept track of for years. That simple fact continues to amaze me, even in people who had spoken and written openly about their intentions to commit acts of terrorism, often for a long time. Has the scale of this phenomenon been taken seriously enough, and understood in time? Certainly not. Covering the jihadi movement among the 'Syria generation' since its inception in 2011 has meant confronting, in television studios, a protean and cosmopolitan form of denial, tinged with ignorance and vanity. The denial expressed by those you could call the 'jihad sceptics'.

In April 2014, the proponents of this 'jihad scepticism' hauled me over the coals on a public channel's late-night TV show, as I tried in vain to explain that many French jihadists had left for Syria with the intention, right from the start, of committing terrorist attacks. A month after the publication of my first book, certain members of a French-speaking jihadist unit based in Aleppo told me anonymously that, as early as 2013, they had planned to return to France to kill as many civilians as possible. And, indeed, these were the very same people who, two years later, constituted the terrorist cell responsible for the attacks of 13 November 2015 on the Bataclan in Paris.

But evoking such a possibility was still taboo. For doing so on that TV programme in April 2014, I was called every name in the book. Having made a distinction between jihadist groups, I began to explain that, as regards the French citizens who formed part of a group as yet unknown to the general public (the ISIL, the Islamic State in Iraq and the Levant, now IS), the logic was clear: 'When you ask them about terrorist acts on French soil', I said, 'they'll all tell you that it's legitimate, they have to do it . . .' At that point, I was interrupted by a sociologist. 'Not at all!' he cried. He mentioned one of his colleagues 'who has been working on these subjects for fifteen years and has never encountered this phenomenon'. 'Wait, let David Thomson finish', said the presenter, with the satisfied smile of someone looking at an oddball whose amusing eccentricities are helping to bring the panel's discussion to life. I tried to continue: 'In their minds, attacking France would be a legitimate act, because its army is present . . .' This was followed by another unanimous interruption. The panel was in an uproar. Without a doubt in his mind, the academic refuted what I'd just said: 'I've never heard the like! Why would they travel so far, if their enemy is already right here? That's what I'd like to know!' He accused me of playing into the hands of the extremists: 'You're painting the same picture that lets some people in France think of this war as a potential terrorist threat to European territory, which gives European populists exactly what they want.' A picture? No. Rather, factual analysis based on two years of work in the field with Tunisian and French jihadists.

It was a lonely moment for me, on live television. And it wasn't over. A female sociologist who, a year later, would become the 'Pasionaria of deradicalization' in France, agreed: 'Their fantasy is to die over there, not to come back here!' Another sociologist then jumped in to warn against the risk of stigmatizing Muslims. 'It's a dangerous path to go down! Won't it allow policies to be put into place that will target the Muslim population even further?' And then came the final blow, by a famous lawyer. 'What does Marc Trévidic say about this?', the camera-friendly lawyer said; 'He doesn't agree with what you're saying at all. I think he knows a bit more about this subject than you. Just because you've done some reporting and met a few dozen jihadists doesn't make you the expert on the issue. I think a bit more humility is in order.'

Very well. Two years later, after almost 240 deaths and three times as many wounded, not counting French victims abroad, terrorism is now part of French daily life. It's on everyone's minds, and will be for a long time to come.

This reminder of the tenor of the debates before the 2015 attacks gives an idea of the level of denial and ignorance on the topic at a time when the general public was just beginning to learn of its existence. It also explains why the public is still so misinformed about jihadism. And politicians as well. Because, even if no one on that night's TV panel had done any empirical work on the subject, every one of them drew on their academic or media credentials to legitimize what they were saying. It is this same alleged legitimacy that they use to market themselves to private and public institutions, parliamentary committees and ministerial offices. This posturing in turn misleads public debate and understanding, and for that reason has significant political consequences.

I am sometimes blamed for humanizing the jihadists. I fully accept this charge. Because the majority weren't born jihadists. It's something they became, often as teenagers. But even this reality is changing. Today, more than 400 French children live in Syria, being conditioned and socialized within the jihadi movement. A third of them were born there. Around 1,100 French citizens have left for Syria since 2012, often in a family group. The number of departures dropped for the first time in the summer of 2016, but almost 700 are still there, half of them women. One fifth have been killed. Another fifth have preferred to come back.

On the site Les Jours, we refer to them as the 'returned', and they've given this book its title. Not only because that's what they sometimes call themselves, but also because they seem to be returning from 'the beyond'. Recording their words allows me not to justify them, but rather to try to explain, understand and dissect these individual stories of French life that have driven their country into a new era of terrorism.

PART ONE
BILEL

Leaving the Islamic State

This phone call between a French citizen and a government official might sound like any other. The man asks for some information and the official responds to his questions. Except for one small detail: this particular telephone conversation took place between a member of the jihadist Islamic State (IS) in Syria and an official in the French consulate in Istanbul, Turkey. After more than a year inside this jihadist group, Bilel,[1] 27, decided to return to France with his 22-year-old wife and their three children: two girls and a 3-week-old baby.

Before crossing the Turkish border, as dozens of French nationals had done before him, he chose to hand himself over to the French authorities. He therefore contacted the French embassy, hoping to prepare his return and to convince them that he wasn't coming back to France to carry out a terrorist attack. Bilel is currently in prison in Turkey, the first French citizen to be prosecuted on Turkish soil for acts of terrorism. As expected, his wife and three children were deported to France, after spending three weeks in a Turkish detention centre.

Of course, Bilel has his own version of what happened over

there. Despite having spent a long period with several groups in Syria classified as terrorist organizations, he swore that he never took part in combat and decided to return to France one week after the killings in Paris on 13 November, because he did not agree with these attacks by the Islamic State. That was also why he recorded the calls he made from Syria with the French consulate in Turkey, before transmitting them to Les Jours. There is no trace of animosity in this phone conversation between these two men, though they are in opposing camps in a state of war. The tone is courteous, even benevolent. Both act as if they're trying to find an administrative solution to an unusual situation.

Bilel: Hello?

Consulate: Yes, hello.

Bilel: Good morning, sir. Mr V.?

Consulate: Yes. Mr Y.?

Bilel: My family contacted you about me . . .

Consulate: I can't hear you very well. The sound keeps cutting out. Where are you now?

Bilel: Right now I'm in Syria.

Consulate: When do you plan on crossing?

Bilel: Well . . . As soon as I get the green light from your side.

Consulate: Okay, we'll give you the green light, but in general terms. Because we can't take responsibility if something happens to you on the Syrian side.

Bilel: No, the Syrian side is fine . . .

Consulate: But as soon as we get confirmation we'll let you know – as soon as the Turks receive our notification about your arrival.

Bilel: No, there's no risk there. To be honest, sir, what I'm more afraid of is the Turkish side. There's no risk from the Syrian side.

Consulate: There's nobody at the border outside the station?

Bilel: No, nobody.

Consulate: There's no IS checkpoint?

Bilel: No. But I'm worried more about the Turkish side . . .

Consulate: No, no. I'll call you back. I'll tell you when the Turks have been notified. But you have to go during the day, okay? Not at night . . .

Bilel: Sure, I know what I have to do on my side . . . My plan is to go around 9 or 10 in the morning . . .

Consulate: That's good, that's good. Well, depending on the feedback I get, would tomorrow morning be possible for you?

Bilel: Yes, I can come as soon as possible, sir.

Consulate: All right . . . Well, listen, I'll get back to you. Stay next to your telephone, I'll call you back during the day.

Bilel: Okay.

Consulate: Okay, good, I'll get back to you, then.

Bilel: Ah, one last question.

Consulate: Yes?

Bilel: I'd appreciate it if you could ask them what procedure I should follow, because I've got young children with me.

Consulate: I understand, yes.

Bilel: I'll have bags of clothes with me, so I want to be sure they don't think I'm carrying anything dangerous . . .

Consulate: The best thing would be to travel as lightly as possible.

Bilel: I have a three-week old baby . . .

Consulate: Yes, about the little one, do you have a birth certificate from the hospital?

Bilel: Yes, I was going to ask about that too. What should I bring along as proof?

Consulate: Well, a birth certificate would be good . . .

Bilel: In French, I suppose?

Consulate: Well, no, it'll be in Arabic. But get it in Arabic and you can have it translated here . . .

Bilel: I think I can get it in French too.

Consulate: You think you can get it in French?

Bilel: Yes.

Consulate: All right, get one in Arabic and one in French in that case, that would be best. And your girls, they don't have any papers, is that right?

Bilel: They've still got their identity cards.

Consulate: Ah, they've still got their identity cards? Ah, I didn't know that. And their mother?

Bilel: She's got hers too.

Consulate: Ah, she's got hers too? Well, that's good news. That'll keep the paperwork down. So you only need a pass for the baby?

Bilel: Yes.

Consulate: Good, that's good news. Try to get a birth certificate for the baby. Do you have any other questions?

Bilel: No, I've got it.

Consulate: OK. Good, well I'm going to check with the Turkish police to see where they're at with things, and I'll let you know if everything is in order.

Bilel: Okay, very good, thanks a lot.

Consulate: Goodbye.

Bilel: Goodbye.

A few hours later, Bilel called the consulate again.

Consulate: Hello?

Bilel: Yes, hello. Mr V.?

Consulate: Yes, Mr Y. OK, well I tried to get some news. I know that you tried to call your sister. Uh, anything new on your side?

Bilel: Uh . . . Well, I went to the hospital, I tried to get a certificate for my son, I didn't manage to get one.

Consulate: Ah. OK. We'll see what can be done. So, for the moment, the only information I have, well actually I have two pieces of information to give you. First of all, the Turkish authorities have acknowledged that they received your notification. Uh, one small and important detail, they're saying: 'We don't know how he's going to cross, the border is closed.' So, I don't know if you've checked out how to cross?

Bilel: Yeah, I've taken a look around the area, I've seen how it is. The Turks have put up a dividing wall on their side. A concrete wall, a big concrete wall. I thought I could walk to the end of it.

Consulate: Uh, listen . . . You see . . . In any case, well . . . Here's their response. They're sovereign in their country, so they have the right to oppose your entry. That said, I don't think they will. Now, if you manage to get through, all the better, at least they're in the know.

Bilel: But what if they shoot at me?

Consulate: No, I don't think they'll shoot at you. I don't think so, but we obviously can't give you a guarantee, we're not them. But it seems pretty unlikely that they'll shoot at you. Because they know you're coming, they've responded to us, that's a good sign. But obviously we can't give you any guarantees.

Bilel: Can you tell me again what they told you?

Consulate: They said they've noted that you might be coming, but they don't know how it's possible, given that the border is closed at that particular spot.

Bilel: And mined, too . . .

Consulate: Ah, I didn't know that.

Bilel: Yes, on the Syrian side, it's mined.

Consulate: Okay. Well . . . Isn't there another place to cross?

Bilel: Uh, it's the shortest way, you see? Because afterwards, further on, there's the risk that the organization might try to catch me.

Consulate: Why, are you currently on the run?

Bilel: Yes, I've been on the run for several months now.

Consulate: But they're not necessarily on your heels right now, right?

Bilel: No, I've dropped off their radar.

Consulate: That's good . . . Well, in any case, with what I'm telling you, do you think it will work for you? I'm thinking maybe not . . . Um . . . Now, I don't know, do you still want to cross, possibly tomorrow morning, is that right?

Bilel: Yes, yes, of course. I want to get out of this organization's territory.

Consulate: OK, so in principle they won't shoot. Do you know how to say 'France' in Turkish?

Bilel: No.

Consulate: Well, they say 'Fransa'.

Bilel: 'Fransa', got it.

Consulate: Ah, like in Arabic too. So just say that, if you encounter Turkish troops.

Bilel: Because they're trigger-happy on the border, right?

Consulate: Yes, yes, I know. Now, they know there's a chance that you'll cross at that specific point. So they're waiting for you.

Bilel: OK. They've got my description. They know I'm coming with my family, they know I've got three children?

Consulate: Yes, yes. They've got the names of everyone, the number of people coming.

Bilel: But has anything like this happened before? Have they ever faced a similar situation?

Consulate: Well, no, because there isn't a border control post there. That's what's new about the situation. But being notified and then waiting for someone to arrive – they've already done that.

Bilel: And how did it go?

Consulate: Fine. Nothing bad. But that was at the border control posts. That's the difference. That means they opened the door, because there was a door there already. In this case, there's no door.

Bilel: Yes, it's a spot I found a while ago. But I hadn't been to the border since then, and when I went back I saw the trenches, the walls . . .

Consulate: Listen, try to walk along it, that might be the solution. So, if they ask, you might try tomorrow morning?

Bilel: Yes. Or tonight, if there's a lot of bombing around me.

Consulate: It's dark there already, isn't it?

Bilel: Yeah, that's the problem, we said during the day.

Consulate: In that case, the best would be stay out in the open as much as possible. But you yourself will see what's best, obviously.

Bilel: And do you know what's going to happen afterwards?

Consulate: Well, afterwards there's the deportation procedure. That could take a long time, three weeks on average.

Bilel: Fine. OK. And, during those three weeks, I'll be in prison?

Consulate: Incarcerated.

Bilel: Will I be with my family?

Consulate: I don't know. No, generally men and women are separated.

Bilel: Okay, listen, I'm going to try tomorrow.

Consulate: OK, well, good luck. But if it goes well, or even if it goes poorly, uh . . . you'll call me back?

Bilel: And what do I do if they shoot at me? How should I call you?

Consulate: No, obviously not in that case. If you manage to cross to the other side, ask if you can make a call and call us.

Bilel: Because that's why I contacted you, to explain my approach, to rule out that possibility.

Consulate: Rule out what possibility?

Bilel: The possibility that they shoot at me.

Consulate: Yes, yes, we're on the same page, that's the idea. Now that they've been informed, that at least limits the risk.

Bilel: Fine.

Consulate: So, good luck.

Bilel: Thank you.

Consulate: And let us know.

Bilel: Okay. Well, listen, if all goes well and I manage to cross without too much trouble . . . But the problem is that nobody speaks French there, is that right?

Consulate: No, nobody speaks French there. You don't speak
    Turkish, do you?

Bilel: Not at all, not a word.

Consulate: With a little luck, there may be some Arabic speakers.

Bilel: Okay. Well, listen, I'll let you know right away, tomorrow
    at 10 o'clock on the dot, I'll be there, Insha'Allah.

Consulate: OK, got it, good luck, sir.

At 10 a.m. the day after this call, as agreed with the French
consulate, Bilel, his wife and their three children managed to
cross the border together on foot, despite the landmines and the
risk of being shot at by both sides. Having been forewarned by
the French consulate of the time and place of the crossing, the
Turks took them into custody immediately. In a long interview
given to Les Jours on the day before his departure, Bilel showed
no illusions as to what was awaiting him in France: 'I'll go directly
to the Turkish authorities. The man [Author's note: from the
consulate] explained to me that then I'll be held in a detention
centre for three to five weeks before being deported from Turkey.
Afterwards, there will be an interrogation, and I know I'll go to
prison in France. What I did was wrong. Something very serious.'

The arrival in Syria

The decision to leave the IS was made over a long period of time. It began, Bilel explains, because of the spiral of violence the group fell into: 'I didn't come to Syria to hurt people, I came to do good. But now I realize that I'm doing more harm than good. I'm part of an organization that's become the world's number-one enemy. I didn't come here to be the world's enemy. And it's getting worse and worse.'

'I had no long-term plans in France'

In France, Bilel, who holds a high school vocational diploma, was living on welfare after a series of temporary jobs. 'I had no long-term plans in France.' He explains that he fell into jihadist ideology after a brief interest in Quietist Salafism. His parents, working-class pensioners born in Morocco, practised a traditional form of Islam, far removed from the jihadist movement. 'They were afraid and shocked when I left; they didn't understand why I was going. But when I got here, I was already a little caught up in the jihadist milieu. In France, I used to follow it like everybody else, in the news, on Facebook. Back then, Facebook was great because everybody was on it and everybody was talking about what was going on in Syria. I had contacts in Jabhat al-Nusra,[2] I had contacts in the Islamic State.'

Bilel says he arrived alone in Syria in the spring of 2014, thanks to a contact from Facebook. He left France for Morocco, then flew from Casablanca to Istanbul. From there, a bus took him to the border town of Hatay, where he joined a contact he'd never met before in person. Upon his arrival in Hatay, Bilel was brought to an apartment filled with what he took to be wounded jihadists, evacuated to Turkey to receive medical attention. Bilel stayed in the apartment for two days before being picked up by someone who helped him cross the border with a group of civilians. They walked through a forest for thirty to forty-five minutes, then they were picked up by a van that brought them to a *makkar*, a safe house for the wounded and for fighters. A call was made to their emir to verify Bilel's identity.

The emir was a member of the Syrian branch of Al Qaeda, Jabhat al-Nusra. He decided to send Bilel to 'do a *muaskar*' – that is, to join a training camp: 'They teach you the basics of how to handle a weapon. They teach you how to take it apart, then put it back together again. They make you run, basic stuff like that. They wake you up at night, they carry out surprise attacks, you've got to get dressed quickly, get warmed up, you dive into ditches, into trenches, and then there's a general inspection to see if you're dressed right or if your weapon is assembled correctly ... They teach you the military life. A new lifestyle, new habits. It lasts a month, but after two weeks I already wanted to leave.' This particular camp was run by Harakat Sham al-Islam (HSI), a group consisting of Moroccans. 'They put me with them because I was of Moroccan descent. It was simpler that way, if only for the language.'

Harakat Sham al-Islam was a jihadist unit composed mostly of Moroccans and founded by a former Guantanamo prisoner, Ibrahim Bin Shakaran, who was killed in combat in 2014, just before Bilel's arrival. The group fought actively against the Syrian regime in the area around Latakia in the spring of 2014, but Bilel considers that foreign volunteers were sent to the front line more often than the Syrians. 'Yes, they used them to fight at Kessab, in the big battle there. I soon understood that when there was fighting, the Syrians would stay behind and send the *muhajirun*, or those who've done the *hijra*,[3] or basically any foreigner, up into the line of fire. That's when I started to understand their mentality.'

Al Qaeda in open war with the Islamic State

At that point in Syria, the brigades linked to Al Qaeda were in an open war with the Islamic State. The jihadist groups were in total discord. The *fitna*[4] had started progressively, a year earlier. It had begun with disagreements over the application of sharia law.[5] Then it was over local influence, such as the control of oil resources. But, above all, because of competition for global leadership between the head of Al Qaeda, the Egyptian Ayman al-Zawahiri, and the head of the IS, the Iraqi Abu Bakr al-Baghdadi.

In the spring of 2014, the IS was pushed back from the front at Latakia where Bilel was stationed. 'At that point, the IS had already left the region. I sensed a lot of hatred against the *dawla*.[6] The people I was with were very much against it. I was neutral, I hadn't yet made up my mind. I had heard of the IS, of Jabhat al-Nusra, and the fighting between them. But it wasn't until I was on the ground that I saw the split, the problems, etc.' Bilel says that he joined Harakat Sham al-Islam out of necessity: 'You have to join a group if you don't want to be alone. I had no money to pay for an apartment, I didn't know anyone who would help me or give me a place to stay.'

Joining the Islamic State

Inside Harakat Sham al-Islam, Bilel met another French national who had arrived a year before him, in 2013: Abu Maryam. Kevin (his real name) converted to Islam at the age of 25. Originally from Toulouse, he was known back home for his consumption of marijuana and his involvement in petty crime, drug dealing and burglaries.

Despite still being active in Harakat Sham al-Islam, a pro-Al Qaeda movement, Abu Maryam, who had grown up in a poor neighbourhood in Toulouse and had been a rapper in his earlier life, dreamt of joining the rival camp, the Islamic State. He soon confided his plans to Bilel. The two men spent Ramadan together, Abu Maryam hosting Bilel at his home for a couple of weeks, and gradually convincing him: the Islamic State was better run, he said, better organized – sharia law must be imposed and it must be imposed right now.

'The war zone around Latakia was like the Wild West'

The Moroccan Harakat Sham al-Islam jihadists' opinion of Abu Maryam started to sour: 'They knew he was pro-*dawla*.' There were important differences between the two jihadist tendencies: 'They're similar in terms of doctrine, but in terms of religious policy, it's not the same thing to want to apply sharia law immediately, afterwards, or gradually.' Harakat Sham al-Islam also criticized the IS for killing Muslims. But, Abu Maryam argued with Bilel, the IS takes care of foreign fighters and finds them a place to live. This turned out to be a convincing argument for Bilel: 'The war zone around Latakia was like the Wild West. There was no order, no faith, no law. [. . .] It was difficult for the foreigners because, well, there was no security, people were being kidnapped.' All the more so because, according to him, the Syrians blamed the foreigners for the war, and for the intervention of the coalition of Arab and Western allies.

Ten days or so after the discussion between Abu Maryam and Bilel, Abu Bakr al-Baghdadi proclaimed himself Caliph of the Islamic State. 'So we decided to join the IS.'

The proclamation of the caliphate in a video released on 29 June 2014, by Abu Bakr al-Baghdadi, from the top of the *minbar* of the Great Mosque of Mosul, drew in the two young French jihadists like a magnet. From that point on, the two men started looking for a way to reach that promised land. The solution came from a group of Chechens also wanting to join the IS, whom they met by chance in a kebab restaurant. 'We left in a convoy with the Chechens and joined the IS. There were about a dozen or so cars and probably sixty of us in total. There were checkpoints, but we got through all the same. We all made it to Al-Bab.' Al-Bab was the largest city controlled by the IS in the area around Aleppo.

No one welcomed them when they arrived. But Bilel describes a general feeling of euphoria, like being on holiday. 'They left us alone. At Al-Bab, there was just one *emni*.[7] He saw us and asked: "What are you doing here?" We just told him: "We're here to join ISIS."'

'It was Ramadan, the atmosphere was convivial'

The *emni* sent Bilel and Abu Maryam for 'registration' to Raqqa, where they spent a week on 'holiday'. 'We would go swim in the Euphrates, at the Tabqa dam. It was Ramadan, the atmosphere was convivial, there was nobody to tell you what to do or to question you. We visited the cities. We weren't Syrians, so we played the tourists. And because the caliphate had just been proclaimed, there were hundreds and hundreds of people turning up, whole crowds! It was enormous, thousands of people. People from France, people of every nationality.'

After a few days of swimming, Ramadan celebrations and relaxation in a country that had nevertheless been in a civil war for the past four years, the two friends finally went to be registered by the IS administration, in the heart of its fiefdom in Syria: Raqqa. Then it was goodbye.

Once they'd registered at Raqqa, the IS sent Bilel back to a *muaskar*, whereas Abu Maryam was destined for other projects. 'Abu Maryam and I were separated and I went back to a *muaskar*. But I have no idea where he went after that. I contacted him a few months later . . . He told me: "I'm going to Iraq in a few days, to do a *dogma*."'

In jihadist jargon, a *dogma* is a suicide mission. Married to two women, the former delinquent from Toulouse had just become the father of a little girl born in Syria. But that didn't stop him from driving a truck loaded with several tonnes of explosives into an Iraqi military base. Before his 'martyr operation', the IS gave him a week's holiday in an expensive hotel in Mosul. On Twitter, Abu Maryam posted smiling photos of himself in the lap of luxury, lounging on giant sofas in the deserted hotel, as well as photos with French jihadists at the Mosul funfair, between bumper cars and a Ferris wheel.

Abu Maryam is still alive, according to friends and relatives

Abu Maryam had fought in the ranks of Al Qaeda at Kessab against the Syrian regime; he had been injured at Kobanî as an IS fighter during the battle against the Kurds, and had become well known on social networks because of the grinning selfies he posted of himself holding a decapitated head. In a posthumous video where he speaks with his thick Toulouse accent, and which shows him standing on the banks of the Euphrates wrapped in the IS flag, along with all of the visual imagery associated with the group's media operations, he claimed responsibility for the attack he would carry out in August 2015.

This French convert had already gained fame on the evening news and 24-hour news channels in France, when, a few months earlier, he was shown in another video burning his passport. His message to his French audience, delivered while holding up a sword and a Kalashnikov, was clear: 'The mujahedin will seize every opportunity to cut off your heads. I call on my brothers in France who haven't yet done their *hijra*: know that combat is a personal obligation. You've been given the order to fight the unbelievers anywhere you find them.'

With no actual proof of his death, his friends and relatives persist in believing that Abu Maryam is still alive. They suspect him of faking his death in order to facilitate a return to France and carry out a terrorist attack there. Indeed, since September 2014, the IS has ordered its partisans throughout the world, by whatever means, to kill citizens of the coalition countries – in particular, French nationals.

Daily life in the Islamic State

Within the Islamic State, Bilel lived in a house in a small village near Al-Bab, the largest city in the Aleppo governorate under IS control. Though he claims not to have witnessed executions regularly, certain violent scenes affected him psychologically, such as heads brought back from battles against Syrian rebels and placed in the middle of the village. As threats or trophies. 'The children would play with them. They found them completely fascinating. But the grown-ups were scared of them.'

Bilel maintains that he never participated in combat. It's a common line of defence, adopted by most jihadists on their return from Syria, once back in France. 'I said to myself: "I'm going to Syria to be able to help people", he repeats; 'So when I got there, I said to my contact: "OK, I didn't come here to fight, I'm here to help."' After joining the IS, Bilel nevertheless went through a second *muaskar*, after his first with the Moroccan jihadists of Harakat Sham al-Islam. 'But this time it was a religious *muaskar*. There were religion classes, sports in the morning . . .'

Inside the Islamic State, Bilel says he drove a minibus

At the end of his *muaskar*, Bilel had to pledge allegiance to the caliphate and decide on his role: 'They ask you where you want to go, if you've got any particular skills, etc. I told them I didn't want to fight, and at some point they needed drivers. I wanted to do my part.' The IS was looking for minibus drivers to move its partisans around, both male and female. Bilel was accepted. Among those who did the same *muaskar* as Bilel, a few left to go to fight in Iraq, he says, others to Syria, while others again joined a *katiba* (a brigade), whereas certain jihadists were destined for kamikaze operations. 'I got onto the bus team', says Bilel.

Within the IS, he explains, there are two categories of people: the *Idari*, the logistics and administrative division, which pays the salaries, houses the jihadists, helps furnish their homes; and the *katiba*, the fighters.

Bilel, considered an administrative worker, tells how he was first put in charge of monitoring the training camps. His mission was to transport new soldiers, once their military training was over, by minibus to their deployment site, depending on the group's needs. 'We were on guard duty for those doing the *muaskar* and then, afterwards, we'd take them to where they were assigned. We'd send them off to Iraq, Syria, or we'd go pick them up at the border.'

Bilel was based at that time in Raqqa, the heart of the IS in Syria, but grew increasingly disenchanted by the way in which the group, which considers itself a State, imposed its authority on the Syrian population. In reality, it was the *dawla* that controlled Raqqa. It had its own police force, its *hisbah* (religious police) and its tribunals. 'I was a little naive, but I needed to come here to realize it. Because that's the thing: there are Syrians who don't want the Islamic State.' But to hear Bilel speak of it, some of them nevertheless preferred the Islamic State over the Syrian regime or other rebel groups, such as the Free Syrian Army, who he claims run rackets at every checkpoint, whereas others collaborate completely and swear the *bayah*.[8]

'Afterwards', says Bilel, 'there's sharia law of course: we'll cut off hands, we'll collect *zakat*,[9] we'll organize, we'll order people to do what is right, forbid what is wrong, but the majority of them don't want it.' He affirms that if another group were to take over the zone tomorrow and didn't impose sharia law, '90 per cent of the women' would stop wearing the veil, '60 per cent of the men would leave the mosque' and 'the stores would open up again during prayers, like before'.

'Sharia isn't just cutting off a hand or cutting off a head'

He confirms that this was another reason for his departure: 'I didn't come to impose sharia; I came to live under sharia. Once you see that the people – not everyone, but a large majority – don't want it, you say to yourself: "Well . . . I'm going to go back to where I came from and you can do what you want."'

On the subject of exactions and the application of sharia by the IS, Bilel says that he has 'mixed feelings'. Sharia law is legitimately applied, according to him, but through its international policies and terrorist attacks, the IS has failed to protect the populations it administers from aerial bombardment. 'I had watched videos about sharia law and read books about it, but I could never recognize the objectives of sharia law within the IS. Because sharia isn't just cutting off a hand or cutting off a head, stoning a man to death or throwing a homosexual off a building. The main purpose of sharia law is to save life, to preserve it. For both Muslims and unbelievers.'

Bilel says that he didn't join the IS 'to carry out global jihad'. 'We came here because there was an Islamic State and we said to ourselves, "If it's the Islamic State that we read about in our books, in the Koran, in the biography of the Prophet, it will be something positive."' Hence his 'mixed feelings'.

The proclamation of the caliphate: a publicity coup for the IS

In August 2014, after a month and a half at Raqqa, everything changed for Bilel with the start of the international coalition and the first bombardments in Iraq. All of the *muaskar* were dissolved, and Bilel's team was sent to the west of Jarabulus, to the Turkish border, to facilitate the arrival of new jihadists.

With his team, run by a Jordanian emir, Bilel had the job of picking up new candidates for jihadist emigration and bringing them into IS territory. The proclamation of the caliphate turned out to be a gigantic publicity coup for the IS, attracting thousands of recruits from across the world. Bilel was overwhelmed with work. 'In the beginning, there were hundreds and hundreds a day. Just after the caliphate was announced, there were hundreds. After that, every day there were around eighty to a hundred people, something like that, for months. But once that coalition was formed, the numbers began to drop, little by little. Within a year, the Turkish border was closed. When we arrived, the Syrians were going in and out of Turkey, goods were going in and going out, the border was open. Now, as I speak [Author's note: November 2015], the border is definitively closed.'

The progressive closure of the Turkish border, coupled with the loss of several IS border posts to Kurdish forces, finally put Bilel and his team out of work. Bilel took advantage of the situation, he says, to drop out of the group's sight. 'Given that the border was closed, we didn't have much work, and the emir dispatched the excess members of our group elsewhere. They gave me a letter and told me: "OK, go see the *wali*[10] in the Aleppo region and he'll tell you where to go."' That's when Bilel managed to disappear, while continuing to live near Al-Bab: 'As soon as they give you your assignment paper, officially speaking you're no longer with the group you used to belong to, so you're no longer linked to anybody until you give that paper to someone else. I let them forget about me. Everybody would see me in the street, but when someone asked me about it, I would say I was still working at the border.'

The rupture after the Paris attacks

'The trigger was the Paris attacks.' After the Bataclan attacks in Paris on 13 November 2015, Bilel decided to leave the Islamic State with his wife and children. Bilel had met his wife through Facebook and brought her from France. It was also through the social network that Nabia[11] discovered the Islamic State: 'She wanted to come and live here. Because in France, with the banning of the headscarf at school, and the niqab in the street ... French public policy is Islamophobic.' This young French woman of Algerian origin was 22 years old. She already had two daughters, with whom she left France to join Bilel and the IS. Upon her arrival, she was sent to one of the homes dedicated to women in Raqqa. Bilel had a document signed by his emir authorizing him to marry Nabia, and their marriage was concluded in a courtroom, before an Islamic judge. In Syria, getting married is 'half a *din*' – that is, a religious obligation for every jihadist.

The Islamic State offers $1,500 for every new marriage

Bilel's role within the IS provided him with stability: housing, a salary ($50 per month, paid regularly), food, etc. Once married, Bilel was able to find an apartment. Within the IS, unmarried fighters live in barracks, in the *makkar*. Couples can move into private apartments, sometimes provided by the IS. The fighters are responsible for the furnishings, and Bilel paid for his with the $1,500 bonus the administration pays for each new marriage. In Syria, the French couple had a little boy. A baby with a birth certificate bearing the stamp of the IS, not recognized by either France or Syria, and who is by definition therefore stateless. 'And that's a problem, because the little one has no papers to return home.' This question was also raised in the conversation between Bilel and the French consulate in Istanbul, before he left the IS.

Three weeks after the birth of their son, Bilel and Nabia decided to return to France. Bilel's family contacted the French embassy in Turkey, which offered to facilitate their return, in liaison with the Turkish authorities. The Islamic State now forbids defections and returns to France. But Bilel, who had been inactive for several months, and who was running out of savings, knew how to disappear. Thanks to his work within the group, he knew the border perfectly and had found a spot near the town of Jarablus that the IS left mostly unwatched. That was where he decided to cross, to flee the IS with his wife and their children.

The terrorist attacks in Paris led him to the decision, Bilel says. The attacks divided the IS internally. Bilel speaks of 'at least' three different strands within the IS. There are the 'exaggerators', the *ghulat takfir*;[12] there's the official doctrine of the IS; and there are 'people who are much softer'. Among the latter, there are the emirs of the IS who consider the priority to be the fight against the Syrian regime, rather than against the rebels. 'In general, those are punished. They're sent where things are worst. Some were supposed to have been sent to the front at Deir ez-Zor,[13] to die at the airport.'

At the other extreme, the *ghulat takfir* have attacked the Caliph Abu Bakr al-Baghdadi, whom they have tried, according to Bilel, 'to turn into a disbeliever'. In political terms, it would be considered a putsch, but the attempt failed: the 'exaggerating brothers' were sent to prison, and the IS gave them three days to change their minds. As soon as the deadline expired, they were said to have refused and several dozen were executed.

'I came for life and I find a reign of death'

Bilel is adamant: it was the attacks in Paris that made him decide to return to France. 'I didn't come here for that.' His French contacts in the IS saw the attacks 'as a response to the coalition planes, which were bombing and attacking civilians: there you go, you attack Islam, you're opening yourself up to retaliation'. And Bilel insists: 'I don't think they deserved it. I don't think that just because you make a drawing or say something, you have to be killed. I'm not here to kill indiscriminately, I didn't come here to live in a world full of killing. On the contrary, I came for life and I find myself in the middle of a reign of death.'

For Bilel, the Islamic State 'will get worse and worse'. He describes a kind of 'spiral': at first, the IS wouldn't attack Syrian rebels, but then it declared that they were unbelievers and began to fight them. At first, the Islamic State didn't organize attacks abroad, but then began to multiply its attacks throughout the world. 'It's a vicious circle', says Bilel; 'I'm not in the virtuous circle in which I wanted to evolve with my family. That's not what I wanted. The Islamic State wants to go all the way.'

Since leaving the IS, Bilel remains imprisoned in Turkey – the first French citizen to be prosecuted for acts of terrorism (another is now being tried as well). Nabia and her children are back in France.

PART TWO
YASSIN

A bullet in his stomach

His jihad was short-lived. Three weeks after his arrival in Syria, in September 2014, Yassin[1] found himself lying on the ground in a makeshift field hospital with a bullet lodged in his stomach. The hospice for recovering fighters was actually an abandoned barracks in Mayadin, a garrison town in one of the remotest areas in eastern Syria controlled by the Islamic State (IS), about 60 kilometres from the Iraqi border.

The young Frenchman was one of about a hundred wounded fighters thrown together there under rudimentary conditions. Many were mutilated or had lost limbs. 'It was a world of pain. Everybody was suffering and moaning. Some would cry, others would shout and get angry. But there was one guy who'd lost an arm and a leg but was completely silent. He had a bone sticking out of him. It had become infected but they couldn't operate on him correctly. He was missing an arm but there he lay, perfectly quiet. He spoke normally. Maybe it was his faith, or resignation.'

Yassin had just undergone an emergency operation. He didn't know whether the men who'd performed the operation had been doctors before they had joined the IS. Part of his intestines had been removed. His hip was broken. He'd lost a lot of weight. 'I had to stay lying down. I couldn't sit up. I couldn't feel my leg because the nerve had been damaged. The nerve was burning.' More than a year after the incident, now back in France, this 23-year-old student in jeans, runners and a polo shirt, with short hair and a youthful, beardless face, tells us his story.

His tale takes him several hours to recount, and gives only an occasional glimpse of his own astonishment as he looks back – as if Yassin can't quite find a rational explanation for it himself. He sits up straight on the sofa in his family's spacious home, in a residential area of a large provincial city in France. Yassin still wears an electronic bracelet on his ankle, imposed under the conditions of his court supervision, but he no longer needs his crutches now and his athletic physique is returning. In such peaceful surroundings, his physical and psychological health is improving. He has travelled a long way. And so has his family.

'No, why would it be forbidden?'

A year earlier, in the heart of Syria. To relieve his pain, the doctors gave Yassin Tramadol. This highly addictive painkiller would later be banned by the IS, but some fighters used it for recreational purposes. 'There were a lot of fights over Tramadol', says Yassin.

Every patient in the hospital, regardless of their physical condition, had to carry out their five daily prayers at the appointed time. Despite his suffering and reduced mobility, Yassin was also required to pray. When he arrived at the makeshift hospital, he couldn't get up to wash himself. So, instead, at each call of the muezzin, a man would bring him a dish of sand to carry out his 'dry ablutions' before praying. 'I couldn't walk to the bathroom, so we did our ablutions like that. The guy would come to me with his plate of sand and tell me: "Do your prayers!" I had to do it.' He sighs. 'I was born a Muslim, but too many rules lead to problems.'

Wounded fighters of all nationalities crossed paths in the hospice, each with their own personal story of how they'd come to Syria. They killed time by playing video games. 'The hospice was full of people. There were lots of kids like me, we were all about the same age. There was an Xbox, and we used to play FIFA. The more religious guys would say: "Video games are forbidden in Islam!" But others would say: "No way, why would video games be forbidden?"'

Shortly after his arrival in Syria, Yassin, who didn't speak Arabic, met three other Frenchmen who came from Lunel.[2] He later learned through Twitter that they were killed in the fighting around Deir ez-Zor airport. The young man raises his eyebrows. 'Looking back, it seems completely crazy. When you're over there, listening to wounded telling you about what happened to them, you start to understand that something's wrong. Sometimes in the morning, three or four planes would bomb the same area. The fighting was fierce on both sides. The IS suffered a lot of losses, but so did the regime. It was a real slaughter.'

The Stalingrad of the Islamic State

The fighting over the Deir ez-Zor airport, about 40 kilometres north of Mayadin, far to the east of Damascus, has been fierce. It had turned into the Battle of Stalingrad for the IS, an unending conflict that even now drags on, and which the fighters prefer to avoid. One of the deadliest battles in the Syrian war. In early 2014, the IS drove Jabhat al-Nusra and other rebel groups from the city in order to take control of its lucrative oil resources. Since then, the group has been fighting the Syrian regime, whose forces are under siege but still holding the city centre and the airport. The control of the airport is a vital strategic point in this bloody war, because it allows the regime to launch bombing attacks and fly in supplies from Damascus.

It was on this front that Yassin was thrown in with other new recruits, hardly ten days after his arrival in Syria. 'There were a lot of us who weren't even 20 years old yet. And they told us: "Until you've sworn allegiance, don't move, and do what we say!" And to those who said: "But we don't know how to fight and you're sending us to the front!" They responded: "You've got nothing to say here, shut up!" When I told them I still hadn't sworn allegiance, they said: "Ah! So, you're not a real brother yet."' None of the men in his group had gone through a *muaskar*, the compulsory training camp for new jihadi candidates, nor had they sworn allegiance to the Caliph of the Islamic state, the Iraqi Abu Bakr al-Baghdadi. On the eve of being sent out to the front, they were given a brief military training. Fighters came with trucks loaded with Kalashnikovs. Each recruit received an assault rifle and one full clip of bullets. Two days to learn to shoot while sitting, standing and lying down. And then they were sent to the front.

Some fighters were ecstatic – others were terrified

The IS needed fighters, but in fact this was also a test. The emir of this zone, a Libyan, wanted to assess the 'sincerity' and the fighting spirit of his new recruits. 'The Islamic state is actually very decentralized. Every emir does more or less what he wants. Ours decided it would happen like that, and that's how it went.' At Deir ez-Zor, the fighting had been fierce for more than three years. 'There was a Libyan there who said: "Deir ez-Zor is worse than Kobanî,[3] except there are no video cameras."' This 'sincerity test' was quick to find its first victims. Yassin and his group were ordered to hold a position in the city centre that had just been taken, and was therefore vulnerable. The first two days were calm. The fledgling fighters used the time to dig themselves trenches in the mud. 'We couldn't see the enemy in the distance, because there were too many destroyed houses. We had no idea where we were. We didn't know what was going on around us. We heard explosions, shots being fired, but we couldn't see anything.'

The situation began to deteriorate on the third day. Trying to take back the position, the Syrian regime started bombarding the area intensely. 'It was violent. Pretty soon it was full-out war. We were being bombed every day. Either by air or by mortar fire. There was shooting everywhere.' Within the ranks of the IS, according to Yassin, there were very different reactions. 'Those who had come to die were electrified: "The battles are incredible, it's great, let's go!" Others panicked: "They're throwing in anybody they can, anywhere they want, just to get massacred."'

The inexperienced recruits were soon decimated. 'Those who had gone there to die', Yassin says ironically, 'found what they were looking for'. A Tunisian and a Jordanian each lost a leg under the air strikes, right before his eyes. The next day, a Lebanese fighter was killed by a rocket. The day after that, it was his turn to fall, struck in the lower back by a sniper bullet that tore through his intestines. It was the end of his jihad: plunged into a state of near-coma, the Frenchman was transferred to the convalescent home in Mayadin.

Yassin remembers almost wanting to die when he was recovering in the hospital. But it was more to lessen his pain than to reach the highest degree of paradise, as the jihadists believe. 'When you're in the middle of all those explosions, and there are bombs dropping every day, faith is more about "coping with reality" than it is about belief. It's more resignation than anything else. In my case, it wasn't faith. I would say to myself: "Well, if I get bombed and I die, at least I won't be in pain anymore."'

$20 bonus for his wounds

On a more practical level, wounded IS fighters continued to receive their salary. 'You're supposed to get paid once a month, but in reality they pay you when they can. But it was something they respected. The fighters would get 100 dollars. If they didn't pay you one month, they'd pay you double the next.' When a member of the IS is killed, his parents receive a bonus of 800 dollars, if they too belong to the group. There is also a bonus paid to fighters wounded during combat. Yassin smiles: 'They gave me a bonus because I was wounded. 20 dollars. Totally crazy. Not even enough for a jar of Nutella.'

It was enough for Yassin to surf the internet, however. In the Syrian territories controlled by the IS, outside areas close to the border covered by the Turkish network, there are internet cafés that offer WiFi service by means of prepaid cards. His family back in France still hadn't heard from him. Yassin decided to contact them via Skype from the hospital in Mayadin. It was their first visual contact since his arrival in Syria.

'Anything to bring him back'

In France, 4,000 kilometres from Mayadin, Syria, and the make-shift hospital where Yassin was lying with a bullet in his belly, Yassin's parents had stopped sleeping altogether. His mother sums up the situation: 'It was horrible. A total nightmare.' The whole family spent their days waiting for a telephone call or a WhatsApp message from Syria. Just after Yassin's departure, one of his sisters received a telephone call from a woman informing her that her brother was in Syria. The dialling code was from Great Britain. Jihadists often use applications that allow them to generate false numbers.

His mother, Nadia, can't hold back her tears. 'We couldn't believe it. It's like falling off the sixteenth floor of a building. You imagine him dead. Everyone who leaves for Syria gets killed. For me it was like I'd lost my son forever. I didn't think I could go on living . . .' She pauses, visibly moved, and takes a deep breath before resuming her story. 'I kept all the numbers, I would send messages: "Please, take pity on me, tell my son to contact me, please." I'd try to make them feel sympathy for me so that he'd contact me. And then, the next day, sometimes, he would send a message on WhatsApp.' News would come in sporadically. 'Our lives became centred on the telephone. We would even take turns going to the toilet, to be sure that one of us could always pick up quickly. He called once when we were driving, we went into a tunnel and he called. Yes . . . Hello? Then we were cut off. He didn't call back afterwards. It was horrible.'

Yassin's parents are practising Muslims. His father, Faysal, a discreet and slender man, frequents one of those French mosques that the jihadists consider apostate. His wife Nadia often finishes his sentences for him. Warm, expressive and energetic, she doesn't wear the veil.

After their son's departure, they hired a lawyer, alerted the French authorities and wondered what they should do. The family lives in a beautiful and imposing house in the provinces, which is where they tell us their story on a winter afternoon, in the midst of a modern, plush suburb. It's a house of large rooms, broad sofas and elegant furnishings. Large bay windows open onto a verdant garden, with a seesaw in the lawn. Their son and his sisters didn't grow up in a working-class neighbourhood. They were pushed to succeed in school and go on to higher-level education. Their Algerian-born parents have lived in France for many years and work as doctors. They make a good living. Yassin had never had a run-in with the authorities. His background was anything but socially challenged.

'Anything to bring him back'

When they saw him for the first time on Skype, five months after his departure, his parents didn't recognize their son. He managed to get online in the IS convalescent home where he was recovering from his wounds. He wasn't alone. They assumed that he couldn't speak freely. Yassin, usually a joking and lively young man, appeared in the dark, very weak, expressing himself painfully in a low voice. He tried to hide his wounds in the shadows. They talked for several minutes. Answering their barrage of questions, he tried to be reassuring, but remained evasive. As doctors, his parents were in no way fooled. His weight loss was blatant. His mother still trembles at the thought. 'He was wounded. He couldn't stand up by himself. I could feel it, I said "No, he needs help. Our son needs us. I'll feel guilty all my life if he needed me and I didn't do anything. I have to go and see what's wrong with him. It was terrible. If I stay here, I'll go crazy. I'll lose my mind, I just can't."'

Yassin is her only son. She speaks quietly, with warmth, authority and assurance. Within the family, her opinion carries weight. At the end of every Skype call, a single and non-negotiable obsession began to take hold of her: to go and get Yassin and bring him back to France. 'I was obsessed with the idea of seeing my son again. And to try to pull him out of there. Anything to bring him back.' Compared to his wife, Faysal is more discreet, but was no less resolved to save their son. She thinks for a moment, laughs and then narrows her eyes: 'I was the one who kept the pressure up.' The couple made up their minds: they would go to Syria and bring their son home.

At that point, Nadia and Faysal began to consider how to carry out this highly dangerous project. In France, among the thousand or so families facing the same tragedy, it's a scenario many have considered. But almost none have dared to act on it. One father had already gone to Raqqa to convince his son to come back. But once he was there, his child refused to come home. A few months later, he was killed in the Battle of Kobanî. Another mother also joined her son in Syria. He managed to convert her to Islam and rally her to the cause of the Islamic State, convincing her to wear a sitar[4] and an explosive belt. She is now imprisoned in France, the oldest person to be prosecuted for terrorism in connection with Syria.

Other parents have also become embroiled with the French justice system for sending money to their children in Syria. The geopolitical context in early 2015 made Nadia and Faysal's project more difficult again. The international coalition had been bombing the Islamic State in Iraq since the summer of 2014. In retaliation, the organization beheaded five Western hostages, including two American journalists, James Foley and Steven Sotloff. These assassinations were filmed by the IS propaganda teams and broadcast around the world. The group adopted terrorism as a global strategy. Its spokesman, the Syrian Abu Mohamed al-Adnani,[5] ordered all of its soldiers or sympathizers to kill 'by any possible means' the nationals of the countries making up the international force he qualified as a 'crusade'. France had just suffered the traumatic *Charlie Hebdo* and Hyper Cacher attacks, and the French authorities were in a desperate situation. The IS was more suspicious of infiltrations than ever before. Its formidable intelligence services, the *emni*, were carrying out investigations to find out everything they could about recruits coming from abroad. When he arrived, Yassin had to fill out a fact sheet about every member of his family. 'They all take down information about you when you arrive', he explains. 'The person to contact if necessary, you give them a telephone number, your level of education, a whole CV . . .'

'I said to myself: "The only solution is to pretend."'

Nadia spent her sleepless nights scrutinizing the 'jihadosphere' on the internet. And that's where the idea came to her. 'At first we thought, "We'll try to go with an NGO." But there was nothing to be done. Nothing at all. It was hopeless. I couldn't sleep anymore at night. I spent my time checking if he was on the list of the dead. I would look on the internet to see if I could see him on a video . . . I don't know, it was a mother's hope. And then I came across some propaganda where they said they needed doctors. So I said to myself: "The only solution is to pretend." We'll come to work with you, we're doctors. You need doctors – well, here we are. And, at the same time, once there, we would try to find a solution to get him out.'

Knowing that the IS already knew everything about them, the

parents had to make their emigration credible to the jihadists. This created a major dilemma: the couple's two daughters. Two long-legged schoolgirls, 14 and 15 years old. Leaving without them would be suspicious, they considered. Leaving with them would mean putting them at risk. 'When we talked to them about it, they said: "We don't want to stay. If something happens to you, what would we do? Imagine if you get there and then he dies? We want to see him too; he's our brother. You have no right to keep us from seeing our brother. Or to deprive us of our parents."'

The leap into the unknown

The decision was made, despite the danger: the whole family would go to Syria, a country plunged in a civil war that in four years had killed more than 250,000 people, and join a terrorist organization which was the enemy of the world and in particular of Paris. 'You're going into the unknown. We said to ourselves: "Let's do it! We'll all go together and see how it works out." If only two of us go and we leave the two girls here, the IS will be suspicious.' They prepared in secret. To friends, family and colleagues, they pretended they were leaving for a few months to the West Indies, to work as medical replacements. 'We didn't know how long we'd be gone. To make it believable, everyone had to think we were really going to work there, for the *hijra*.'

They packed their bags with medical supplies. Here again, the goal was to make their intention of working as doctors for the Islamic State more credible. They contacted their son by WhatsApp and asked him to recommend them to his emir, in order to facilitate their trip. The next day they booked their plane tickets and flew to Turkey. A leap into the unknown. A return to an earlier time.

'Salam alaykum, my son is in Mayadin'

The Islamic State's reception of the emigrants began in Turkey. The jihadist emigration system was by then well oiled. Upon their arrival at the airport, Yassin's family, who had made the unheard-of decision to go and rescue their wounded son and brother, was greeted by an official of the Islamic State. An Egyptian. Foreign candidates for jihad are typically housed in *madafa*, or transit houses, in Istanbul. One floor is reserved for women, another for men. But the family refused, preferring to stay in a hotel before going to the Syrian border. The Egyptian accepted and led them to a hotel. 'He wouldn't let us out of his sight. He saw where we were, in which hotel. He checked everything. Watched everything. He had a mission. He led us from one place to another. Afterwards, he would give a report to someone else. That's how they communicated. They have a whole network.'

The parents weren't worried about the intrusion of this bearded guide into their family circle. They used the opportunity to do some sightseeing in Istanbul, even taking their daughters bowling. Faysal, the father, took it upon himself to keep the mood light. 'We had to reassure our young daughters. We couldn't let them feel like they were in danger. They sensed the danger a little, but we protected them so much that they weren't really afraid. They were with their mum and dad. I was thinking of my son. To be honest, there wasn't anything that scared me. When you're in that state of mind, when you've got a purpose, everything else is secondary.'

The Egyptian led them to a bus station in Istanbul and instructed them to travel to Gaziantep, a city close to the Syrian border, where other IS agents were waiting for them. When they got off the bus, they were picked up by two Syrians from the IS, each about 30 years old. 'They were very happy. For them, having two doctors was a godsend.' The two men accompanied them to a hotel and took their photos, in order to make them fake Syrian ID cards. All their clothes were taken away and replaced by Syrian dress, to help them cross the border more discreetly. They would be conveyed by minibus. 'They brought us some old, ugly bags', Nadia recalls. 'We had nice bags, we had left with a suitcase we'd bought in Dubai. They just took it! He even wanted to take my handbag. But I said "No, that's mine!"'

Another surprise, at the border: the emissaries of the Islamic State announced that they would have to lay out a large sum of money to pay off the Turkish customs officials. 'We had already paid 600 euros for the fake identity papers. We also had to pay the Turkish captain 1,000 euros per person not to shoot at us and stop the monitoring of the border for one hour. There were four of us, which came out to 4,000 euros. And we had one hour to run across.' The family, which left France with 10,000 euros in cash, had little choice but to pay the illicit customs duty. There remained a 'no man's land' of about 1 kilometre to run across. The ground was muddy. A smuggler from the Islamic State accompanied them and helped with their baggage. 'They gave us special treatment because we were doctors. They sent a young man in his early twenties to help us cross.'

After their efforts, they were greeted by the sight of a large black flag bearing the seal of the Prophet Mohamed. The family

approached the Islamic State border control, on the Syrian side.
'The reception was cold. It was strange.' The checkpoint was
guarded by a young fighter wearing a camouflage qamis[6] and
armed with a Kalashnikov. While the first questions were being
asked of Faysal, his wife and two daughters had to put on a black
sitar, a whole-body veil which, unlike the niqab, also covers the
eyes, and which also has gloves to hide their hands. Nadia laughs
about it today. 'It was impressive. It was like we'd been thrown
back into another century. By a time machine. It was another
world.'

'They were bearded men, and they spoke Arabic well. But I don't speak Arabic at all'

At that point, an off-road vehicle filled with armed fighters
stopped at the checkpoint. Faysal addressed them: 'Let me intro-
duce myself: Salam alaykum. My son is in Mayadin. I explained
the situation. They were bearded men, and they spoke Arabic
well. Literary Arabic. But I don't speak Arabic at all.' His wife
spoke the language better, but she wasn't allowed to speak to men.
The IS considers that Islam forbids a man from hearing the sound
of a woman's voice if she is not his wife. Nadia gently mocks her
husband. 'He's a Berber. He can't speak literary Arabic at all.' It
didn't matter. The jihadists knew who they were. They had been
sent to pick up the family and take them to the IS authorities to
have them registered. The family was separated. Faysal climbed
into one car, Nadia and her daughters into another. They headed
towards the women's home in Mayadin: 'The House of Horror'.

Within the Islamic State, all women must pass through the
madafa, also known as the *makkar*. New female arrivals, unmarried or divorced women and widows, are all grouped together
with their children. For the first category of women, the dura-
tion of their stay corresponds to the amount of time needed by
their husband to get to the IS and find an apartment. Unmarried
women must wait to find a husband, or for the man who had them

come to Syria to pick them up, with his emir's authorization. Widows must observe a waiting period of four months and ten days, as do divorced women. Women are forbidden from leaving the *madafa* unaccompanied. Women of all nationalities cross paths in such homes. Jihadist women live in seclusion there, sleeping on simple mattresses on the floor in large common rooms. Cleaning is done by Yezidi slaves captured in Iraq. The houses are considered unsanitary. Each home houses a hundred or so women, grouped together in close quarters, cut off from the outside world and without internet access. From time to time, the television screens broadcast videos of executions by the Islamic State. The conditions are deliberately Spartan, in order to encourage marriage. Indeed, the only way to leave the *madafa* is by religious union with a member of the IS.

Every day of the year, jihadists wanting to find a wife (or another wife) knock on the door of the *madafa* in order to take part in *mouqabala*, a practice equivalent to speed dating. Fifteen minutes to get to know each other and choose one's partner. It's the only time a woman is allowed to uncover her face and speak to a man. All under the watchful eye of the woman in charge of the *madafa*. The main house for women in Raqqa was tightly controlled by a Moroccan woman, the much-feared Oum Adam. Very influential in the IS, perfectly francophone, this intellectual jihadist was the widow of a very well-known Al Qaeda terrorist. He was a French-Moroccan veteran of the jihadi movements in Bosnia and in Afghanistan, responsible for several terrorist attacks, who, with their 8-year-old son Adam, was killed in an assault on their house in Riyadh by Saudi forces in 2005.

'The worst enemies of women were the other women'

Nadia and her girls didn't stay in the *madafa* in Raqqa, but in Mayadin. During the five days of their stay there, the two daughters, aged 14 and 15, received an unending flow of marriage proposals. Nadia says: 'The whole problem was the *madafa*.

That's where everything happened, that's where the women would show their faces. The worst enemies of women were the other women. They were terrible. They were the ones who would come to assess the new recruits, the new arrivals. They'd see if the girl was pretty and, afterwards, they'd tip off the men. Then the men would come. I had lots of proposals. I always found an excuse: "Wait, they're going to study at the university. Wait, we're going to Raqqa, so I can't marry my girls." But I couldn't just say no categorically. Because after a while, if you say no two or three times, it starts to look suspicious, it might have come back to bite us.'

The most unbearable part of their five days there was the waiting. Because Nadia no longer had any contact with her husband, who had left to find their son in the hospital. She became convinced that Faysal had found Yassin dead, but didn't dare tell her.

'He weighed less than 40 kilos'

Under the strict authority of the Islamic State, each province is administered by a *wali*, and each city by an emir. The position is held by a fighter, often from Iraq or Syria, usually in his thirties or forties. When Yassin's father arrived, his identity information was taken down and he was led to the office of the emir of Mayadin. 'So', he tells Les Jours, 'I presented myself, I explained the situation: "I'm here to see my son." The emir called someone and told him: 'Take him to see his son.'"

Jihadist insurrection considers itself to be, and sells itself in its propaganda as, a functioning State. Since taking power, the group has imposed a rudimentary but effective proto-state administration on its territories, both by force and by the fear its army arouses. That administration has a pyramidal hierarchy which is divided into provinces, and which has a *wali* (the equivalent of a prefect) in each capital city. He relies on the *marqama*, the Islamic courts, which apply a literalist interpretation of sharia law, and a kind of 'three-headed' police force, largely composed of foreigners: the *hisbah* for petty offences, the *shorta* for offences the IS deems punishable by the death penalty, and the *emni*, its intelligence service, which is in charge of tracking down spies and instilling fear within the organization itself.

The *wali* also rely on the Islamic jurisprudence of the 'house of the fatwas', based in Raqqa. It was this organ, led by an Egyptian, which gave religious legitimacy to the burning alive, inside a cage, of a Jordanian pilot whose F16 had crashed. All filmed with multiple cameras, with slow motion, close-ups, sound effects, and a staging inspired by Hollywood horror films. But for real.

'Over there, it's not like here: there's nothing'

On the emir's orders, the jihadists led Faysal to the convalescent centre. He pushed open the door and, in midst of the other wounded, he finally found his son, lying on a mattress, and in a pitiful state. The two men hadn't seen each other for months. 'He was tired, thin and sick. He'd been shot in the stomach; his pelvis was fractured. There were a lot of problems, major lesions. He couldn't move, and he weighed less than 40 kilos, rather than his usual 65 kilos. That really made me worry. My first concern was to figure out what was wrong with him, and especially how to get him out of there in that state. 'Over there, it's not like here. They have no surgeons, no proper care, no health care system . . .'

Yassin couldn't believe that he'd dragged his father, his mother and his little sisters into such a dangerous and hostile place, so far from France. He says: 'What were they doing there? I'm happy because we were very lucky, but I was very worried about them. In the state I was in, I was no longer aware of what was going on. They arrived just after I'd had a failed operation. I was in a bad way, very bad. Just lifting my head made me dizzy. But their arrival made me start eating again. I started to get better quickly.' His father began to take care of his son, seeing to his bandages, his food and his physiotherapy.

After five days, the IS provided him with an apartment. 'We received housing quickly because we were doctors. For free. A no-frills apartment: a fridge, a hotplate, mattresses on the floor.

It was clean, there were no problems with the electricity, and we didn't have to pay anything for it.' Having the apartment allowed him to go and rescue his wife Nadia and his daughters from the *madafa* – to their relief. 'Five days of mental torture. I had no news; I was going crazy. When I saw my son, I didn't recognize him.'

Although reunited, the family was now stuck in the middle of the IS quagmire. How could they get out of the jihadist-controlled area safe and sound? Just then, becoming paranoid, the organization had banned any returns to 'lands of the unbelievers'. Accusations of espionage were commonplace. Many within the IS had been sent to its prisons, and some executed for spying or for 'witchcraft'. To get out, the family would have to be smart. In his physically diminished state, Yassin couldn't cross the border clandestinely. The first step would be to get him back on his feet. So, for one month his family devoted themselves to this task, in Mayadin. But Yassin needed medical care not available in that remote village, which was being bombed regularly, with the front lines only a few kilometres away. They would have to go to 'the capital', Raqqa, because 'in Syria, the best health care is found in Raqqa. At least there's a hospital there.'

Faysal explained that he had asked the emir for an official document authorizing him to go to Raqqa and, in exchange, had made him a proposal: he would agree to work for the Islamic State. 'What they wanted were doctors. Raqqa is their capital, there's the big hospital there with a lot of health care facilities, and there's a university with a medical school. They needed us. So I spoke to the emir who was in charge of Mayadin. I told him it was to help my son, but also to work in the hospital there.' The emir accepted the deal.

The French doctors in Raqqa

The Islamic State doesn't only make use of ultra-violence in its propaganda videos. As part of its attempt to portray itself as a functioning government, the group also floods the social networks with images of pre-existing infrastructure, seized by force during its conquest phase, between 2013 and 2015: urban planning services, bread-making factories, pastry shops, butchers, road repair facilities, electrical installations, garbage collectors and hospitals. The organization's media branches regularly present these health care services as state-of-the-art facilities, free for all Muslims, in which specialists from all over the world, especially from the West, contribute their know-how in the service of the Baghdadi's caliphate. Yassin's parents, who had gone to find their wounded son, worked there and experienced it from the inside. What they discovered, they said, was very different from these images of a well-functioning IS city.

The IS busses in surgeons from Damascus

In addition to its dilapidated medical equipment, the large hospital in Raqqa was faced with a shortage of qualified doctors. Most of the Syrian staff had fled when the IS progressively took over the city, from the end of 2013 to early 2014. According to Yassin's family, the IS resorts to a surprising practice to address this labour shortage. The organization, they say, brings in surgeons by bus from Damascus – the enemy camp – in return for high pay. And the doctors are not required to be members of the group. 'We couldn't understand how they were able to cross the border. They're paid very well. These are Syrians who aren't members of the Islamic State, but who help with operations and care for the wounded, but they have to be paid. It's win-win, but their work isn't well done. If they were with the IS, they'd only get the 50 dollars.' Nadia and Faysal, on the other hand, received the same 50 dollars as a monthly salary, as administrative workers.

The group has announced several times the institution of its own currency, the gold dinar, without ever actually succeeding in doing so. Ironically, all salaries paid by the group, like all of its other transactions, are paid in American dollars, the currency of one of the countries most hated by jihadists. This dollarization of their economy, and the influx of foreign fighters, is even said to have increased the cost of living in Raqqa. 'Life is expensive. Why? Because people in the IS are paid in dollars, so they can buy what they want. Whereas a poor Syrian, with his Syrian pound, can't.'

'Abu Claus' – a kind of IS Santa

On arriving at Raqqa, Yassin's parents were put under the authority of the emir of health, the equivalent of an IS government minister. Like most of the group's top executives, he was an Iraqi. A man of about 60, trained as a physician, easily recognizable with his white hair and beard. Out of derision, or perhaps simply to dedramatize his personality, Faisal and Nadia soon came up with a nickname for him: 'Abu Claus. Because with his long white beard, you'd have thought he was Santa Claus.' A Santa Claus of the Islamic State variety. In numerous videos depicting violence, he is the one who supervises the public amputations, stonings and decapitations. Faysal and Nadia say they were spared the spectacle of such violent acts, committed in the name of Islamic law. 'Abu Claus' had them not only work in the hospital, but also give classes at the University of Raqqa, so as to train new doctors for the caliphate. 'We said yes, of course. We couldn't refuse. We responded to everything he would say to us with: "Yes, no problem."'

Within four days of their arrival in Raqqa, they had become doctors and professors for the Islamic State. In the morning they worked at the hospital, and during the afternoon they taught. These activities would later raise the suspicions of the French intelligence services. But they insist they only treated women, children and elderly people, never wounded jihadists, except their son. 'The jihadists needed war surgery. Bullet wounds, fractures, etc. It wasn't my speciality. We're not surgeons. For wounded soldiers, you need surgeons. It's true that we worked there. That was part of the plan.' Their plan was to move their son from Mayadin, which they considered too close to the front lines, and take care of him in Raqqa, by offering to work for the Islamic State.

The hospital was special in a number of ways. One part of the building was strictly reserved for men, another for women. Yassin's parents were, they say, the only French people on the staff, amongst whom an atmosphere of mistrust and suspicion reigned. Nadia refused to be separated from her two daughters for even a moment, and they would follow her everywhere, dressed in their sitar. 'I was suspicious of the nurses, I was suspicious of everybody. So I kept a close watch on the girls. It was a state of war. You couldn't trust anybody.' They were also afraid of being kidnapped, and then sold to Syrian-regime forces. 'You're part of the IS, you're a *muhajir*, meaning someone who has come from abroad. They sell you to their soldiers. And a doctor was worth a lot of money. So we were afraid of the Bashar people, and we were afraid of the Islamic State finding out that we wanted to leave. We were afraid of everybody. So we had no contact with anyone.'

Their mistrust also applied to their evenings at home, in a building inhabited by Syrians. Even though many locals have joined the IS, according to Yassin's parents the majority of inhabitants consider it a force of oppression. 'Most of them hate the Islamic State. Especially the women. It was like they were being invaded. They considered them as foreigners coming to take their place. They didn't accept it. Even we, as *muhajirun*, were viewed poorly. Living with Syrians made us very afraid.' The family almost never left the house. Armed jihadists patrolled the entire city. Everything was under surveillance.

'We had France 2, we would watch Nagui'

As French doctors, they were treated particularly well. The family was quickly provided with a car (a Kia) and an apartment. The first thing they did was have a satellite dish installed. The IS had just issued a fatwa prohibiting satellite television channels, but Nadia insisted on having the French channels. 'The guy who came to install it said: "It's forbidden, you have to set it to the Arabic channels." But we just told him: "No, we want the French channels." So he put in a Hotbird [Author's note: the satellite for French channels]. We had France 2, we would watch Nagui',[7] tells Yassin's mother. 'The first time we turned it on, I was happy to see François Hollande. It was strange because we'd gone a month and a half without TV, without seeing France. We'd watch programmes that showed the French countryside. It was unbelievable, we were so nostalgic, it made us so happy to see France.' That was when the family began to hatch a new plan: their escape from the Islamic State.

Running backwards

Since arriving in Syria, the family had managed not to arouse suspicions. In the eyes of the jihadists, the two parents and their daughters were model emigrants. Despite their solid reputation, however, they still needed a good excuse to obtain official authorization to leave the territory. By that point, all departures had been forbidden. Expressing a desire to return could have been considered espionage. Those convicted of spying within the IS could be put to death.

Their excuse, Yassin's parents explain, would be that they were going to the Turkish border to pick up their third daughter, who was pregnant and who, they claimed, also wanted to join the caliphate. For this trip, Faysal obtained the authorization of his emir, 'Abu Claus'. The emir's assistant wrote up the official document. He even offered to accompany them to the border. The road was dangerous, and simply making a wrong turn risked leading them into the arms of the enemy camp, behind the pro-Bashar lines. Faysal politely declined.

This first document made it possible to obtain a second one, this time from the 'Office of Emigration and *hijra* of the Raqqa *wali'*. This newly invented administrative body within the IS was responsible for fighting against desertions, which were becoming more and more common. According to the figures from the French Interior Ministry, more than 200 French nationals, disappointed by their jihad experience in Syria, have made the return journey to France. That's almost 1 jihadist out of 5. An official document from the caliphate's emigration authority was needed to cross the border at Tal Abyad. Located 90 kilometres north of Raqqa, this small town was at that stage the main crossing point between the IS and Turkey. Everything crossed the border there: goods, fighters and refugees.

The guards paid less attention during the prayers

The family notified its lawyer in France. 'We told her: "We're leaving tomorrow." She contacted Mr V. He said: "OK, we'll meet you at 11 a.m. at the border, at Akçakale."' 'Mr V.' was an official[8] at the French consulate in Istanbul, with whom the family's lawyer in France had been in contact for several weeks. He wanted to help as best he could, and suggested that he wait for them on the other side of the border, with the Turkish soldiers in Akçakale. The city is located opposite the border post at Tal Abyad. The next morning, in Raqqa, the entire family loaded themselves into the Kia the IS had loaned them. But nothing went according to plan.

The first difficulty arose when they arrived at the IS border control post. Faysal presented his pass to a jihadist in front of the barrier. But it was Saturday, and the Turkish border was closed on the weekend. In the car, under her sitar, Nadia felt the first waves of stress. 'Oh my God! There was no hotel and we'd run away. Above all, we couldn't go back.' Returning to Raqqa would necessarily raise suspicions, because Faysal had no reason to take his wife, his two daughters and his wounded son to the border. They had no choice. 'We had to leave', Faysal insisted to the jihadist and pretended that a smuggler was supposed to bring his pregnant daughter to the Turkish side on that very day. 'He said to me: "It's not possible, give me the smuggler's number." Faysal pretended not to have a telephone. The jihadist told him to pull his car over to the side. He complied. They waited. Then came the hour of prayer. The guards gathered in a barracks and stopped paying attention to the family. Faysal decided to try his luck and take advantage of the situation to cross without being noticed. 'Come on, we're going. I drove slowly, I passed through them. They didn't realize what I was doing.'

Except that, behind a last turn in the road, just 10 metres before the Turkish border post, a second IS checkpoint came into view. 'There, I saw a giant gate, ten or twenty metres high. Very high and closed. And two guys came running at us with Kalashnikovs. "Hey there, where do you think you're going?" So I showed them my pass. He looked at me and said: "Who let you through?" "Your colleague at the first roadblock." "Wait here, I'm going to call him." Uh oh . . .' Inside the car, panic ensued. But at that very moment, a Syrian refugee tried to climb the border wall, but fell and hurt himself. The family owes him their lives. 'The guard saw him, he hung up and said: "Wait here!" And he left to go to him. If he had contacted the first roadblock, we were dead, we would have been imprisoned.' Faysal didn't wait for him to return and immediately turned around. Back towards the Islamic State.

'We couldn't go back to Raqqa. Faysal and Yassin would have been put in prison, perhaps even killed. The girls and I would have been married off'

The family drove around Tal Abyad, moving from street to street without stopping. 'It was a really small city', Faysal explains. 'We stuck out, especially as a stranger with three women.' They called Mr V., their contact in the French consulate. 'And that's when he told me that the Turkish authorities were going to contact the IS checkpoint to allow us to pass. So I told him: "No, anything but that! You'd be signing our death warrant!"' Nadia saw only one solution. She told Faysal: 'Drive down along the wall, along the border, there's got to be a way through.' Along the way, an old Syrian shepherd told them about an abandoned border gate that had been closed for a long time, used by illegal immigrants. They finally managed to find it in the late afternoon. Nadia was 'close to going crazy'. 'We couldn't go back to Raqqa. Faysal and Yassin would have been put in prison, perhaps even killed. The girls and I would have been married off. We didn't even want to think about it. We absolutely had to get out that day.' The situation was critical.

They called Mr V. again. The consular representative travelled to where they were in person, coming with the Turkish military. 'He came and found that large gate closed, surrounded by barbed wire, and tried to figure out where to cross', Faysal recalls. 'He called me back and said: "Where are you?" I told him: "We're five minutes away from that gate by car!" Yassin was on the telephone directing us. "Go papa, go!" We drove along slowly, spotted the gate, and that's when I hit the gas. We drove up to within two or three metres of the barbed wire, to get Yassin as close as possible. We stopped the car. The Turks and Mr V. pulled the barbed wire back. The girls and Nadia were let through. A soldier carried Yassin on his back and then it was my turn. And then, phew! The girls were shouting. We felt like we were alive again.'

In Turkey, the interrogations began. The family had to explain their actions. Faysal started smoking again. A few days later they were expelled from Turkey and forbidden from ever returning. In France, when he arrived at the airport, the police brought Yassin in for questioning. And from there, predictably, on to the DGSI[9] and prison.

'Now you're going to tell us what really happened'

He was in Turkey on holiday, took a taxi to Istanbul, fell asleep in the back seat and then woke up a few hours later in the town of Akçakale, on the Syrian border . . . Once back in France, the first explanations Yassin offered the investigators made them smile. The stories told by jihadists from Syria are often far-fetched, but this young man raised the bar a notch with his tale of being unwittingly enlisted in the Islamic State. Today, Yassin admits that his tall tale didn't hold water. 'It wasn't a great story. I just couldn't come up with anything better at the time.'

Yassin now admits to having succumbed to the sirens of the Islamic State. It was 'a big mistake, to put it mildly. I'm very grateful, I know I put everyone in danger. It's hard to admit.' How did the jihadist propaganda manage to take root in this young Frenchman's mind? The factors driving this phenomenon are multiple and protean, and affect people with different profiles – some from very different social backgrounds – in different ways. Jihadism offers bruised egos the possibility of becoming heroes of Sunni Islam. The IS sees itself as part of Muslim eschatology,[10] and offers jihadists a higher status within a utopia – that of an ideal home for all Muslims.

At the time, Yassin was suffering from a sense of failure and frustration. 'It was a time when I didn't feel great with who I was as a person.' After graduating from a scientific high school with good grades, he began studying medicine, just like his parents. But he failed the second-year entrance exam twice. So he then tried pharmacy. But he gave that up quickly, and tried another training programme, with disappointing results again. Coupled with this was the stress of being a member of an Arab-Muslim family living in French society. He had been extremely close to his sister, but she had just married and was now expecting a baby, and he found that hard to accept. He was no longer getting along with his parents, stopped going out, and spent more and more time in front of his computer, watching videos about the Islamic State on the social networks.

'There's a difference between being at home eating crisps in front of your computer and being over there in a trench'

'There are a number of things that attract people to it', Yassin explains. 'For me, it was the possibility of having a status, of being someone who counts, and even more than that. You go there, you have a car, you've got everything. You get to be part of something big. They show you videos of shining knights saving the world. I wasn't very religious at the time. I didn't go to the mosque very often. I would pray with my father from time to time. I was at a pretty low level in terms of faith. I didn't read. But it was something slightly mystical, like a prophecy that people were waiting for. There was a kind of madness to it, almost a collective trance, that convinces you to do it and that everything will be fine. I used to watch a lot of propaganda videos showing normal life. There were lots of people over there saying: "Life is wonderful here, we go fishing, we all eat together in the evening. Then we go to the hospital to bring the sick what they need; afterwards, we take turns policing calmly." The more puffed up it was, the better. When you're in France and you hear about life over there, it sounds like a dreamland you absolutely have to visit. But there are two different realities: being at home, quietly eating crisps in front of your computer, and being over there in the mud, in a trench, with bombs going off all around.'

Today, Yassin's new version of the facts still leaves the DGSI investigators somewhat perplexed, because he insists that Turkey forcibly 'swapped' him with the IS. 'In France, the first words of the interrogation were: "We don't believe your stories about a swap, it's a load of bullshit. Now you're going to tell us what really happened."' In the summer of 2014, the Islamic State had just seized Mosul, the second-largest city in Iraq, with little resistance. The West was terrified. During its triumphant conquest, the IS seized all of the financial and military resources in the city, but also took hostage about 40 Turkish diplomats from the consulate. Ankara quickly began negotiations, which led to an exchange of prisoners. At the end of September, the intelligence services released 46 Turkish citizens in exchange for 180 jihadists detained in Turkey. According to the British newspaper *The Times*, 2 Swedes, 2 Macedonians, 2 English, 1 Swiss and 3 French citizens were on the list of jihadists. Yassin, who had been arrested by the Turkish police shortly after his arrival near the Syrian border, with his wheelie suitcase, insists that he was one of the 3 French citizens exchanged.

He now claims that Turkish police came to the police station where he was being detained with other jihadists. These police officers, he says, led him to believe that they were bringing him back to the city of Urfa to be expelled to France. Yassin told them that he didn't want to join the IS, but wanted to return to France. He made several calls to his parents and to the French Embassy in Turkey from the Turkish police station. He claims that he didn't realize what trick was being played on him until he crossed the border with dozens of other youths on Turkish buses, and saw the black flag of the Islamic State. 'At that point, I understood what was going on.'

Electronic bracelet on his ankle, confiscated identity papers

Is his version of events credible? Contacted by Les Jours, another French jihadist, detained at the same time but in another Turkish detention centre, insists that this exchange was organized on a voluntary basis. He says he himself refused. But Turkey does in fact appear to have exchanged jihadists with the IS against their will. At the beginning of 2016, the Belgian Abu Saif was handed over to the IS by Turkey in exchange for hostages, even though Belgium (where he had been sentenced to twenty years in prison for terrorism) had asked Ankara for his extradition. The rumour of his execution by the IS, who accused him of helping deserters flee its ranks, remains unconfirmed to this day.

After seven months in Syria and four days in police custody in France, Yassin was placed in pre-trial detention in the prison hospital in Fresnes (Val-de-Marne). Wearing an electronic ankle bracelet, and with his identity papers confiscated, Yassin is now trying to resume a normal life, navigating between family and judicial obligations, in particular 'going to see a psychiatrist to combat [his] radicalization'. He still practises his religion a little, 'to keep my parents happy', has resumed his studies, and three times a week visits a physiotherapist to work on his rehab. Yassin doesn't yet know the date of his trial for 'criminal association, for the purpose of preparing acts of terrorism'. He faces up to ten years in prison.

His parents and sisters risked losing everything for Yassin. On their return to France, they too were suspected by the police of having ties to the IS. Why did they leave for Syria without informing the authorities? Why did they stay almost three months, agreeing to work for the Islamic State? Why did they put their two daughters at risk, exposing them to the possibility of being indoctrinated, married to a jihadist or even killed in a bombing raid? To all these questions, Nadia and Faisal respond with the same answer: their goal was to save Yassin. In the end, no charges were filed against them, although they know that a long and trying legal process is still ahead of them. But it's nothing to what they've already been through. 'We're just trying to make the most of life now. Your life can change overnight, so quickly and so cruelly, that you have to know how to make the most of it. When it's for one of your children, you can't rely on anybody but yourself. The past has become so dark and painful that we don't want to think about it any more. It's time to look to the future now', says Nadia.

'Just sit there and wait for someone to bring him back to me? No.'

She has no regrets. She lived in the heart of the Islamic State for nearly three months, risking her family's life. 'It's a new life for us now. When I wake up in the morning, I say to myself: "Oh my God, he's here." Sometimes my nightmares wake me up. I couldn't have gone on living without him. Life seemed unimaginable without my son. It's what's known as the "empty nest syndrome." I just couldn't accept it. Nothing could console me. I had one single goal, to see and find my son again. And I thought: "Even if I go and find him dead, I have to pray at his grave." I needed something concrete. "I have to touch my baby, I have to touch my son. Just sit there and wait for someone to bring him back to me? No. That's not how we are." It was our problem and our pain, no one else could experience what we were going through. No one else could feel that unimaginable pain.'

PART THREE
ZUBEIR

Zubeir, 20 years old, the repentant jihadist

The meeting takes place in a small group setting, without a microphone or a camera, in a neighbourhood education centre in the outskirts of Paris. On this spring morning in 2016, Zubeir knows that he's putting himself in danger by speaking out against those he now considers his 'enemies', after a year spent in their ranks in Syria.

'I don't want a *fatwa* on my head', the young man says worriedly. Inside, he sits down shyly at a table where coffee and hot croissants have been set out. Tall and thin, with short hair and a sparse beard, Zubeir has a half-smiling, half-scowling look on his face, common to teenagers. He has just turned 20. Two years ago, he was in Syria with a Kalashnikov slung over his shoulder, in the company of some of the same Belgians and Frenchmen who would later carry out the attacks of 13 November in Paris. Six months ago, he was sitting in a prison cell in Fleury-Mérogis, having decided to return to France, 'disgusted' with his experience in Syria. 'It was a huge mistake', he says today. Out on parole, with his name on the 'S list',[1] he has come here voluntarily to speak this morning to a group of troubled youths about his disillusionment.

In front of Zubeir[2] sit two young men and two young women between the ages of 14 and 17, all of whom are having problems at school and have been chosen by their teachers to listen to his story. Sipping Cokes, the two youths with the faces and voices of school-boys crack jokes, and talk about a YZ motorcross cycle they dream of buying one day and about tickets one of them has to a David Guetta concert at the Eiffel Tower, but which he wants to resell at his school for fear of a terrorist attack on the eve of the Euro football tournament. Their teachers are concerned about the two young men only because of their poor academic results and regular absence from class. One of the two young women, on the other hand, has been asked to attend today because, in the eyes of one of her teachers, she shows certain 'warning signs'. However, as if to excuse herself for having 'raised a red flag', this young woman immediately tries to play things down: 'There's no need to get hysterical about it. After the attacks, you'd hear people say: "Nice job, they got what they deserved." But just because you're not mourning for *Charlie* doesn't mean you support the terrorists.'

Not too long ago and these 'weak signals' would surely have passed by unnoticed

In recent weeks, this bright-eyed teenager, whose father is of Algerian origin and whose mother is Italian, began to wear long dresses and a black turban. She started frequenting the mosque more assiduously and the opinions she expressed were more conservative than usual. France had 'no future', and only offered her the opportunity 'of washing other people's toilets' or being a 'cashier at Carrefour during the summer'. 'I can't stand it any-more', she says. A year or two before, such 'weak signals' would probably have gone unnoticed. But with the departure of more than a thousand young French men and women for Syria since 2012 and the attacks of January 2015 in Paris, the French social services, terrified at the idea that another Kouachi or Coulibaly might pass through their hands, are paying closer attention now.

Florence, a mother also present at this morning's meeting, knows something about the phenomenon. One day, her 14-year-old daughter ran away from her suburban family home to join the Islamic State in Syria, together with her companion, who now threatens France in videos posted on the internet. Over a period of two years, the mother has spoken on the phone only three times to her daughter, who has already had two children. Like hundreds of other French parents, Florence hadn't noticed any warning signs. Now she is infuriated with the school services for not having warned her of her daughter's conversion or of the fact that she had started wearing a veil at school, taking it off just before coming home in the evening. 'Our children managed to deceive us under our own roofs', she admits. That was in 2013, the year the first French citizens left to join the ranks of the jihadists, before intelligence services and the media realized the magnitude of the problem. It continued until early 2014.

'I don't agree with those people any more'

'Hello, my name is Zubeir. In 2013, I left France to go to Syria . . .' From his first words, all eyes are fixed on him. Silence. He speaks softly, lowering his eyes slightly towards the table. This is a first for him. It's the first of its kind on a national level as well: after their time in police custody, those returning from Syria are often asked by the internal intelligence services to tell their story in order to help construct an anti-jihadist argument, which the authorities call a 'counter-discourse'. Until now, almost everyone has refused.

'When they come back, most people may be disappointed, but don't regret what they've done. Not at all', explains Zubeir. 'They're still in favour of jihad. That's why most of them don't want to speak out against these people. They've got a lot of information on the people in the IS, but consider France a country of infidels, an enemy of Islam, fighting against their Brothers, so they don't want to help.'

So far, Zubeir has been an exception. Not only did he accept, but he even asked to tell his story in person to dissuade others from leaving for Syria. 'Because I don't agree with those people any more. I'm completely against them ideologically. I want to help those I consider to be more just. I will always consider democracy a more just system than those people.'

Although resolutely hostile to the jihadists, his story doesn't fall into the usual traps of institutional counter-propaganda. He doesn't use any easy clichés gleaned from the mass media. He doesn't talk about Captagon,[3] regularly (and falsely) presented by the press as 'the jihadist drug'. 'At least if they were drugged we could forgive their actions, but we can't even do that. They're just stupid', he jokes in front of the adolescents, without underestimating his new enemy.

Zubeir breaks down the main lines of the worldview promoted by the videos of the Islamic State or Al Qaeda that prompted him to leave for Syria, by telling what he saw and heard over there and in French prisons. His Kafkaesque tales about those he calls 'jihadi deadbeats' call to mind scenes from the comedy film *Four Lions*.[4]

To illustrate the paranoia that reigns within the IS, Zubeir tells of a misadventure that happened to a Belgian Al Qaeda member he met in Syria. Having quit Jabhat al-Nusra for the IS when the caliphate was declared at the end of June 2014, this Belgian had the bad idea of complaining about the food. 'All he did was criticize a meal. He said: "The food over here is terrible, I prefer what we ate back at the al-Nusra Front!" And they threw him in jail for three weeks!' Those around the table laugh. Once he got out, however, the young jihadist opened a restaurant in Raqqa, with a menu written in French for his jihadist customers from France and Belgium, most of whom don't speak Arabic.

There are fewer smiles when he tells of the 'hundreds of IS members who have disappeared, apparently executed without their deaths ever being announced. The pseudo-caliphate where people are supposed to be free is actually a dictatorship. Criticizing

Baghdadi can get you thrown into prison. And chances are you'll never get out again, that you'll die in there, but more likely from a jihadist bullet than from a Bashar soldier.'

Zubeir describes a 'gangster culture' among the French jihadists

During his time with Al Qaeda partisans, Zubeir said he met with French emirs who taught the Koran without speaking a word of Arabic, who felt they had more military legitimacy than veterans from Afghanistan, 'even though all they'd ever done in France was commit robberies'. He describes a 'gangster culture' within the IS, and 'fights over nothing' between Frenchmen who spend their time isolated from fighters of other nationalities. 'They get into arguments, sometimes there are fights, they're proud of carrying weapons.'

He also recounts witnessing the arrival of 14-year-old girls 'who think they're on their way to meet Prince Charming, but all they're going to do is stay at home 24/7. And when their husband is killed, the IS will propose another husband to them. They'll have no choice: if they say no, they'll have to stay in a women's home.' Zubeir describes these groups as being 'like a mafia of jihadist criminals. The way they understand their religion is that everybody else is an unbeliever except for them.' Zubeir continues: 'The leaders lived in luxury, with beautiful cars, beautiful houses, while the rest of the population starved. My idea of the group was people united together, but they weren't united at all. They all said that they're fighting Bashar's regime by providing a better model of life than in France. But in reality most of them were fighting for oil and against Sunni rebels. They didn't give a shit about how the Syrians lived, that was all just talk.'

Zubeir explains that he eventually became disgusted with the jihadist project, even though it had been a dream for him while still in France. His break with jihadist ideology is the result of a personal evolution, however. In his view, no counter-discourse developed by an institution could produce the same effect. The young man doesn't believe in what the French authorities call 'deradicalization', which has become a profitable business for some, without obtaining convincing results. In France, more than 1 million euros of public money were spent on such programmes between the end of 2014 and the end of 2015. 'Money thrown out the window', he quipped in an interview with Les Jours; 'I don't see how we can deradicalize these people, knowing that they don't see themselves as radicals – rather, as Muslims living in accordance with what they believe, that is, according to the Koran and the Sunnah.[5] And we're not going to deradicalize these people using imams who call themselves republicans, whereas the religion is completely opposed to the French Republic.'

After experimenting with such programmes for two years, the civil authorities in France appear to have resigned themselves to the impossibility of governmental deradicalization. A semantic shift has gradually taken place in institutional discourse: the word 'deradicalization', increasingly contested, has been replaced by the less ambitious but perhaps more realistic discourse about a 'disengagement' or 'withdrawal' from violent behaviour. After several unsuccessful initiatives, the hope is no longer to turn an individual away from religious radicalism by presenting him with a normative vision of Islam, but rather, more modestly, to draw him out of a violent form of radicalism using support and evaluation programmes.

However, the first deradicalization programme, which had been entrusted – without independent supervision – to the CPDSI[6] by the French Interior Ministry in 2014, was not renewed in 2016, after a widely publicized failure was revealed by the French radio station Europe 1. A young woman whom the courts had entrusted to this centre after she'd planned an attack against a synagogue in Lyon in 2014, and who was presented in many French and international media outlets as a model for deradicalization in France, was arrested at the end of 2015 on her way to Syria to join the Islamic State. She is currently in detention.

'Stop Jihadism', a drop in the bucket compared to the IS's strike force

At this stage, the counter-discourse is something of a pseudoscience. In 2015, the government launched the programme 'Stop Jihadism', managed by the privately owned public relations company, Publicis. A drop of water in a daily ocean of content on the social networks. That same year, the Islamic State alone claimed to have broadcast 800 videos, 15,000 photos, 18 magazines in 11 languages, and tens of thousands of daily tweets. The French government's counter-discourse amounted to 2 video clips and 1 Twitter account.

Despite the terrorist attacks, the violence, the bombings, the deterioration of the military situation and reinforced border controls, departures from France to Syria continued to increase from 2012 to 2016. According to official figures from the public authorities, in July 2016, 689 French nationals (including 275 women and 17 minors) remain in Syria or Iraq, to which must be added 420 children, one-third of whom were born there, remain undocumented, and are being raised and socialized under jihadist ideology. In France, close to 1,000 individuals are considered by the intelligence services to have shown signs of 'inclination to depart', within a population of sympathizers estimated at about 3,000 people, who are under various degrees of police surveillance; 195 French nationals have been reported killed in the region, and about 203 have chosen to return to France.

After one year in Syria, and another year in prison, Zubeir presents himself as having 'repented' of jihad. However, his unorthodox vision of the Muslim religion retains a radical inflection. The young man now considers himself an apostate or an ex-Muslim, because in his eyes the rejection of jihad, and the acceptance of democracy and the French Republic, necessarily imply a rejection of Islam. 'Religion has never been compatible with democracy. So you're not going to deradicalize people by showing them others who say the opposite, by making them

believe that the correct form of Islam is republican and democratic, whereas the texts say the opposite. They're not going to be
deradicalized by that, nor by helping them find housing. We've
got to admit that when people fall into radicalism, it's very complicated to get them out again.'

On the other hand, by promoting a counter-discourse, Zubeir
believes that it may be possible to prevent certain individuals
from embracing jihadism. 'Yes, there are ways. The first thing
is to make them love their country. People who've fallen into
terrorism don't love their country, they denigrate the country
in which they live. They are already strongly anti-system, and
very much into conspiracy theories. They see the Islamic State
as a good, righteous government that enforces its laws, whereas
the complete opposite is true. They see France as a country that
has colonized other countries, and continues to colonize them,
while waging war against the poor, Arabs and Africans. They see
France as a racist country. So the counter-discourse has to start by
making them love their country again.' How? Neither Zubeir nor
the French government has found the answer yet.

Being a jihadist means feeling important

Our first meeting with Zubeir after his release from prison takes place in his neighbourhood, at the foot of his apartment building, in the fall of 2015. But we've been in touch with him via the internet since 2013, even before his departure for Syria. This tall and discreet young man, who never goes out without his little waist bum bag, wants us to taste his favourite kebab. According to him, the best kebabs in the entire Parisian region are found in his neighbourhood: he refuses to eat anywhere else. Indeed, he explains that the first thing he did when he got out of prison was to treat himself to a kebab with ketchup and mayonnaise. But 'more seriously', it was to visit the family he had left abruptly two years earlier to go to Syria. He acts nonchalantly but shows himself to be funny and extremely quick-witted, expressing himself precisely and critically, capable of explaining objectively the process that led him to become a jihadist, in order to feel important.

As a teenager, he was a pretty good student

To him, his social background isn't the determining factor for understanding the path he took. Zubeir describes himself as coming from an 'upper-middle-class' family. That said, he grew up in Seine-Saint-Denis, in the tower blocks of its public housing estates, beside its eight-lane motorway. Originally from the Maghreb, his parents are self-employed in intermediary professions. They live together with their children in a three-bedroom, 80-square-metre apartment. Not everyone has their own room. When he left for Syria, he was still a minor, and a pretty good student. 'I had never seen the inside of a police station in my life. I'd never been in trouble at school. I'd never been punished.' He was a discreet and solitary teenager, sometimes with a sulky look, but always with a little smile in the corner of his mouth. He didn't go out very often and never had a romantic relationship. He spent a lot of time alone. 'My life wasn't really that great at the time. I only had two or three pals, we used to play video games together – *Call of Duty* [Editor's note: a successful video game series]. I read manga and listened to rap music.' He found life in France boring. Extremely boring. He was looking for something else.

Since Zubeir's release from prison just under a year ago, Les Jours has been meeting with him twice a month in his neighbourhood, in coffee shops and fast-food outlets, accompanying him to court dates or during his attempts to reintegrate into society. Dozens of hours of interviews, in order to understand and tell this French story.

Unlike many francophone jihadists, Zubeir speaks Arabic (*darija*, the Moroccan dialect), as well as literary Arabic, and has a real understanding of Islamic culture. As a child, he received a very structured religious education. From the age of 6 to 15, in the same way that others would go to catechism, he would attend a Koranic school once or twice a week to memorize the Koran. His parents are practising Muslims, but do not adhere to any particular current of Islam. Zubeir grew up in a religious environment and incorporated the values that go along with it. 'A Muslim has to be strong. He always has to be the best in everything. He can't let himself be brought down, he's got to stay proud. Never imitate the unbelievers. It's not an extremist viewpoint, but it's nevertheless conservative.' At home, for example, they don't celebrate birthdays, because these are regarded as a 'religious innovation'. The term refers to any human invention unknown to the Prophet, absent from the Koran and the Sunnah, and therefore forbidden. His twentieth birthday was spent like every one of his other birthdays: no party and no gifts. Zubeir spent the day walking the streets of Paris alone, enjoying a relaxation of his probation. 'That doesn't bother me, but because I never celebrate my birthday, sometimes I forget my birth date. It's not normal to forget your birth date.'

'We are driven to consume and consume . . .
But . . . there's much more to life'

After turning 16, Zubeir embarked on a quest for spiritual absolutes, something he couldn't find in contemporary society. 'We are driven to consume and consume . . . But after a while, you realize there's much more to life. Some people need a different project. When you see that the only thing Western democracies do today is enable people to buy more things, you realize that it's meaningless, it doesn't make you want to keep living. Just consuming things is boring, it's like we're all dead. We're like robots.' Between his family's values and those of a secularized France threatened with political apathy, the teenager felt lost. 'I felt there was something missing. I had a spiritual void to fill and I filled it with religion.'

Around then, the young man began to admire a group in a neighbourhood mosque who were not afraid to display their piety, and wore their kamis with pride. Their 'prophet-like' beards, long with a shaved moustache, seemed to correspond to the description of the companions of the Prophet he read about in the scriptural texts. 'When I looked at the believers in the mosque, I began to consider them as different from the others. They had a very particular way of life. I started to ask them questions and I found out that they were trying to return to a purer understanding of Islam. "This is how the Prophet was, and so we're going to be like him." That interested me. If you practise a religion, you should practise it in its purest form. You have to try to imagine how people like that think. They think about heaven and hell. What they want isn't the Islam of France, it's just Islam. They're looking for a door that leads to heaven.'

Within a few weeks, Zubeir had integrated into this group of believers, of the Salafist Quietist[7] tradition. Contrary to popular belief, this current, as proselytist as it is rigorist, is an enemy of the jihadists. Firstly, because of its ties to Saudi Arabia – it is guided by Saudi mufti who are linked to the Saud monarchy. Jihadists despise this power, because they believe it usurps the holy places of Islam while living in opulence and corruption.

Another reason for this mutual animosity is Riyadh's cooperation with the United States, on both economic and security fronts, in an increasingly intense fight against terrorism, since the September 11 attacks. While they share a common doctrinal foundation and both follow certain scholars, they are at odds on the issue of armed jihad. According to the Quietists, who have developed a theory of submission to temporal authority, war can be decreed only by the 'governor'. In France, Quietists often help the police by denouncing the jihadists they consider *takfiri* or *khawarij*. They also regularly report those jihadists' Facebook pages in order to have them taken down.

Zubeir has definite views on the debate about the Salafist question in France. In his opinion, this rigorous ideology, advocating fundamentalist values in complete opposition to those of the French Republic, was a decisive step in his religious radicalization. These two branches of Salafism are, of course, violently opposed, but Zubeir now considers that for him, as for a majority of the French nationals he met in Syria, Quietism prepared the ground for, and constituted a stepping stone towards, his embrace of jihadism. 'It had a big influence on me, because it was the first picture I had of Salafism. Little by little, I started to think that it wasn't ever enough, and that the highest level was jihadism. That's where you cut all your ties, where they tell you that you can't just live quietly, so you have to die quickly, you have to fight – it's actually a form of suffering. I don't think there's anything above that. In terms of humanity, it's the most dehumanized ideology in the world. I always wanted to go further, so that's where I ended up.'

The tipping point

As is often the case, Zubeir's first exchange with a jihadist sympathizer didn't take place in a mosque or in his neighbourhood, but on the internet. 'It was on a forum that had nothing to do with jihadism. I was looking for information about political Islam and I came across it completely by chance. It was the first time someone told me about his vision of Islam and jihad. He was a French jihadist.' This first discussion took place in April 2013, when Zubeir was only 16 and considered himself a Salafi Quietist. He left for Syria barely seven months later, in October.

Once he became more interested in the jihadosphere, he quickly broke with the Quietists. On Facebook, Zubeir began to subscribe to pages advocating the *hijra* – leaving France and emigrating to the land of jihad – such as Wake Up Ouma, which no longer exists. As often occurs in this dynamic of ideological isolation on the internet, he established his first contacts with jihadists on this mainstream platform. Then he made others on a social network reserved for the initiated, a kind of jihadist Facebook that has since disappeared: Ansar Ghuraba.

After the virtual exchanges, the first meetings

Among Zubeir's bookmarks to the most important ideological websites, there also appears the former francophone forum Ansar al-Haqq, which was shut down in the summer of 2015. 'I got to know them when I was looking for answers to questions like: Is jihad part of Islam? Are we required to do it? etc. When I was still with the Salafists, I read a lot about their scholars and their ideology on the internet. You don't have to travel 3,000 kilometres any more to have a scholar answer your questions, now you just go online. You ask questions, they give you answers.'

Then came the first real-life meetings. After his exchanges on the social networks, Zubeir finally met 'IRL' – or 'in real life', in internet lingo – the person with whom he would later leave for Syria. They met at a demonstration held to denounce attacks on women wearing the niqab around Paris. 'They showed up with the black flag of the *shahada*,[8] the same one used by the Taliban. They just stood there, looking good. I'd known him for a few days on Facebook, we'd spoken once or twice before. Back then I hadn't yet embraced the jihadist ideology. He told me: "We've got to demonstrate, to show our anger." He used to preach and distribute leaflets. He called it "street *dawa*". I liked that and I offered to help.'

After this first encounter, his ideological network, at first purely virtual, consisted of a small group of about fifteen people who would meet at least once a week in one of the only mosques that jihadists frequent in Paris, despite its being directed by the Tablighi[9] movement. The members of the group were all between the ages of 17 and 25, and mostly came from various Parisian suburbs.

'It felt like being in a Muslim country'

Despite not sharing their ideology, this mosque served as a meeting point for the group's members, whose discussions revolved around the jihad in Syria and how to get there. 'It felt like being in a Muslim country when we'd go to the mosque. We weren't even in Paris any more. There was a restaurant and a fast-food place next door. We could eat and then go and pray. We knew that the police wouldn't bother us there. When we talked to anyone, it felt like he was one of us, and everyone spoke openly about jihad in Syria.'

The group became more and more convinced of their obligation to leave for the war-torn country, but they still hesitated between Al Qaeda and the Islamic State of Iraq and the Levant (ISIL, now the IS). Via the social networks, the team was already in contact with two charismatic leaders based in Nice and Lyon, who were very influential in the jihadosphere. The group was fascinated by their online videos, whose calls for jihadist emigration relied on Muslim eschatology. These videos helped prepare the ground. The real tipping point, says Zubeir, was the civil war in Syria and Bashar al-Assad's repression: 'I started thinking about it after seeing their videos on YouTube explaining that *hijra* is an obligation for every Muslim.' These two men were considered the main French recruiters for Syria. In June, in a small apartment in Paris, they met Zubeir and his group for the first time, five months before their departure. One of the recruiters left the following month to scout out the path leading to ISIL. He was the one who opened the door to Syria for them.

Losing interest at school

At that point, the French intelligence services began to take notice of Zubeir. The group's repeated meetings near their favourite mosque had attracted the attention of the police. They'd been aware of this place of worship since the 1990s, when it was still a stronghold of the Armed Islamic Group. The mosque was under some of the heaviest surveillance in France. Zubeir's father was even summoned to the police station. An official warned him about his son's acquaintances. Back at the family home, a heated discussion ensued and his father decided to confiscate his computer and tablet. But it had little effect. A model student up to that point, Zubeir now began to slack off at school. He was unable to pray at the appointed time, and as a result became less and less diligent. Above all, he could no longer stand the way his teachers spoke about Islam, particularly the way they would insist that Islam and jihad should not be conflated, whenever there was a terrorist attack somewhere in the world. The effect on Zubeir of such an approach was the opposite of that desired, only reinforcing his convictions. 'The more they told me that that wasn't Islam, the more I was convinced of the opposite. For those believing in this ideology, the more their enemies – that is, the West – tell them that that isn't Islam, the more they're convinced that the opposite is true. They say it's just a line to keep people asleep, to encourage you to be obedient, to be completely passive towards what's going on in the world. At that time, I had read something in a book by Ali ibn Abi Talib, one of the first Caliphs, that said: "If you want to know where the truth is, follow the direction of the unbelievers' arrows."'

One day in a philosophy class, his teacher referred to a particularly bloody attack committed by the Somali Al-Shabaab in Kenya against the Westgate shopping centre in Nairobi.[10] 'He just started talking about it, saying, "That right there has nothing to do with religion, it's more a war against Western values." I couldn't take it any more, hearing that it has nothing to do with Islam, that it wasn't motivated by religion.' That was the day Zubeir decided to walk out of the classroom and drop out of school.

'I've always supported people and parties that were against the system, like the Front National or the far left'

Even today he has an aversion to what the journalist Jean Birnbaum has dubbed the 'nothing-to-do-with-it' discourse, which claims that such attacks have 'nothing to do with Islam or with religion'. Because, in his opinion, this media and political paradigm, designed to avoid conflating terrorism and Muslims, is useless and counter-productive. 'I don't like it when people try to discredit them by saying: "No, that's not Islam, it's not written in the Koran." Even if you tell a young person: "no, it's not written there", he's still going to go and find out about it. He's not stupid. He's going to look and see if it's written there and he'll see that that is indeed what is written. He'll get an exegesis of the Koran, he'll pick up Ibn Kathir or Ibn Abbas, one of the Prophet's companions, and he'll see that yes, he legitimizes fighting against people who have fought against us, and there's no point in saying it isn't written in the Koran and that it's got nothing to do with Islam. Those people attract a lot of attention by using religious arguments, by citing the Koran, by using *dalil*.[11] For those who see them as a sect outside of Islam, it looks like indoctrination. But for those who regard those views as an integral part of Islam, they just see someone who wants to live in conformity with what he believes.'

Zubeir confesses that he has always had a penchant for political radicalism. 'I always had this revolutionary side to me: I wanted to be a politician, I've always supported people and parties that were against the system, like the Front National or the far left. Then, when I added Islam to the list, I said to myself: "I believe in Islam, and I have this revolutionary side of me. So in Islam today, who is trying to change things? For me, it was clearly Al Qaeda. They were the only ones offering an alternative and attacking everyone else. It was a return to strong moral values. In France, there are same-sex marriages and everything. We are against that. That's what attracted me – the fact that their discourse was different from everyone else.'

Without knowing it, Zubeir embodies the concept of the 'Islamization of radicalism', as theorized by Alain Bertho after the *Charlie Hebdo* and Hyper Cacher attacks. According to this anthropologist from the University of Paris VIII, this development is driven by the disappearance of twentieth-century ideologies and the 'collapse of the modern trope of politics, which understood the taking of power to be the lever of collective trans-formations'. In retrospect, Zubeir now considers that he was in need of a project at that point in his life. Secular modernity no longer offers all young people hope in the future. For some, it is jihadism that offers a response to this contemporary ideological vacuum and this need for radicalism.

In this sense, Zubeir also embodies the need for transcend-ence identified by the American anthropologist Scott Atran.[12] 'We were bored, there was nothing to do, we were in a rut and life lacked spice. I used to say to myself that we weren't created just to work and have fun. I considered life as something you had to endure, something complicated. For me life was supposed to be dangerous, because in the Koran it's written that human beings were created to struggle in life, with trials and tribula-tions. Life isn't about just working, drinking and eating quietly and avoiding seeing the poverty in the world, people being mas-sacred, and so on.' Without his religious upbringing, his quest for meaning could have pushed him towards some other form of engagement, in the way that other French nationals have joined the Kurds of the PKK, for example, or, in another age, have turned to revolutionary communism. 'I wasn't looking for reasons to live in communism, because that wasn't how I was brought up. I was brought up with religious values, so I turned to religion.'

Zubeir acquires a certain notoriety within the jihadosphere

By espousing the principles of jihadism, the solitary adolescent was no longer invisible. He gained in self-esteem and began to walk tall and with pride. Previously, he was hardly noticed in his neighbourhood or high school. His life had been neither fulfill-ing nor particularly happy. His new-found convictions, however, gave him a new social environment, one he perceived as fraternal, and which helped to bring him out of his social and existential isolation. On the social networks, Zubeir quickly acquired a certain notoriety thanks to his provocative and vindictive postings. He felt less lonely and his need for social recognition was satisfied. 'When I was younger, I wanted to become famous, and that's why I liked to post on Facebook.' His notoriety within the jihadosphere[13] gave him social capital and, perhaps for the first time in his life, this young man who'd forgotten his own date of birth had the feeling that he really existed, that he was someone important. 'Embracing this ideology meant entering into a community. Every time I would post something on Facebook, I had 30 "likes" from people I didn't know and who would then start talking to me. I felt like a cocoon was forming around me, and that I was no longer alone. That helped me get out of my hermit lifestyle.' This new community created a mimetic group effect – a closed-minded ideological context where any questioning of the project was considered an act of apostasy. Which also played a key role, as part of a collective movement, in his decision to leave for Syria.

Once the decision to leave France had been made, the question remained as to how to finance the trip. Zubeir was a high school student with no income. His partner in jihad, a convert to Islam, tried to take out a consumer credit loan, like many jihadists. His application was rejected because he didn't have a job. In the end, however, the solution more or less dropped out of the sky, thanks to the Ansar Ghuraba jihadist social network. An anonymous correspondent contacted him to ask if he intended to do his *hijra*. He responded that he wanted to go but didn't know how to do it without money. His contact offered to pay his way – because for those who can't leave to wage jihad, funding the cause is also considered a means of earning 'points' for heaven. Several jihadist ideologues, such as Anwar al-Awlaki, the media spokesperson of the AQAP,[14] have written about this, and those works have been translated into French.

'I'd never been so handsome in my entire life'

The meeting was scheduled in Paris. The day after their discussion on the internet, a thirty-something bearded man Zubeir had never met before handed him an envelope in a kebab restaurant. Inside was several thousand euros in cash. For Zubeir and his group, it was a sign from God. 'It was unbelievable. I'd only spoken to the guy once on the internet, and then he showed up. I couldn't believe it. We were sure it was a sign, because things like that don't happen to just anybody. It was absolutely incredible, some guy you've never met showing up and handing you several thousand euros in cash. That meant it was written, that you had to go. There's a verse in the Koran which says that he who fears God will always find a favourable outcome. So I said to myself that it was because I was on the right path that God made this happen for me. We understood it as a sign, that God wanted us to go and save the community.' After handing over the cash and finishing his kebab, the unknown benefactor got up and left. Zubeir never saw him again. Now more determined than ever, he went to the first travel agency he could find and bought two tickets to Turkey.

His departure for Syria took place just seven months after his first virtual contact with a jihadist. No one in his family knew about his project, which he had planned in secret. On the day he left, he dressed up as if for a great event. 'I'd never been so handsome in my entire life. A nice shirt, nice cardigan, nice pants, nice bag, suitcase . . . I looked great.' His travel partner opted for a more hip-hop outfit, trading his turban and kamis for a pair of baggy pants and a baseball cap. Zubeir was only 17 years old, but France had just lifted the obligation for minors to have parental permission to leave the country. The requirement was reinstated two years later after a flood of departures. Everything went according to plan. After live-tweeting their trip and geolocalizing their position on Facebook, they arrived in Syria the next day and were welcomed into an organization linked to Al Qaeda. Zubeir had absolutely no contact with his parents during his entire year in Syria.

Jihadist seeks YF for marriage

Zubeir had a strange feeling of power when he arrived in Syria: did being a jihadist suddenly make him more handsome? He had never been much of a lady's man back in France.

At 17, he'd never had an intimate relationship with a woman. 'I was a pretty frail person, and I used to get sick all the time.' Once he joined ISIL, after a brief time spent with Al Qaeda, his Facebook inbox began to be flooded with marriage requests. 'Women would see my photos. I got marriage proposals every day.'

Zubeir learned how it worked from a Frenchman, well known among the jihadists, who had arrived a few months before him. 'He told me: "If you want to get married, take a photo of yourself holding two Kalashnikovs like this." And he added: "You'll see, you'll be scoring in no time." He got married like that with four women over there. Three French women and one Tunisian. Because he had four wives, he got two apartments. ISIL provided them. He posted a lot about himself on Facebook: either to act like a playboy and show his friends back in France he was there, or to taunt the anti-terrorist services in France, or to attract women to come to Syria.' This charismatic French jihadist was killed in 2014 during the fighting between the IS and Jabhat al-Nusra in northern Syria.

According to Zubeir, foreign fighters would spend a good deal of their time flirting on the internet in Syrian cybercafés. 'They were all connected 24/7 just for that. 24/7 looking for women. Every one of them got what they wanted; they all got married in the end.' In his view, in most cases the religious aspect is fundamentally important in a jihadist relationship, but sex appeal is also a motivating factor, even if the subject is often taboo. 'They don't talk about it, but a lot of them left France with that in mind. When you've got a bunch of guys together, they start talking to you about marriage. You see they left France just for that reason. But they won't say it like that. Because in their minds if they're emigrating for something other than for God, they won't be accepted into paradise. So they'll never tell you that they emigrated for women. But that's how ISIS has managed to attract so many people.'

The attractiveness of the *houris* in paradise

According to Zubeir, the attractiveness of the *houris* in paradise,[15] 'with their black eyes overflowing with white', is also a very important factor for the candidates for martyrdom and suicide bombings. 'They were obsessed with the *houris*. When a lot of them thought about their deaths, that's what they had in mind for when they arrived on the other side. They'd say it wasn't forbidden to die for that reason, because it meant dying to go to paradise. In terms of motivation, on a scale of one to five I'd give the *houris* a three.'

With a jaded laugh, Zubeir remembers an anecdote told by a Frenchman from the Islamic State after the death of one of their comrades. 'He said he'd seen white spots on his underwear. He said he ejaculated after his death because he'd seen the *houris*. He said: "*Hashakoum*,[16] brothers, he ejaculated, *soubhanallah*, that means it's true! The *houris* in paradise are real, my brothers!" And the others actually believed his story.' The teller of this anecdote was 'droned' by the United States in December 2015 in his car in Raqqa, Syria, because of his alleged links with the perpetrators of the 13 November attacks in Paris.

One day, a young woman aspiring to emigrate decided to put the piety of the French nationals in Syria to the test. Within their ranks, any form of mixing between the sexes is formally prohibited. Men and women are kept strictly apart. When a fighter marries, he leaves the barracks and has to move into a private apartment with his religious wife (or wives). Women are obliged to wear the sitar outside the home. Some groups consider that even a woman's voice shouldn't be heard by a man who isn't her husband. This rule is also meant to apply to private exchanges on social networks. In reality, however, that isn't the case at all.

From among his many admirers, Zubeir made the acquaintance of a young woman who was more enterprising than the rest. To his surprise, she had no qualms about sending him naked pictures of herself. 'She was flirting with the jihadists. She would send pictures of herself wearing almost nothing, or even completely naked. The guys around me she'd send those pictures to were crazy about her. She sent them to me too. A lot of girls would send photos of themselves, but she was the only one who would send pictures of herself completely naked. The others wouldn't. There were women who'd loosen up a little, but she was the only one who'd do that. What surprised me was that, despite everything we knew about her, she still managed to find a husband over there. Even though everybody knew what she was up to on the internet.' Zubeir wasn't the only one to receive such racy photos. Having made up her mind to leave for Syria, the young woman had made contact with other men too.

A revelation during an unusual trick

Her story was unusual, to say the least. She explained that she used to work as a prostitute, despite being only 18. She had also suffered sexual violence in the past. The young Frenchwoman, of Catholic origin, told Zubeir how she had had a revelation during an unusual trick, which led her to convert to Islam. 'She was an escort girl. At first I was shocked, I said to myself: "Who is this girl?" Afterwards, I told her to stop sending me photos. But I wanted to know why she did it. She told me her story, saying that she used to work as an escort girl before she converted. In the beginning she was *minhaj salafi*.[17] But then she became interested in jihad and everything, the "true ideology", and said she would eventually like to emigrate. She told me that she once had a strange client who refused to sleep with her. Apparently it was a bearded guy, very chaste. It was a little weird, this deeply religious client who hired a prostitute but wouldn't do anything with her because he was too chaste. Whatever. And she told me that that was what set her off. When she saw how chaste he was, she wanted to learn about Islam.'

Zubeir is embarrassed to admit that he hoped to marry her in Syria. But when she arrived with her brother, with whom she had converted two months before, he wasn't able to pick her up at the border. The young woman agreed to be the second wife of another French jihadist. But a few weeks later, her husband was killed. After the prescribed period of mourning had passed, the young woman remarried a local fighter in the Islamic State. 'She was fed up with French men. She said they were sexually obsessed and didn't know how to behave themselves. She wanted a pure Arab.' She has since given birth to a child in Syria. Her brother is fighting in Iraq.

Zubeir then switched his hopes to a French teenager. 'We sent messages to each other every day, she was mad about me. Every time I posted a photo of myself, she'd "like" it, or put hearts on my photos. I think those women are really naive. She was 15 years old. They're living in the clouds, dreaming of a Prince Charming in a fairy tale. She contacted the group in April and a month later she'd joined us. She said she didn't want to do any housework, and that she wanted to fight. She couldn't understand that women don't fight in Syria. The poor girl found herself in a difficult situation. In the end, she didn't want to stay in Syria any more, but they forced her to stay.' The group's emir finally decided to marry her off to one of his relatives, who wanted a second wife. She had managed to get to Syria by her own means, despite only being 15. Her new husband was 30. 'Everybody is bothered by that except the jihadists. They'll tell you that Mohamed married Aisha when she was only nine.'

'LOL jihad'

For the first few months of Zubeir's time in Syria, at the end of 2013, the French jihadists had little involvement in the fighting. The ISIL, which had just announced its formation in Syria, had not yet imposed its authority or its administration. The first French jihadists had very little contact with the front line in their daily lives. At most, they were assigned guard duty from time to time in a *ribat*, one of the guard towers on the checkpoints between the belligerent parties. Most of the French jihadists were then living in the same towns, sometimes in the same neighbourhoods, in the Aleppo suburbs. They lived in large houses abandoned by wealthy Syrians fleeing the war. According to Zubeir, after two weeks or a month in a training camp, the French nationals would spend their time like a group of friends: going on walks, visiting cybercafés and fast-food restaurants and carrying out their five daily prayers together.

Thanks to numerous consumer credit scams, some of them had arrived in Syria with large amounts of cash, sometimes even with luxury cars purchased on lease agreements in France. Several jihadist sheikhs have declared this practice 'lawful under Islam'.

To finance jihad in Allah's footsteps, stealing from disbelievers is now no longer considered theft, but rather *ghanima*,[18] or the spoils of war. Two Frenchmen in Zubeir's group arrived in Syria with 80,000 euros in cash. They had come by road all the way from France in an Audi Q7. Having had no problem passing through an official Turkish border post, the vehicle was resold in Syria to pay for a pick-up truck mounted with a heavy-calibre machine gun for the group. In the early days, however, it wasn't uncommon to see jihadists carrying weapons and posing as if in a rap video in front of luxury vehicles registered in France.

The first French 'star' of jihad 2.0

This was the time of 'LOL jihad' and selfies posted by smiling, gun-toting jihadists in Syria. In those days, the daily lives of the French nationals in Syria were followed on Facebook like a reality TV show, and a photo of a vanilla ice cream in Raqqa could receive the same number of 'likes' as a selfie with a decapitated head. Their viewers exhibited the same fascination, the same addiction and the same processes of identification. All were invited to join this Syrian version of *Big Brother*, where one leaves not by being voted out by the other participants but by being killed, with the certainty of reaching not the relative glory of celebrity magazines, but heavenly bliss itself.

In 2012, the 20-year-old Abu Tamima began to post selfies of himself in Syria, wearing a Lacoste tracksuit and holding a Kalashnikov. His Facebook page had almost 2,500 subscribers. This handsome, smiling young Frenchman, full of gangster humour crossed with jihadist culture, became the first French star of jihad 2.0 thanks to the photos and videos he posted on the internet. One such video would show him going through the pockets of a decaying corpse from the enemy camp to get a wad of dollars; another would show him joyriding in an upmarket sedan. Sometimes he'd have fun spray-painting *DAWLA BAQIYA*[19] on an abandoned car, the same way he might have tagged 'Fuck the

Police' on the side of a train, back in his old life in France. In other photos, he could be seen writing the name of Mohamed Mehra with the shell casings of his Kalishnikov, as a tribute to the terrorist responsible for attacks in Toulouse, or sitting in his room, planning an attack, surrounded by automatic weapons and grenades, with the Eiffel Tower drawn on the wall behind him. He also appeared proudly bearing arms together with the Belgian Abdelhamid Abaaoud, coordinator of the 13 November attacks in Paris and of the attack in Verviers, Belgium, in January 2015. He regularly tweeted photos of his shopping sprees in Raqqa, smiling in Ray-Ban sunglasses and a Vuitton shirt, with a Glock holstered under his arm. His fans could see him on beach outings on the banks of the Euphrates, or eating hearty meals in the large hotels he squatted with other jihadists. Even his funeral became a media event, with a final photo showing him lying in his grave. Since his (presumed) death was announced in 2015, his photos continue to fascinate his supporters and are shared throughout the jihadosphere. From 2012 on, this was the openly terrorist yet very attractive image they sent via the social networks to their friends back home in France – the image of a 'five-star jihad', as Zubeir calls it.

Often at the bottom of the social ladder in France, they joined the group in power in Syria

Like Abu Tamima, everyone became a sales rep to his network in France for this new land of emigration, seen as an outlet for the conflicting ambitions of modern life. Syria under jihad took on the allure of a land of material and spiritual plenty, where the oppressed finally became the oppressors, where class relations were reversed, and where young French nationals, most of them from minority groups, assumed for themselves the State's legitimized use of violence – all for the price of a one-way ticket to Turkey. Often at the bottom of the social ladder in France, they joined the group in power in Syria. Subject in France to laws of which they considered themselves the victims, in Syria they became the guarantors of the extremely violent imposition of laws of their own. It was the bloody revenge of the humiliated, the remedy to all frustrations, leading exponential numbers of people to leave France for Syria from 2013 on, even at a time when the phenomenon remained unknown in the media and underestimated by the intelligence services. Jihad in Syria was sold and experienced as an individualistic and collective experience of joy, legitimized religiously, offering new arrivals the chance of becoming knights of Islam and of wiping away all their sins.

Everything that was impossible in France became possible in Syria. With Nike Airs on their feet, an assault rifle in one hand and a latest-generation smartphone in the other, these French nationals hadn't left capitalist consumerism behind. Everything they couldn't have in France was there for the taking in Syria, as 'spoils of war', and all in the name of a cause their propaganda presented as fundamentally noble, rewarding and redemptive: defending Muslims by creating an ideal city, together with the promise made to the chosen few to reach the highest level of paradise. 'You see them in videos, swimming in pools, having fun, eating ice cream, Nutella. They take pictures with cats, they go to amusement parks. They're having a great time and they feel free. No more constraints, no more submission to what they consider a corrupt system', says Zubeir. 'They are living in the best of all worlds, free to enjoy themselves without feeling guilty. When they had fun in France, they'd say to each other: "Yeah, but what we're doing here isn't right, we're having fun while other people in the world are being killed." But now that they've gone to fight those oppressing their brothers, they no longer have a problem enjoying life.'

Like being at summer camp

Jihad regards itself as the most radical possible response to social determination, or to psychological, familial or identity problems, by means of a liberating experience amplified by a project at once playful and transcendental. Zubeir admits to having 'had fun' in Syria, and even enjoying a certain level of comfort. 'It was disturbing sometimes. We no longer felt like we were in a country at war. We felt like we were having fun, it was like we'd gone to the beach, or were on holidays. It was really "LOL jihad", yes, that's the right expression for it. We had it easy, we'd hang out on the internet, making jokes. We'd troll the forums; we'd play with cats, that was how it was. It was cat jihad; it was a little weird. We ate really well, it was crazy, there were fruit juices, I could order a cappuccino every morning. There were times I ate better over there than here.' Zubeir notes a 'surrealist contrast with what you'd see on TV. Sometimes we'd be going 200 kilometres an hour in a pick-up with our buddies, eating ice cream. Always laughing. It didn't seem like jihad at all. It was more like being at summer camp. It was comfortable jihad, a jihad of luxury. Five-star jihad. A jihad where you could shoot at people and eat ice cream at the same time.'

Over the course of several months, Zubeir increasingly felt that the French 'LOL jihad' culture was an import of 'gangster culture' into Syria. The middle classes were also affected by the phenomenon, of course, and in much rarer cases even the upper classes of French society. Nearly a third of the prospective jihadists come from Christian families – sometimes even Jewish. But the converts themselves often come from Christian homes among minority populations in France: from Portuguese, Asian or sub-Saharan immigrants, or from Travellers' communities or, in many cases, from the French West Indies and the French overseas territories. Rural areas are no exception. The dynamics can't be completely explained in terms of immigration – delinquency – poor suburbs. Sociologically speaking, however, the French jihadist phenomenon is mostly to be found amongst young people with a low level of education, brought up in a Muslim culture and living in the country's working-class neighbourhoods.

Zubeir believes that only a minority are driven by a sense of piety – that is, engaged in a genuinely religious struggle and rejecting all form of ostentation online. He believes that, behind the fundamentalist varnish, most French nationals continue to behave in Syria as they would in France. They don't change their lifestyle so much as 'Islamicize' it, while at the same time taking revenge for frustrations suffered in France, by unleashing their will to power in an armed struggle. 'This gangster culture really exists in the IS. To be honest, the gang habits haven't changed that much. The language is the same. The jihadists have Islamicized the words used to describe criminality. Before they would have called somebody a "faggot", today they say "*murtad*", an apostate. But it's the same way they used to insult people before, during their period of ignorance, the *jahiliya*.[20] The language is Arabicized, or Islamicized, but the behaviours stay the same. They trade insults, they deliver punchlines like in a rap song, but now it's for the glory of the Islamic State. Even over there, they're always drawn to everything that glitters – gold, women, guns . . . They're into the same things as in the inner cities back home, the same pleasures.' Except that, Zubeir explains, 'they'll say that anything they steal is taken as spoils in war. They do a *ghanima*. When they lie to people who aren't like them, they don't call it a lie, they say they're being cunning. When they talk about insulting others, they say that God has given them permission to speak ill of the unbelievers. They do the same crap as before, but with a little more Islam in it.'

When the coalition goes to war

From 2014 on, jihad became less and less LOL. The beginning of that year saw the start of the *fitna*, the discord – that is, the fratricidal battles between Sunni rebels and jihadists. French nationals who had left together for Syria suddenly found themselves in enemy camps. Once the international coalition entered the war in August 2014, with its bombings and the targeted strikes from American and British drones, the jihadists' use of the internet changed profoundly. For military reasons, the emirs imposed a communications blackout on the fighters. The jihadist selfies – a great source of strategic information for the enemy – were forbidden and gradually disappeared. Only the official media branches of the Islamic State were allowed to make any public communication about the group. The content broadcast by the jihadists themselves had to be validated by the hierarchy of their media brigades. It was the end of 'LOL jihad'. Postings openly promoting terrorism on Facebook between 2012 and 2013, and on Twitter from 2014, gradually vanished from public platforms, which were deleting thousands of accounts on a daily basis. From 2016 on, they moved to more anonymous and discreet parts of the social web, such as Telegram,[21] the Russian messaging service that offers encrypted exchanges.

On the ground, the Frenchmen were increasingly ordered to fight and to die. Often in suicide missions. Zubeir remembers the arrival of two friends from Martinique. As soon as they got in, like everyone else they filled out their fact sheet, which included a check-box for fighter (*muqatil*) or for kamikaze (*inghimasi*). They chose the latter. 'Those who will carry out suicide operations are put in a special *maqqar* [Author's note: a house for fighters]. They stay there until somebody comes and gets them to go to blow themselves up. That's what happened to the pair from Martinique. They saw something about Syria on YouTube. They converted to Islam, then off to Belgium to meet somebody, then straight to Syria. When those guys showed up, they didn't even know how to pray, they didn't know anything about Islam. They learned how to pray when they got to Syria. One of them blew himself up in a suicide mission in Iraq with ISIS. They were really nice guys, the poor bastards. I felt bad for them.'

That was when Zubeir and several other Frenchmen decided to leave the ISIL to join a pro-Al Qaeda brigade. Disgusted by the group's excessive violence and the behaviour of the French nationals who were part of it, they hoped to find more religious orthodoxy in Jabhat al-Nusra.[22] But they quickly experienced the same disappointment, and his cell, consisting of French and Belgians, broke up as the air strikes intensified. Zubeir found himself isolated in a small border town near Turkey, risking arrest for desertion. 'When you're in France, you want to leave, but when you're in Syria, you get bombed every day and you miss France. You start to think that your life in France wasn't actually that bad. I can thank ISIS, because what they did really disgusted me.'

He had a glorified idea of the jihadist project before leaving France. But dealing with its reality gradually disillusioned him. The religious piety put forward by the group's propaganda seemed to him a mere pretext, and the military situation became more and more complicated. Zubeir had no desire to end up in an IS execution video, dressed in the orange uniform of their prisoners. And he had started to miss the country he came from. After a year in Syria, he contacted a member of his family.

He explained that he wanted to return to France. The French and Turkish authorities were alerted. From Syria, it was only a few kilometres on foot to reach the Turkish side. He crossed the border and went to the first Turkish customs post he saw. When he told them his identity, he learned that his name was on an Interpol wanted list. The customs officers were watching a football match. At the time, the Turks still welcomed foreign fighters warmly. 'They offered me tea, biscuits. I watched the game with them. I used their computer and logged into Facebook.' His 'LOL jihad' was over.

'I found ISIS at Fleury-Mérogis'

A bit embarrassed – even ashamed – Zubeir rolls up the leg of his jeans to give a glimpse of the black plastic ring attached to his calf just above his tennis shoes: his ankle monitor. Since his release from prison in 2015, the first months of Zubeir's probation have been relatively strict: he is forbidden from leaving Seine-Saint-Denis, and must check in every week at the local police station. Some nights his sleep is still disturbed by memories of the bombardments. A psychological counselling programme, included in his probation, helps him to externalize his fears and sleep better. 'In Syria, I saw people crossing the street and then, Bam! a barrel of TNT drops on them out of the sky. We'd find an arm on one side of the street, a leg on another. It was disgusting. I still have nightmares about it, but I'm not psychologically traumatized.'

Zubeir is happy to have been released on parole, after his incarceration in Europe's largest prison, in Fleury-Mérogis, France. 'It was honestly the worst time of my life. Worse than Syria. And compared to Moroccan or Tunisian prisons, French prisons are a luxury resort.' Zubeir acknowledges that being deprived of his freedom had a beneficial effect on him, forcing him to do some soul-searching. 'If I hadn't gone to prison, I would have been in a worse state. It allowed me to be quiet for a while, like when you go on holiday. It gave me time to rest, with no stress. At first, I didn't understand what I was being blamed for, and prison helped me understand.' Zubeir is convinced that going to prison helped him to leave jihadist ideology behind. But he has no doubt that most of the others went in the opposite direction.

General euphoria after the *Charlie Hebdo* attacks

Through peer pressure, most of the detainees he met in prison were locked in a violent form of religious radicalism. Some became even more hardened in their convictions and in their intent to carry out acts of terrorism once they got out of prison, or even within its walls. Zubeir remembers in particular the general euphoria after the *Charlie Hebdo* attacks, which occurred while he was still incarcerated. 'They yelled, they made *takbir*,[23] you could hear shouts of "Allah Akbar" everywhere. The whole building was full of people yelling it. It was incredible. That's why I think there really are a lot of them. It was like they were everywhere. They were all shouting in unison, delighted, and not ashamed to show it. I said to myself: "These guys are crazy."'

At the start of his prison stay, he sent us a handwritten letter. The handwriting was neat, with no spelling mistakes. This on its own made him stand out from other jihadists. The essence of what he wrote might seem surprising. 'I couldn't take the barbarism of the IS and the useless struggle of Al Qaeda. I was sick of trolling on Facebook from Syria, I'd been much better off on my couch [Author's note: in France]', he wrote from his prison cell. 'You could say I've repented of Salafism, jihadism, radical Islam and all those other terms that refer to the doctrines of Ibn Abd al-Wahhab, Sayyid Qutb and Osama bin Laden. To be honest, I don't practise religion any more, I'm an "apostate", I don't believe in Islam any more.'

These words would be a surprise to those who knew this young man in 2013 in Syria, flitting from one rebel group to another – first an ardent proponent of the Islamic State, then of Al Qaeda. At that point, Zubeir was better known for the photo of himself he'd posted on Facebook, wearing a kamis and a turban, index finger raised and a satisfied smile, with his weapons and his cat. The photo was taken at the jihadi base of the French nationals, some of whom have since committed acts of terrorism in France. The impression given is fundamentally different from the one he'd like to give today.

Zubeir's rejection of the Islamic State led him to quit Syria a year after he'd arrived. But, back in France, 'I found ISIS at Fleury-Mérogis', he says. He was put in with prisoners returning from jihad zones or who had attempted to reach them. The way he tells it, the majority of these 'PRIs' (prison jargon for 'Persons Radicalized by Islamism'[24]) remain deeply attached to jihadist ideology. In prison, he ran into several men he had met in Syria and who had come back, just like him. Networks created in or prior to Syria were re-established behind bars. The relationships, reputations, feats of arms and stripes earned on the street continued to determine and structure the group hierarchies in the prison cells, the exercise yards and throughout the prison wings where jihadists were brought together. Whereas some had been trapped by family or friends 'visiting' Turkey, and others arrested while returning to France in order to commit terrorist attacks, most had come back voluntarily. Disappointed by the Islamic State or by Al Qaeda – but not by jihadism.

'Some even say they'll carry out jihad all by themselves'

The majority hadn't repented of jihad, says Zubeir. Caught up in the ideological echo chamber specific to prison life, the convictions of many had only hardened further. 'Most of them were still stuck in it. Maybe one or two were against it, but most were for it. There were a few who were against the IS in Syria–Iraq, but who were for the IS in Libya,[25] for example. There were those who said they were disgusted by the IS, but not with Al Qaeda. Some even said they weren't for anybody, neither the IS nor Al Qaeda, but that they'd carry out jihad all by themselves: they'd get a gun and just go for it, commit an attack as soon as they got out. Then there were others saying that if they couldn't get out of France, they'd do the same. They were all really excited about it. Even if they only killed one person, they'd do it to die as martyrs. That's why they wanted to hit France. All they want is to be martyrs. They're sick of this life.'

The Islamic State, prison ward

We conducted interviews over the course of a year with seven 'PRI' detainees, including Zubeir, incarcerated in different prisons. One of them, imprisoned after returning from Syria, told us about his daily life, spent with a young man who had tried several times to reach the country without success. Our interviewee had spent his first months in prison alone in his cell. Then, 'they put me together with a nitwit. He was a real superstar, that one.' Life with his cellmate didn't go well, for ideological reasons. 'He used to say to me: "No, don't watch the weather report, it's a prediction about the future, so it's *shirk*."[26] He didn't want to watch the evening news either, because he'd say: "It's not true what they say. You can't watch the female newscaster, she's practically naked." He removed the TV cable. If he heard music playing outside, I had to close the window. When the cell above us asked me to pass them up some cigarettes by the window, he didn't want me to do it. He drove me crazy. I told him: "Go to bed and smother yourself with your pillow, please. You want to die as a martyr, right? So do it now and leave me in peace.'"

His cellmate steps into the public eye in Saint-Étienne-du-Rouvray

This 'superstar' had just turned 18. Originally from near Rouen in Normandy, he had never been to Syria, but had tried to get there several times (only two attempts gave rise to criminal prosecution), without success. Arrested in Turkey, he was deported to France and imprisoned. Our interviewee, who had just returned from Syria, considered his cellmate even more radical than those he'd seen over there. 'In prison, I saw guys like him, worse than what I'd seen in Syria. Some of them had never set foot in Syria, but they were worse than ISIS. They took it up another level again.' Every morning he was woken up at around 4 a.m. by his cellmate for his dawn prayer (*salat al-fajr*). At night, the young man would sometimes wake up in tears and begin chanting. 'He talked to himself, he'd say: "I have to stop sinning. I have to stop sinning."'

At the time of this interview, our interviewee's cellmate was still unknown to the general public. He was just one more 'PRI'[27] among nearly 250 in the Paris area. A few months later, in July 2016, in a church in Saint-Étienne-du-Rouvray, he put himself in the spotlight. In the middle of a mass, he entered the church with an accomplice, threw himself at an 86-year-old priest named Jacques Hamel, and forced him to kneel in front of the altar, before cutting his throat with a knife before the horrified eyes of a few nuns and worshippers. It was Adel Kermiche. When his identity was released to the press, those who had known him in prison couldn't hide their astonishment. How could a detainee whose radicality had been so well known in prison have managed to deceive several magistrates to such an extent that they decided, against the public prosecutor's recommendation, to release him with an electronic surveillance bracelet?

'Many brothers would rather have Trévidic as a judge'

The terrorist had initially been placed under detention by the former anti-terrorist judge Marc Trévidic, who was then transferred to another department against his will, in line with a rule requiring specialized magistrates to change posts every ten years. He was a judge whose understanding of jihadism had paradoxically won him a form of esteem among some of them, as another detainee explained: 'Many brothers would rather have Trévidic as a judge', he explained in a telephone call from prison. 'He understood things better and was a better judge for it. It's like if you gave a judge who specializes in fraud a paedophile case. It doesn't make sense, you have to understand the psychology and all that goes with it.'

It's an opinion Marc Trévidic himself seems to share, not without a certain bitterness. Nine days after this terrorist attack, which the Islamic State would later claim as its own, in an interview with the Belgian public television station RTBF, he allowed himself a subtle dig at his former colleagues: 'I had someone in front of me who wanted at all costs to go and wage jihad in the Islamic State. I could see that little glint in his eye that tells you he's never going to change his mind. Every judge is free to make his or her own decisions. But I want to say one thing: it takes years of experience before you can begin to distinguish those who are pretending from the rest.'

Even so, on the social networks, Adel Kermiche had never made a secret of his intentions. After eighty-six people were mowed down by a 19-ton lorry in Nice on 14 July 2016, in the name of the Islamic State, he commented on Twitter: 'That makes me feel "Nice".' The day before, he also tweeted: 'Wallahi I'd cut the throats of all the Kafir, even if there were billions of them! Ya Allah.' On his private Telegram channel, where he had met his accomplice Abdel Malik PetitJean online four days previously, he announced, the day before their attack, that 'a big thing is going to happen, share it with everybody [. . .]. We're here, my brothers, you know that the hijra is pretty complex, so let's say hello to [President François] Hollande, here's a kiss, smack, smack, and let's do what we've got to do here, bismillah.' All 140 of his followers understood the message: France is preventing us from going to Syria, so let's hit them here.

'Even when they pray, they try to hide it'

Such a clearly terrorist discourse could only be expressed openly amongst prisoners. A completely different façade would be shown to the prison authorities, and especially the CPIP,[28] whom the prisoners regarded as maintaining a certain humanistic empathy for them. Yet the magistrates' decisions on whether or not to release a prisoner rely on the reports and evaluations made by these same CPIPs. If the detainees' accounts are to be believed, deception and cunning are particularly prevalent amongst those ordinary prisoners detained for non-terrorist acts, but whose subsequent radicalization in prison goes undetected by the authorities. 'There was one guy who'd been in prison for a few years for murder, he was crazy about ISIS, and ISIS didn't even exist yet when he got sent down!' Zubeir recalls. 'He told me how they do this inside. "We hide, we pretend, we act like your average Joe so we don't get singled out." Coulibaly[29] was able to do what he did because he lost himself in the crowd like everybody else, and then *Boom!* he struck. They considered it a "*taqiya*". But they didn't use that word, they just say they "outsmarted" them.' According to Zubeir, outsmarting the authorities can take different forms: 'Out on a walk, you see them smoking, but they're real jihadists. They wear sweats like everybody else. They even try to hide it when they pray, so the guards don't see them. Most of them have never even set foot in Syria. I've seen maybe ten guys just waiting to get out of jail in order to do something. There aren't a lot, but there are one or two of those ten who are going to carry out terrorist acts.'

Until now, the somewhat caricatural idea of prison as a 'jihad university' has been qualified by certain statistics. Upon their arrival in prison, more than 70 per cent of the 'PRIs' had never been incarcerated before. Which is to say that it wasn't in prison that the majority encountered this ideology. On the other hand, many prisoners' testimonies suggest that an increasing number of those incarcerated for terrorism tend to become more attached to their ideology during their imprisonment. Moreover, the constant increase in this prison population threatens in time to transform prisons into real jihadist incubators. As of the summer of 2016, there are 325 'terrorist detainees' in France, of whom nearly 250 are incarcerated in the Paris area, including 25 women. And among the 68,800 prisoners nationwide, almost 1,400 of those detained for common law crimes or misdemeanours are considered by the prison administration as 'currently undergoing radicalization'.

When contacted by phone, several other 'terrorist detainees' confirmed this analysis. Such as this one, imprisoned at Fleury-Mérogis after returning from Syria: 'What's sure is that, of those getting out, I guarantee that, of the 300 incarcerated, three-quarters will go to Syria or will do things here in France. Only a handful will reintegrate into normal society. Every door is being closed to them, so the only door that's been left open for them is that one. We've been isolated, like guinea pigs in an experiment. I'd never been in jail before, I'd never dealt with gangs or organized crime. Why is the system always coming down so hard on us? It's the system that's turning us into radicals.'

Though mobile phones are officially forbidden, most inmates have one. Such devices are regularly confiscated during cell inspection and even full body searches, but others soon take their place – miniature mobile phones, known as 'earpieces', or smartphones with internet access.

Adel Kermiche, one of the murderers of the priest Jacques Hamel, explained on his private Telegram channel that he had studied '*aqidah* and *fiqh*' (Islamic belief and jurisprudence) in his prison cell with a sheikh based in Mauritania. It isn't unusual to see public exchanges on Twitter or Facebook between a French jihadist active in Syria or Iraq and a jihadist detained in France. Everything going on in Syria and Iraq is followed in French prisons in real time, just as those in the IS follow what's happening in those prisons holding its supporters and fighters. While incarcerated, some go as far as giving religious classes to sympathizers on the outside, via Facebook or private Telegram channels they manage from their cells. The telephone also allows certain detainees to conclude religious marriages with women who in turn are being held for terrorist acts, or with women outside of prison who share their ideology.

'Even those in for drugs or burglary would start shouting "Allah Akbar!"'

Contacted by Les Jours on those same phones, many confirm these practices. And they provide a few anecdotes from everyday life that show an administration somewhat overwhelmed by the magnitude of the phenomenon – by its rapid behavioural changes and by the new communication possibilities the internet has created.

An inmate in another prison, for example, sends a video showing him installing speakers on his windowsill, facing outwards. Turned up as loud as possible, the loudspeakers play the most well-known *anashid*,[30] or the famous *a cappella* war songs of the IS, heard throughout the prison block and other buildings. 'Ah! Ah! Ah! You could hear it all over the prison. Even those in for drugs or burglary would start shouting "Allah Akbar!"', laughed the prisoner, who was being held for a highly publicized jihad affair. 'The atmosphere was fantastic, to be honest. Sometimes you'd hear gunshots and explosions in the *anashid*; it was like the war was going on in here. The guards are too stupid to understand what the *anashid* mean. They don't get what it's about, but the Muslims understand', he joked. The lyrics of some of these war songs are very explicit, even for someone who doesn't speak

Arabic. The pro-IS prisoner even plays the Al Qaeda *anashid*, which sends the name of the terrorist organization resonating throughout the prison. 'That was the best. The *nashid* repeats "Al Qaeda, Al Qaeda" over and over. With the volume all the way up! We have the whole compilation in here! I think the only ones who don't get it are the guards.'

Prison, jihadist territory

Like a quick death, spending time in prison constitutes an essential part of every jihadist's career. 'Some people say it's a *ni'ma*, a blessing', Zubeir explains, having himself been imprisoned in France after his return from Syria. 'It's the government that's imprisoning them and they hate the *taghut*.[31] And why are they thrown into prison? Because they're telling the truth, they think. Either they're killed or they're locked up. So the longer they're locked up, the more determined they'll become. They'll feel even more hatred for those they call the *"taghut"*.'

Prison as a beneficial ordeal

Most of the movement's key international ideologues have spent time in prison. Indeed, many jihadist organizations are born in prison. Such was the case of Ansar al-Shariah,[32] whose leaders founded the group in Tunisia while in Ben Ali's prison cells, before being freed as part of the general amnesty after the 2011 revolution. This was also the case of the current Islamic State, a large part of whose leadership, including its emir al-Baghdadi, spent time in US prisons in Iraq, such as Abu Ghraib and Camp Bucca. Abu Loqman al-Sury, the current Wali of Raqqa – and perhaps also Abu Mohamed al-Jolani,[33] emir of the former Jabhat al-Nusra – spent time in Syria's Sednaya prison before the revolution. In these circles, time spent in prison can become a mark of distinction and help to determine one's place in the social hierarchy. While it remains a difficult test, it is nevertheless a positive test for those contemplating jihad. Firstly, incarceration by the enemy is experienced as a natural response to one's ideological framework, which is strengthened by that very fact. Being 'tested by the disbelievers', then, comes to be seen as beneficial, and also earns one 'points' towards entering heaven.

Most of the jihadist inmates we interviewed over the course of a year played down the idea of a higher level of proselytizing in prison. But they admit to calling on other inmates to practise their religion. One prisoner said that he would even give classes on religion while being held in solitary confinement in the disciplinary ward. During a search of his cell after the terrorist attacks of 13 November, prison guards found a telephone among his personal possessions. But the inmate had a second phone: 'My telephone, an S3 mini, was in my cell when they were searching me. I prayed to Allah, I asked Allah to blind them. I did four *rakats* [Author's note: prostrations] and they didn't find it.' In prison, mobile phones sell for between 300 and 400 euros. They are smuggled in by way of care packages from friends and family, sometimes even with the knowledge of certain guards. They're also thrown in over the prison walls. They land in the exercise yard, where they're picked up. 'A call is made with another telephone saying: "Ok, do it now, throw over the package with a nickname on it."'

'Is it permitted to steal from the *kuffars*?'

This converted inmate used his five days in solitary confinement to reread *The Sealed Nectar*,[34] the version of the Prophet's biography preferred in conservative circles. And in the evening, when the guards weren't paying attention, he says he 'taught classes to those in solitary' by speaking loudly through the walls. But the teacher was sometimes disappointed by how his message was received. 'I called on them to accept the unity of Allah above all and to disavow democracy. I preached in particular against democracy. They listened a little, but the problem is they weren't sincere. They're the ones who have to come to religion, not religion that has to go to them. I would explain it clearly. I didn't lie to them. I'd say: "You are unbelievers." Al hamdoulillah [Author's note: 'praise be to Allah'], some of them admitted it. I said to them: "You don't do the *salat*,[35] you don't know anything about the Koran or the Sunnah." They were too attached to the *dunya*.[36] I was in a building where there were only thugs and hoodlums from the inner cities. They're locked up for petty crimes, most of them young men between 18 and 20. They get out, they come back. I used to do *dawa* [Author's note: literally the 'calling', preaching on a daily basis to call non-believers to Islam], but it was hard because the window was really small. Most of them asked me dumb questions like: "Is it permitted to steal from the *kuffars*?" I said to them: "Look, for me, taking their property is permitted. Allah says so in the Koran."'

He explains that these petty criminals were looking for religion to legitimize their delinquent behaviour. 'These guys just wanted to know if it was hallal, because they're basically just thieves', explains this improvised jihadist preacher. 'I would say to them: "OK, first learn your religion. You're just stealing because you're criminals." They interpret the verses or the *hadiths* to justify their actions. They just want to know if it's allowed to continue stealing.'

Beyond the problem of proselytizing, the other factor that makes jihadist detention an intractable problem is that it is also regarded as a means of deepening ideological knowledge. 'That's what I love about being in prison', explains another 'terrorist detainee' over the telephone. 'The only thing I miss is my family and my wife. Apart from that, prison helps me take a step back from things. You know, to understand why people get radical-ized, you should ask yourself: what pastimes can keep our minds fully engaged? Other than sport, nothing. So the majority of the prisoners read, pray and study the Koran. And the rest follows naturally. Allah takes care of everything. One brother said to me: "The harder they are on us by throwing us in prison, the more comfort we take in our path." You can see proof of that in the prisoners who get out of Guantanamo after undergoing the worst kind of treatment, and then return to jihad in Syria.'

We passed around a book by the No. 1 in Al Qaeda

In his cell, the prisoner was reading a French translation of a book by the leader of Al Qaeda, the cover of which had been torn off so it wouldn't attract attention, and so it could be passed around. In this work, the Egyptian ideologue and intellectual Ayman al-Zawahiri, former right-hand man of Bin Laden, theorized this idea perfectly: 'Yes, detention can be extraordinarily fruitful when someone committed to a cause, or a mujahid, manages to put it to good use, in order to obey God, devote himself to Him, learn His book by heart, study and preach, learn from the trials he under-goes and emerge from them stronger, deepened in his faith, and even more committed to waging jihad.' Not forgetting one last, important point: for those tempted to carry out terrorist activities after their release, time in prison helps them to establish relation-ships with criminal networks, which can be useful for procuring weapons on the outside.

In prison, a shared opposition to the French State tends to attenuate ideological boundaries, which allows links to be formed between worlds that at first sight ought to be opposed. Jihadists often admit to having good relations with other 'terror-ist detainees'. 'Here in prison we've got good relationships with the Basques and the Corsicans', one of these terrorists explains, as do several others. 'When we're together on the football field, we play together. The Basques play hard. Even after eight or ten years in here. They make their political demands every month while walking the yard, carrying posters and signs. I admire their patience. We respect them and they respect us, but we know that someday, on the outside, we might be enemies. But that doesn't keep us from respecting each other's struggles and values.' This type of terrorist osmosis can be seen at work in the women's block too. 'The Basques are so nice, they made me a surprise cake for my birthday', Les Jours was told by a young French woman who was back from Syria.

Jihadist hostility towards symbols of the State can also target the prison administration. Even in little everyday things. 'There are brothers here who carry out jihad on the water and electricity', one prisoner tells us, only half-joking. 'They turn the taps and the lights on, to push up costs for the prison administration. Personally, I feel bad about the water, because I like to respect the environment.'

More seriously, the prospect of an attack within a prison, or a concerted takeover of part of a building by a large group of organized and mutinous jihadist prisoners, does seem credible. In June, the former 'terrorist detainee' Larossi Aballa called for the killing of prison guards and police officers, in a video where he claimed responsibility for the murder of two police officers at their home in Magnanville, France. 'They consider the guards legitimate targets', Zubeir confirms. 'One day they might attack them. Especially the prisoners doing long sentences. At some point they're going to go and lose it and kill a guard, saying to themselves: "Since this is where we are, we might as well wage jihad in prison."'

Aballa's call to arms, broadcast on Facebook Live directly from his victims' home a few minutes after having killed them, immediately made the rounds of the prisons. And its threat became a reality less than three months later, on 4 September 2016, when a 'terror detainee' at the Osny Prison (Val-d'Oise, France) attacked a guard with a handmade weapon, clearly intending to kill him. And this despite the fact that the jihadist prisoners kept at Osny are considered the least dangerous, whereas those for whom the administration sees no hope of rehabilitation are sent to the Lille-Annoeullin prison complex. The 24-year-old inmate used a 20-centimetre-long iron shaft pulled from his cell bars to attack a guard who had just opened his cell door, at exercise time. Wounded in the neck in particular, the guard was only saved by a colleague firing a Flash-Ball. The attacker came from Trappes, one of the cities most affected by the jihadist phenomenon in France, to the point that jihadists refer to it as 'Trappistan'. He had been sentenced to five years in prison for attempting to go to Syria, where two of his brothers had already been killed fighting for the Islamic State.

The inmate who attacked guards in Osny

This was the first jihad-related attack in a French prison. Inmates who knew the assailant told us that he acted after learning that his wife – who was expecting a child conceived with him in prison – wanted a separation. Even if psychological distress was the trigger, the motivation behind the attack was nevertheless politico-religious. Afterwards, while awaiting the arrival of the prison's specialized 'immobilization' unit, he drew a heart with his victim's blood in his cell. 'He just cracked. He was a bit depressed, and he was weak and easily manipulated', explains an Osny detainee who knew him well. 'He wanted to provoke an assisted suicide. But he was unlucky, because it wasn't the RAID[37] unit that intervened, and he wasn't killed.' He was 'unlucky' because, as a jihadist, he had hoped to receive the heavenly favours accorded to a martyr killed by the police. Having taken place in a prison wing housing twenty jihadist detainees, this attack relaunched a debate about the use of such units.

Since 2014, the number of individuals returning from Syria and Iraq has steadily increased, and incarceration is now systematic for the men amongst them. Because of the unprecedented scale of the problem, the stakes involved are only going to rise.

Confronted with this crisis, the French prison administration is currently experimenting with various possible solutions. But their options are limited, given current prison overcrowding and the lack of resources – both material and in personnel. In an attempt to counter proselytization, a project launched in Fresnes (Val-de-Marne) which gathered together 'terror detainees' was extended to three other prisons in 2015: Osny, Lille-Annoeulin and Fleury-Mérogis. Approximately one-third of the 'PRIs' have been gathered together in these dedicated prison units. The most dangerous – those best-known in the media – are completely isolated. The others are mixed in with ordinary inmates, as part of a 'dilution' policy. This controversial measure allows these atypical prisoners to be kept under much closer surveillance and monitoring. They are offered the opportunity to join discussion groups where outside speakers come to give talks about geopolitics or religion. Two-member teams consisting of a prison educator and a psychologist are charged with constantly assessing the degree of their radicality. While some complain of being turned into 'lab rats', others are not unhappy with their 'preferential treatment', including having individual cells. But grouping such inmates together into separate prison wings also allows them to organize themselves, thereby reinforcing the jihadist project. Just like in Syria, emirs have been named inside the prison walls, with parallel organizations structured hierarchically in a pyramidal form. Despite the sanctions incurred, group prayers are sometimes organized. But these activities would occur whether such dedicated units were in place or not.

According to Zubeir, it makes no difference whether the jihadists are grouped together or mixed in with common prisoners: the problem remains the same. 'There's a lot of personal isolation in prison. The people who turn to religion will look for a familiar environment. So who are they going to turn towards? Straight away they're going to turn to ISIS, because the people in ISIS are just like them, they're not so different, they've often followed a similar path, they come from a violent background, young guys with the same fantasies, who speak the same way.' Zubeir points to the Islamic State videos that take their visual cues from Hollywood: 'That really gets the attention of the guys in prison. And when they see ISIS fighting alone against a coalition that can't manage to beat them – that gets their attention too. Add in the fact that they're in prison and already hate the French justice system and you've got an explosive cocktail on your hands. People in prison feel alone and vulnerable. Whoever is the most determined will encourage the others to stay strong. And he'll incite them to wage jihad once they get out.'

'I'm afraid that people are afraid of me'

It is now two years since Zubeir's departure for Syria, which ended when he chose to give himself up to the French consulate authorities in Turkey. After a year spent in prison in France, he now appears before the Paris criminal court, with an electronic bracelet around his ankle. His entire group, about fifteen people, has also been summoned to appear. Some are present in court, while others are still in Syria, where they follow the trial on the internet. The young man with whom Zubeir left France is thought to have been killed in a suicide bombing mission for the Islamic state in Iraq. But because the French government has no documentary proof of his death, he is tried *in absentia*.

Not everyone appearing before the judge has been radicalized to the same degree. In the witness stand, one of the defendants begins by announcing that the only justice he recognizes is that of God, not that of the judge. He dismisses his lawyer and chooses to defend himself. Questioned by the presiding judge, he swears allegiance to the emir of the Islamic State, Abu Bakr al-Baghdadi. As the prosecutor begins his questions, the witness cuts him off. It's the hour of prayer. He begins to pray in the witness stand. 'Great, this guy is going to be our lightning rod', whispers Zubeir's lawyer at the break.

Indeed, his own client looks like a teddy bear in comparison. Despite the extremely tense security climate in France, there's plenty in Zubeir's file in his favour. He is very young, his remorse is credible and he has been cooperative with the authorities. The court gives him a light sentence. To his relief, he's not being sent back to prison.

'You're never proud of doing something stupid'

His friends were surprised the first time they saw him back in the old neighbourhood, his tall frame wrapped up in a winter jacket. 'They were shocked to see me again. They were happy.' To those who know of his past, he prefers not to mention it. 'It's not something I'm proud of. You're never proud of doing something stupid. I'm disgusted with myself for what I've done. I'm afraid that people are afraid of me.' For a year now, Zubeir has been trying to 'live a normal life again'. He visited his old high school, hoping to sign up again for his last year of classes. But the school principal knew about his past and refused. In the end, Zubeir managed to sign up to a professional training programme for the coming academic year.

After the initial euphoria of seeing each other again, his relationship with his parents has become tense, and there is conflict on the question of religion. Zubeir now totally rejects it. Like many Muslims, his parents see nothing religious about ISIS, but see it rather as a Zionist plot. 'They're still in denial. It's never the fault of the Muslims, it is always the West's fault. Always the Jews' fault, or the Zionists'. It always the Jews who are financing it.'

He can no longer stand this refrain of 'that-has-nothing-to-do-with-Islam', so often repeated in the media and in politics (see above). In his opinion, jihadism has everything to do with Islam. 'For me, this religion meant emigration, armed struggle, jihad and living under sharia law in an Islamic state. And I got sick of it. I decided to give up this religion because jihad, for me, is an integral part of it. That's why I gave it all up. It has nothing to do with religion, it has nothing to do with anything at all. But there's a logical connection between that and Islam. If you're being realistic, the connection is there to see.'

Wearily, Zubeir once again quotes the truism that 'Islam and terrorism are not the same thing': 'They've got nothing to do with one another, Islam has never told us to do that, Islam has never said to be violent like that. So they think it's either an educational problem, which in some cases is true, or it's a misunderstanding. Yes, they've killed, yes, they've fought. The Islamic references used by the Sunnis advocate armed jihad, the struggle against the unbelievers, the institution of sharia law everywhere. It's obviously not just something they made up. Even burning people: the Islamic State didn't come up with that themselves, it's in the texts. There were companions, one of the so-called "well-guided Caliphs" who burned people – Abu Bakr al-Sidiki, the first Caliph of Islam and a close friend of the Prophet, and Ali Ibn Abi Talib, the Prophet's nephew. If it wasn't written down somewhere, they wouldn't have done it.' Zubeir recalls the Camp Speicher massacre in Tikrit, where the Islamic State shot 1,500 Iraqi army prisoners and threw some of the bodies into the River Tigris: 'There's a reference to that. They didn't just make it up. Killing people and throwing them into a lake, or into water – that's a reference back to a specific event. They didn't just make up the idea of cutting people's throats either. They justify what they do with a verse from the Koran that says to strike their necks. In a war, to strike their necks means to cut off their heads.'

Convinced of this fact, Zubeir no longer prays, no longer frequents the mosque and hides himself so as not to have to fast during Ramadan. 'I'm very discreet. I don't talk to anyone about it.' Such things are not done in a conservative household. 'They tell me I have to be careful, because in hell ... It's always the same: it's hot in hell, in hell you'll be all alone, in hell there'll be nobody to help you. There's also the threat of knowing that there is no other truth than this one. Even what may sometimes seem bizarre has to be accepted, it can't be discussed. All these threats.' Grown tired of the religious pressure within his family, Zubeir now dreams of being independent. But it won't happen soon.

Zubeir can't leave Syria behind

Back from Syria and out of prison, he finds himself back with his family, back in his bedroom and alone again. He still spends a lot of time in front of a screen, glued to his Samsung phone and his Twitter feed: 'Hey, see what happened in Aleppo? Intense.' He still follows every military surge, every shifting of the fronts, down to the last millimetre. 'It's so I'll have arguments to throw back at them', he explains. He can't put Syria behind him. His past keeps catching up with him. Coming out of the metro in Belleville in Paris recently, a man called out to him in Arabic and slapped him on the back. 'Hey, Abu Zubeir, salam alaykum!' Turning around, he was surprised to find himself face to face with a Syrian he'd known well over there. This family man had welcomed him when he first arrived in Syria, back when he was still a jihadist. It's a surreal encounter in the middle of Paris between a former French jihadist and a Syrian refugee who, having crossed Europe on foot, is now applying for political asylum in France. Their roles were now reversed, ironically. The Syrian was now a migrant who'd fled the Assad regime, taking the opposite path from the one taken by Zubeir two years earlier.

PART FOUR
THE WOMEN

After jihad, a 'quiet' return to classes for Safya

Safya smokes. On the platform of a train station in a large French city where she told us to meet her, she inhales one cigarette after another. Tobacco is one of the most important items banned in Raqqa, a central city in Syria administered by the Islamic State, where the young woman has just come back from spending eight months of her life.[1] 'I used to smoke before I left. And I smoked a little in Syria. Well, actually a lot. I used to smoke the whole day. In Syria, I'd go through a pack in a single afternoon. A sister and I used to sneak off to smoke. It would have been a disaster if another sister had found out: she would have told on me immediately.' To keep others from finding out about her vice, she would spray her sitar with perfume several times a day. Because Safya knew the 'legal penalty' for smokers: 40 lashes of a whip. For the masters of the city, however, the punishment remains purely theoretical. According to her, members of the IS enjoy greater indulgence in this regard than the Syrians. 'Once I witnessed a French brother arresting a Syrian for smoking. The man was crying. He was begging him to let him go. He was saying: "I promise I'll never do it again, please forgive me."'

Safya doesn't wear a veil. This plump and pretty 23-year-old wears her hair long and untied. 'I got sick of having my ID checked by the police', she explains. Meaning no outward signs of religion. She even has a piercing on her chin. 'It was an impulse decision', she says, bemused. 'I walked past the shop and I said to myself: "OK, let's do it!" It's pretty, don't you think? I love tattoos too, but that's totally *haram*.' It was an adolescent act of coquetry that would have been very out of place within the Islamic State where she had been living just six months before.

Released after 96 hours of police custody

Safya smiles. She says she's just come back from a morning spent shopping. The rapidity and ease with which the young woman returned to her normal life in France is disconcerting. Despite living inside a terrorist organization that regularly carries out bloody attacks in France, and despite her well-entrenched jihadist convictions, Safya is free and no legal proceedings have been taken against her. She simply spent 96 hours in police custody at the DGSI facility in Levallois-Perre once she stepped out of the plane in France. The interrogation by the police rankled her. 'They asked me to identify some people. They were taking the piss out of me, asking me questions about religion. They asked things like: "What is jihad? What are the five pillars of Islam? What does it mean to die as a martyr?" They want to find out if you went for religious reasons or something else, because they want to prove that most of the people who go over there have no idea about their religion. So I told him: "The three possibilities for martyrdom in Islam: dying in combat, being eaten by a wild animal or dying from a stomach illness." They just broke out laughing, they were taking the piss out of me. I was shocked. They thought they knew my religion better than I did.'

Safya was anything but cooperative with the police. 'One morning they asked me: "You look like you're a little bored. Do you want to go on the internet? You can go on Facebook if you want." I just wanted to laugh. They really thought that I was going to connect to Facebook at the DGSI![2] They're so stupid. I think they really thought I was an idiot. A total idiot. They asked me if I wanted to give them my passwords for Facebook and email. I was like: "Uh, no way." And I'm thinking: "This is the DGSI!" They didn't just graduate from high school, they studied at the university for this!'

At the end of her police custody, Safya expected to be brought before a judge to be placed on probation at the very least. But no. 'At the end, the investigator came to see me in my cell and she told me: "Pick up your things, we're not pressing any charges. You're free." I was super-happy but kind of shocked. But then I told myself it was fine.' She now considers that it would have been wrong to incarcerate her. 'Well, I didn't do anything wrong', she says spontaneously. Before letting her go, however, the police asked her if she would agree to meet young women who were thinking about leaving for Syria, in order to convince them not to go. She refused categorically, because of her attachment to the IS, which is still very strong. 'Frankly, I've got better things to do. Knock it off with that crap. And it's pointless anyway. If I was in their shoes I'd just think I was an apostate.'

So far, the French authorities have been rather lenient

Like most women who have returned from Syria, Safya appears to have benefited from a form of gender bias, a sexist prejudice that leads French authorities to consider female jihadist engagement more leniently, because it is considered more as the result of a victim's submission to male domination. It is understood as a kind of indoctrination into a sect, in which a woman's free will disappears. Male and female motivations for the jihadist emigration are, however, relatively similar. In institutional circles, this radicalization is often seen as a form of psychological pathology, unconnected with any possibility of rational choice. Female jihadists are, therefore, victims.

For Safya, however, this way of understanding the problem is too psychiatric and gendered, and avoids other objective considerations which apply also to men. And it takes away the responsibility of women who are often in complete control of these processes. 'If a girl wants to go to Syria, it's her decision. It's not some guy who is trying to grab her in the street and say: "All right, go to Syria or I'll beat your face in." No. They're the ones who want to go to Syria, it's their decision. If a girl in France doesn't want to leave, she doesn't have to. But there are a lot of girls who go to be with their husbands. Yes, it's true, most of the girls go for that reason. One of them told me: "Well I came here because my husband is so hot." And yes, let's be honest, the brother was a good-looking man. Hot even. That's how she said it: "I left for my husband's good looks." I was shocked. But at the time it made me laugh.'

Before deciding to return, Safya looked into how women returning from jihad were treated in France. 'When I was over there, I talked about it a little with my mum. I told her that if I was going to be locked up when I came back, it wasn't worth it. And she told me that she had spoken with the Dounia Bouzar's organization and they told her I wasn't really risking anything.'

Before the spring of 2016, jihadist women were not considered a threat to national security. Particularly because women in Syria, unlike men, were not allowed to take part in combat. Unless there is evidence of propaganda activity online, or the recruitment of other women to go to Syria, most are not prosecuted. Moreover, for these young women, who are often psychologically unstable and sometimes traumatized by their experience and who usually have no criminal or prison history, detention tends to be perceived by the judicial and prison authorities as an aggravating factor in their radicalization. While in prison, they are also more likely to engage in the jihadist proselytism of ordinary prisoners who may be open to it.

Impossible to escape from the Islamic State without a husband or guardian

Of the 200 people who have returned from Syria, only about 20 have been women. Leaving the jihadist ranks is infinitely more complicated for them than it is for men. Without the accompaniment and authorization of a husband or guardian, it is virtually impossible for women to flee. There are a few exceptions: some have been smuggled out by rebel groups hostile to the IS and active in its territories, and resisting it in the form of underground operational cells. Only 3 of the 20 or so women who have managed to get out of Syria have been placed under arrest in a dedicated prison block, in Fresnes, France, unlike the men, for whom incarceration in France is now automatic. The oldest of these, nicknamed 'Granny Jihad', around 50 years old, was converted and radicalized by her son, a well-known figure in the IS. Another, much younger woman known as the 'ISIS match maker' by the media was released on parole under court supervision. The third was none other than Oum Hafs, the wife of 'Bilel', whose story is told in this book.

This legal doctrine is evolving, however, in the face of the increasing number of thwarted attacks that have been planned by often very young women (even minors). In August 2016, the French anti-terrorism prosecutor's office in Paris announced it was going to increase the severity with which it treated them.[3] Things began to change when the first failed terrorist attack using a car filled with gas cylinders was uncovered in central Paris in September 2016. The attack had been planned by three women.

Since then, Safya has returned to the life of a not-so-diligent student. 'I went back to my classes quietly in my old university.' When she finds the time, she attends classes for the master's degree in education she interrupted when she left for Syria. She holds a vocational diploma, but she suspects that her past may well complicate the exercise of a professional activity in this area. During her detention, an internal intelligence investigator reminded her of this fact. 'They knew my whole background at the DGSI. They asked me: "So you're studying education?" I said "yeah." And they asked: "You think that you're going to find a job in education after what you did?" Frankly, it was quite demoralizing.' She had always dreamed of working as a special needs teacher, but she finally gave up on having a professional project. 'I'm just not interested in working. Maybe working from home, but not going to work with men. It'll be hard, financially speaking, but I know how to get by without much money.' She currently gets by on welfare and with the support of her parents. She lives alone in a small apartment in the city centre. Her baby, only a few months old, was conceived and borne in Syria but was finally delivered in France. A nanny helps her watch it when she's attending classes at the university.

Her child shows signs of psychological problems that worry her. She has also consulted an infant psychologist. 'I made an appointment for my daughter – she wakes up suddenly, she tenses up and she starts screaming and screaming. So I went to see a psychologist because I was really scared, and the psychologist asked me how my pregnancy went, and whether there were things that bothered me during it. I told him: "No, it went really well", because I wasn't going to tell him . . . I didn't want to go into it. But afterwards I realized that's what it was. A baby feels everything. I'm really pissed off with myself.' Despite this, for the first few weeks Safya thought she had made a huge mistake returning to France. At first, she was even angry at her parents for pushing her to come back to the country she despised. But she has gradually changed her mind since. Nevertheless, she still doesn't regret the time she spent inside the Islamic State, which she looks back on with the same casual attitude as she would a year spent studying abroad.

'Sharia is sharia, that's all!'

Safya left the IS more for economic and family reasons than because she now disagreed with the group's ideology. Her baby is the main reason for her return to France. One day she went to the hospital in Raqqa for an ultrasound scan and witnessed a childbirth. At the end of a hallway, she saw a young woman in pain, supported by her mother. She had to bring her baby into the world without an epidural. It was like a wake-up call for Safya. She couldn't imagine giving birth under such conditions, without her mother and without an epidural. 'Quite frankly, I admire the women who give birth in Syria. There are lots of women who have their babies delivered over there. They don't all die. But they don't really know how to give epidurals over there. Everybody warns against it, so the women give birth without an epidural. But I couldn't. I was afraid. In terms of hygiene, it's very far from French standards. And, psychologically, it was too hard to hear my mum crying, begging me to come back. I was expecting, and she was telling me that I was going to deprive her of all of that, and I didn't have the right to do it. Those things really get to you.'

After this realization, Safya confided her fears to her husband, a French fighter, and urged him to find a way to return to France as soon as possible. 'We had asked the *dawla* to let us leave. We wanted to be honest about it, but they said no. So I said to myself: "I'm a free woman, I can do what I want. If I want to leave, I leave. I'm not in prison." We decided to go into hiding and leave. But it was forbidden and super-hard to leave the *dawla*.'

Her husband had just made a video celebrating the terrorist attacks on *Charlie Hebdo* and the Hyper Cacher grocery store in Paris, calling for new attacks in France. He had associated with some of the most dangerous and most sought-after French nationals within the IS. The couple shared an apartment in Raqqa with a man from Belgium, who was a close associate of Abdelhamid Abaaoud, the coordinator of the 13 November attacks in Paris. The jihadist was well known for his videos, in particular of the beheadings of prisoners. 'He was so nice, he made me laugh so much', Safya says. 'But he was messed up in the head. When you talk to him you think he's a really calm guy. But he's totally into *dawla*. You don't notice it when you talk to him. He had cut a *murtad*'s throat and decapitated him in a video, and he said to the people of Belgium: "Yes, we're going to do that to you." But when you talk to him, he's a super nice guy. Calm and collected.'

Safya's husband knew that the French authorities would be waiting for him, but he went ahead with it. The couple managed to escape by mixing into the flood of refugees with a group of migrants. In Turkey, after a few days of tourism in a hotel in Istanbul, they went to the French consulate, who had them arrested by the Turkish police, who proved to be relatively kind to the couple. 'The Turkish cops were so cool with us that we got scared. They didn't put handcuffs on us, and one of them said to us: "Yes, the *dawla* are right." He said that France was full of assholes. We looked at each other and said: "Damn, this guy is *dawla*."' And, in fact, they were real Turkish police officers who took them to an administrative detention centre before they were sent back to France, where the police were waiting for them. Unlike Safya, her husband is currently incarcerated in France, presumably for several years.

'I had everything I wanted in terms of clothes and perfumes, so it was perfect'

Safya feels guilty for making her family suffer, but she doesn't regret her commitment to jihadism. If she hadn't gotten pregnant she probably wouldn't have considered returning. First of all, 'because, quite frankly, yes, I had it good in the Islamic State. I was with my husband, we had our apartment, we had everything we needed. And as a woman, I had everything I wanted in terms of clothes and perfumes, so it was perfect. I had French sisters I could talk to. I was never alone.' She stayed with her husband in a large apartment that belonged to an upper-class family in Syria before the arrival of the jihadists, who took over what would become their capital city in early 2014. Safya knew this because the owners left their home so quickly that they didn't have time to take most of their photos and personal belongings with them. 'They left all their papers. You could tell they'd left in a hurry. There were clothes in the closets. It was clear that they took the bare minimum with them and rushed out. It was a great apartment. Really big. It had a big living room, a big kitchen with the most modern appliances, like an American-style kitchen, a bathroom and two bedrooms with a shower.'

Taking over the apartment, still filled with the belongings of its previous occupants, didn't trouble Safya. 'Well, no, because I was told that the previous owner was a *murtad*, an apostate.' A few months later, when leaving the IS, a smuggler who knew the former owners before they had fled, told her another story. 'It turned out that they weren't apostates after all. The man was a professor of Islamic studies, but who didn't support the *dawla*, who said that it wasn't the true Islam and he had had his property taken away. They told him to get out of his home and leave. And that his house didn't belong to him any more. The smuggler told me that he had taken refuge in Turkey with his family.'

Nor did Safya complain of the food in Syria – except for her brief stay in Fallujah, Iraq, where conditions were much more frugal. 'I lost eight kilos in two months. I didn't eat anything. They'd serve us birds they'd shot out of the sky. It was disgusting. So I said to myself: I don't care, I'm just not going to eat any more. When I got to Syria I was elated. I made up for it in no time. When we got back from Iraq, they had almost all the products you could get in France: lasagne, Barill pasta, Snickers, Kinder. You could get whatever you wanted.'

Safya is released

While in detention, a few weeks after returning to France to see her family and give birth, Safya is still openly in favour of the Islamic State. She even regrets having returned. She swears that she never hid her convictions, even from the investigators. "In terms of sharia, they do it right over there because they really apply it', she says without hesitating, 'and no Muslim can dispute that, because otherwise he's not a Muslim. We had all the videos before they were released. So I saw everything. Like *Salil Sawarim 4*,[4] where they cut off the heads of all those pilots. It was very well done, like in a film. It showed brothers walking by to the music of *dawla*, each of them holding a knife. They had them kneel down and then the guy dressed all in black spoke and then they cut their heads off. I thought: "They're brave to do that, I couldn't do it." I explained that to the DGSI, but they didn't want to listen. I told them that sharia is sharia. I wasn't the one who made it up. Sharia is part of the Muslim religion, so I won't change what I think about it. And they asked me if I agreed with those acts and if they had to be killed. I told them: "It's part of sharia! It doesn't matter if I agree or disagree, OK? Sharia is sharia, that's all!" There you go. What else could I do? That really got their attention . . . But I don't know, they were idiots.'

The unambiguous nature of her position didn't keep her from being released from custody. It did, however, warrant her remaining under police surveillance. Safya is regularly summoned to the police station. She believes that her telephone is tapped, and that she is tailed by a car belonging to the intelligence services. Her parents, who don't share her ideas, also keep a close watch on her.

Six months later, when we met Safya for another interview, the young woman had changed her position somewhat. Since that time, there had been the attacks of 13 November 2015 in Paris, leaving 130 dead. She now says that she has rejected the Islamic State and has returned to a Salafist Quietist approach to Islam, while still bearing strong ill will towards France and feeling herself closer to the 'sisters of the *salafya*'. Safya, nevertheless, stays in daily contact with her French sisters in Syria through the internet. Her relations with the more determined members are sometimes electric. 'When I came back to France, they thought I was a piece of shit.' But many others contact her because they too want to flee the IS. 'Yeah, there are a lot of them. Most of them because they didn't think their lives would be like that over there. But it's almost impossible to come back now.'

Her friends from before jihad have turned their backs on her. 'They call me "the terrorist". I had one friend I was very close to, but she's mad at me because she saw how my mother was when I left. She told me: "A normal person couldn't do that to her parents. I can't be friends with someone like that."' Safya understands her. She spends her time immersed in religious books of the Salafist Quietist persuasion. 'Even in the lecture hall at the university I sit in the back and study. Right now I'm working on the *Tawhid* by Ibn Qayyim[5] translated into French.' This self-taught learner, who doesn't speak Arabic, refuses to step into a mosque in France. 'The people in the French mosques are completely out of touch. They hang the French flag outside. Wait, excuse me? That's way out of place. They're nuts. There's no democracy in Islam. Should I go and talk to a French imam so he can tell me to become a good citizen? No!'

She continues to reject the French Republic and French mosques as a whole. She still can't imagine her future in France. Her unease hasn't gone away. She now speaks of her desire to undertake *hijra* – no longer in Syria but in Yemen this time, an important destination for Salafist Quietists. 'Some sisters talked to me about it. There's a group of sisters who wants to leave. I can't stay in France any longer. I hate France. I don't feel at home in France.'

Lena, the women and the desire to kill

Lena,[6] too, has returned to France, but still dreams of the Islamic State and even of terrorist attacks in France. She spent more than one year in Syria before returning. She was disappointed with her experience, but remains attached to the ideology. 'If I could do it again, I'd pack my bags and go back', she says without hesitation. In France, this student came from a working-class family with Algerian parents. She had only worn the niqab for two months before abandoning her studies to leave for Syria to join a French jihadist whom she had met on the internet a few weeks before her departure, at the end of 2014. Despite financial difficulties in the beginning, she says that they were very happy and 'fell in love'.

But six months later, her husband was killed in battle and the complications began. As a widow without a protector, she was placed against her will in a women's home. Her property was taken away from her and she ended up being imprisoned on suspicion of espionage. She managed to escape a few months later under confused circumstances. She says that she was 'terribly mistreated' within the IS, and was subjected to physical and psychological violence. And yet she remains deeply enamoured with the organization and its project.

The group's rank-and-file members, according to her, are responsible for its problems, especially the French fighters, who have 'imported their gangster form of *jahiliya*', whereas the upper hierarchy has retained its purity. In fact, after her experience with the mother cell in Syria, she is considering leaving again, but this time to go to the Libyan branch of the IS, located in the former Kadhafist bastion of Sirte. In that city, there are fewer French nationals, who are well known for their bad behaviour – perhaps no more than thirty. This new IS franchise has, according to her, learned from the errors committed in the Levant. But the offensive launched by the Libyan forces in Misrata in May 2016, supported by American bombing operations, ruined her hopes of a second *hijra*. Her identity papers have been confiscated and she is currently free under court supervision, in a France which she hates, awaiting her trial for 'criminal association for the purpose of committing acts of terrorism'.

Jilbab, black gloves, make-up and a little Chanel bag

Wrapped in a long jilbab[7] and wearing black gloves, this short woman doesn't go unnoticed in the streets of Paris. At the ripe age of 22, she would like to wear the full niqab, but French law prevents it. On the other hand, she allows herself to wear make-up and one beauty accessory: a small Chanel bag in quilted black leather, hanging from her shoulder on a gold strap. 'It was a gift', she explains, showing its certificate of authenticity. Behind her elegant looks, her plump cheeks and her clear voice, Lena doesn't hide her penchant for terrorism for very long. 'Targeted attacks like *Charlie Hebdo* are very important. The day *Charlie Hebdo* was attacked was one of the most beautiful days of my life', she says with a broad smile. Then in an angry tone: 'I'd be so happy if something like that would happen again. And I hope that the next targeted attack will be done by a sister.' During the *Charlie Hebdo* attack, which was claimed by the Yemeni branch of Al Qaeda, a rival of the Islamic State, Lena was in Raqqa, a bastion of the IS. 'Everyone was happy. The cars were honking in the streets. It was Al Qaeda, but the next day the IS hit the Hyper Cacher[8] and all of a sudden we were all united. There were no more differences.'

In Syria, she had daily contact for months with the French women of the Islamic State. She is perfectly aware of their iron determination in support of jihad. The stories she tells are highly informative. She remembers meeting a mother of a large family of eleven – including her husband, his daughter and three sons – who had all left together in a camper-van from Strasbourg to join the IS. On that day, the French mother, who had already lost her husband and her 12-year-old son (the youngest French national killed in Syria) in fighting since the family's arrival, had just learned that another one of her sons, 14 years old, had also been killed. She received a bonus of 800 dollars from the IS for his death. 'When we saw each other, we took off our sitars. She was wiping away tears. She kept repeating "Alhamdulillah, Alhamdulillah." And I said to her: "It's okay, stay strong", and so forth. And she responded: "No, on the contrary, Alhamdulillah, I'm so happy." She was actually crying for joy because her son had been shot dead at a *razoua* [Author's note: an attack] in combat. I'm sure she was sad too, because her husband was gone and she'd lost her sons. She only had one son left, who was 11 or 12, and she had married her 13-year-old daughter to a 22-year-old fighter. But she was surely thinking about her son's martyrdom', which would help her to be absolved of her sins.

The main mission of the women

According to data provided by the French authorities, of the 700 French citizens active in Syria and Iraq in the summer of 2016, 280 were women. In addition, there are currently approximately 420 French children in the area. One-third of them were born there. Within the IS, the main mission of the women is to raise the next generation of jihadists. This situation is unprecedented. It is the first time in the history of contemporary jihadism that children have been born and been socialized within this ideology. Children raised to kill, in the love of jihad.

According to Lena, these children are trained to fight from the age of 7. 'I saw a lot of young children, babies, 5- and 6-year-olds. They're always with their mothers. Normal schools – ones with history, geography, maths and all that – don't exist over there at all. But they're starting to open Koranic schools. The little ones don't start fighting right away, but they go through a *muaskar*, that is, military training with weapons, which they start sometimes at the age of 7, but normally starting at 10 or 11.'

After their military training, some of these little French jihadists, known as the 'lion cubs of the caliphate', are used to execute prisoners in videos and are sent to the front. Safya also knew some of the French children who were killed in combat. 'They put them on the list of *inghimasi*.[9] They send them there first. The emir tells them: "You guys are *inghimasi*, you have nothing to worry about, you're going to heaven. I hope you won't die, but if you die, don't worry because you're going straight to heaven."' For the women, the death of a husband, a brother or a son is often experienced as a divine blessing. They believe that he will reach the rank of martyr and therefore be granted divine favours. They also hope that he will absolve them of their sins by opening the doors of paradise for them, as part of the promised intercession for seventy people of their choice, once they have reached the afterlife.

Between 2014 and 2016, the Islamic State claimed between sixty and eighty suicide attacks per month, on average. Since the first French kamikaze attack carried out by a Toulouse convert in Syria in 2013, at least forty of the 200 French presumed dead in Syria and Iraq have chosen to carry out suicide operations. According to another Frenchman, a convert to Islam of Caribbean origin, interrogated in February 2015 shortly before carrying out a suicide attack in Iraq, such highly murderous sacrifices are thought to be 'a consecration' by the jihadists. He explained: 'I'm in a hurry because I want to meet my lord and kill as many *murtadin* as possible. I want to be killed and to add the *kuffar* (unbelievers) to my body count. We're the only ones to do that because we sacrifice for our religion. The *kuffar* and the *murtadin* know deep down that they're fighting for their passions. They're enjoying their earthly lives, while waiting to burn in the flames in hell. The French are really determined in that regard. Among the Europeans, they're the ones who do the most *dogmas*.[10] My mission is to open up an area with a Hummer loaded with three tons of explosives. It's to allow the brothers to move forward by inflicting enormous losses upon the enemy and spreading fear. But we're driven by our faith. It's not because we've had a bad life here. Why would I be afraid? It's bi'idnillah [Author's note: 'by the grace of Allah'], a key to heaven.'

A waiting list for kamikazes

The morbid smiles seen on the face of suicide bombers before their bombing missions comes from their fanatical conviction that they are doing good by killing those they consider to be enemies of their religion. And from their assurance that both they and their loved ones will reach paradise. The wives of those about to carry out a suicide attack will sometimes remind their husbands not to forget to intercede in their favour with God in the afterlife. Such requests, however, are not always well received in the jihadist circles: in order for a sacrifice of one's life to be considered valid, it must be done only for God, and not for the attacker or his loved ones. It is the intention that counts, at the risk of losing the favours granted to a martyr.

According to several testimonies from those who have returned from Syria, and from jihadists still there, candidates for suicide attacks for the Islamic State must sign their names on a waiting list. All suicide bombers are volunteers and are selected by the organization. They're brought together in a *maqqar* or barracks reserved especially for them, and they go through a specific training programme. The Islamic State ensures, in particular, their determination, in order to avoid choosing a candidate who might hesitate at the last moment before blowing himself up. Not only would such a hesitation lead to the failure of the mission, it would also risk discrediting the group's claim to hard-line terrorism.

When an emir is looking for a kamikaze, from any area controlled by the IS, the candidates are often given a week on 'holiday' at a large hotel in Mosul or Raqqa with their relatives for a final farewell. Some record videos to be broadcast on the internet after their death. Others prefer to go to their deaths in secret, without any form of ostentation, sometimes without even informing their family back home in France.

The women demand the right to carry out suicide attacks

Women are still prohibited from fighting and, as yet, are not allowed to carry out *dogmas*. Many of them are frustrated that they are not allowed to participate in what they consider a priceless opportunity: reaching heaven through a suicide bombing. 'The waiting list for *dogmas* is huge', Safya confirms. 'Several sisters asked to be added to it, but their emirs refused.' Lena remembers that when the Strasbourg mother learned of the death of her second son she wrote a long letter directly to the emir of the IS himself, Abu Bakr al-Baghdadi, to beg him to allow her, exceptionally, to carry out a suicide attack. 'She told me that because her sons and husband had been killed, and because her family was so well known, she might get Baghdadi to agree to make an exception for her. She thought she could convince him to let her carry out a suicide mission near Baghdadi's city in Iraq. That's what she wanted. She left the very next day. Since then, no news.'

Almost no activities are organized for the women. French women, most of whom don't speak Arabic, spend the majority of their time with Belgian women. As they would back in France, they go on shopping trips to Raqqa, or visit each other in their apartments to drink tea when their husbands are off fighting, often for several days or weeks at a time. Most of their conversations revolve around terrorist attacks in France. Many of the women dream of carrying out such attacks back home. Most carry a Kalashnikov and wear an explosive belt under their sitar. 'They're proud of their weapons. They completely support their husbands. When there are terrorist attacks, they're the first to shout for joy and rejoice', says Lena. 'There was one sister who used to say: "I'll go back to France, bi'idnillah via Greece, and I'll cut all their throats." We weren't allowed to go back home, but she would say to me: "If I tell them what I want to do, they'll let me go back through Greece." I'm just waiting for the order from Baghdadi to go fight.'

In the evenings, Safya recalls that some women 'would even rehearse terrorist attacks. We'd return to France with fake passports for the 14th of July, go into the crowd, take off our jilbabs and start shooting. One woman said she was going to use a pillow to make it look like she was pregnant. She said she'd fill it with dynamite to blow herself up when François Hollande passed through the crowd.'

Safya and Lena both agree that, even though women might not have the right to take part in combat operations now, this won't always be the case. Lena explains that by the time she left the IS at the end of 2015, training camps for women had already been set up. 'The women have been trained. When I left the Islamic State they had just created a *muaskar*, a training camp for women. It was just starting. Weapons and religion. There's no doubt they'll be allowed to fight someday. They're going to start running out of men and the borders are being closed. A lot of men are being stopped at the border or even at the airport before leaving. And many are being killed in combat. They've got to be replaced.' Safya also confirms this trend. 'All of the *dawla* sisters want to fight. When I came to Syria I wanted to take up arms too.

I don't know why. Maybe it was stupid, but it gave me a feeling of power.'

An early version of the car bomb terrorist cell in Paris

They would be proven right a few months later. The role of women in the IS began to change in September 2016: first, a terrorist cell comprised of three women was arrested in France by the anti-terrorist police after failing to detonate a car loaded with gas cylinders in the middle of Paris. They had been encouraged to do so by a Frenchman based in Mosul, Iraq, and they applied his instructions (sent by the Telegram messaging service) down to the letter. At the time of their arrest, the youngest of the terrorists, only 19 years old, attacked the plainclothes police officers who were keeping watch over them, wounding a civil servant with a knife. The judicial authorities, who had previously considered such women as victims, understood that jihadist women had been benefiting from a gender bias.

Described as 'fanaticized' by the Paris public prosecutor François Molins, they are at least as determined as the men, if not more. Soon after this event, the Islamic State officially claimed credit for a failed attack organized by three women against a police station in Mombasa, Kenya, indicating a shift in the group's strategy. Presented as 'sympathizers' by the group's propaganda arm, *Amaq*, these women had simply been encouraged to act on its behalf, without having received any military training. This official recognition demonstrates that the group's hierarchy no longer prevents women from carrying out attacks in its name. The time when the women of the Islamic State were not allowed to fight is now over.

However, the only currently known example of a female paramilitary unit within the IS is the Islamic police force for women. At the end of 2014, in order to ensure the application of sharia to women while maintaining a strict separation between the sexes, the organization set up a brigade made up exclusively of women, known as the 'women's *hisbah*'. This armed body within the jihadist proto-state is composed mostly of foreigners and is responsible in particular for enforcing the obligation to wear the full-length veil on Syrian women. But after a few months, the local residents began complaining about the violence with which the police force carried out its activities. The IS finally decided to end the experiment to keep the local population from turning against it. 'The women's *hisbah* was created so that women could correct women, and not men', says Lena. 'But the women turned out to be too violent, so the men said stop. Generally, it was the Tunisian women who carried out the punishments. They used to beat the Syrian women. They'd kick or slap them in the street. For example, a Syrian woman in a niqab who wore lots of make-up or tried to make her hair look long – she'd get smacked. The Tunisian women had bad reputations, just like the Chechen women. Every time there was a problem someone would say: "We're going to get the Tunisians." They were considered to be the meanest. There were lots of complaints about them for hitting too hard. It's just supposed to be a little smack, you're just correcting her: "Take off that flower or lower your niqab or put on a sitar." You don't just beat a girl down to the ground for it. That's why the women's *hisbah* was disbanded.'

In France, jihadist women are as difficult to dissuade from the ideology as the men. On her return from Syria, Lena, free but still marked by violent radicalism, has no faith in the 'deradicalization' programmes run by the French Interior Ministry that she is obliged to follow. 'I just went once. And never returned', she says. 'I've never been an alcoholic in my life. But that's what it felt like. When you show up wearing a niqab or a jilbab, somebody pipes up with a "salam alaykum." They talk to us like we're old alcoholics, squinting their eyes and asking us in a quiet voice: "So, what led you to ISIS?" That's really how it is. It's so funny. They talk to us like we were lost, things like: "So your family didn't take care of you?" And then for me it was: "Hey, would you mind going on

BFMTV[11] with us?" I felt like a little lab rat. De-radicalization for me is a neologism that they just made up out of thin air. What's it supposed to mean, anyway?'

Clearly, the programmes have had no significant effect on this young woman's level of radicalism. She may have left behind the Islamic State, but not their ideology.

'I felt powerful. Better than everyone else'

Before joining the Islamic State, they were students in France like so many others. They've returned, but they still want to leave France, and consider jihad as something positive. How did this happen? Safya and Lena agreed to meet with us and tell us their stories over the course of several months. They don't know each other, but both have similar sociological profiles and motivations. They're both under 25, grew up 'on housing estates' in provincial France and have non-divorced parents and several brothers. Both were born in France to parents born in the Maghreb. Both hold high school diplomas – a vocational diploma for one, and a general diploma with distinction for the other. They were both rather good university students before joining the IS. Lena is also passionate about classical literature. Both women received a religious education – Lena even went to a Koranic school as a child – before moving away from Islam as adolescents, only to return to it in a radical and sudden manner, just after turning 20.

'We've all had a traumatic experience at one point in our lives', Lena confesses, trying to explain why women embrace jihad. Well, perhaps not all, she explains, but many of the women she met in Syria had had chaotic moments in their lives. 'Not all of them, but many women, sure. I knew girls who had difficult pasts. One of them had been molested and raped by her father, another spent time in a psychiatric hospital because her parents beat her. And then there were lots of women who had problems with their parents after converting to Islam. Their parents just didn't agree with the religion.' Did Lena herself convert to the ideology after a particularly traumatic event? 'No', she says, hesitantly. 'I had a problem when I was a teenager, but it wasn't the kind of thing to make me pack my bags and take off. I got over it pretty quickly. Nothing serious. One of God's tribulations.' She refused to elaborate further.

Safya, who claims never to have suffered anything particularly traumatic, seems less convinced by this interpretation. 'A girl who gets raped and manages to talk about it is strong. Especially if she talks to a man', she concedes. While no general law can be derived in the total absence of statistics, the numerous interviews we have conducted confirm this empirical observation: many of the women who have joined the jihadi movement have experienced domestic or sexual abuse, parental abandonment, prostitution or drug addiction. In these cases, an ideology promising paradise and atonement for sins for oneself and for one's loved ones after a life of earthly tribulations offers the hope of redemption.

Wearing a full veil as a 'liberating' experience

However, female jihadism can't be completely explained from this angle alone. Many different factors are at play, often identical to those for men. Nevertheless, Safya's and Lena's stories reveal troubled relationships with men, and problematic positions in French society determined by gender and ethnicity. Both describe wearing a full veil as a 'liberating' experience. 'You can't understand if you're not a Muslim and if you're not a woman', Safya explains, 'you cover yourself up and it makes you feel freer. You feel like no one can touch you.' They describe their decision to wear the full veil firstly as a response to an existential malaise, and only secondly as a religious prescription.

The full veil protects them against the judgements of men. 'All those clichés about a blonde girl in a miniskirt. People ask immediately: "Who is this girl? Why is she dressed like that?" So, of course, they're going to judge her. I think the veil frees us from all those stereotypes. People in France will always judge you on your physical appearance. I figured that in an Islamic State where everyone is veiled from head to toe, and where people don't look at the shape of your body or the clothes you wear – that means we're all equal. Yes, I liked that. Right now, I can't deal with being judged by my physical appearance.'

Safya shares exactly the same opinion. 'It's really a religious thing. When you put on the niqab, people won't judge you, they'll say "you're an extremist", but they won't say "she's easy".'

Both women say they were timid and not particularly social before jihadism. 'I was a pretty normal girl. I mean the kind you can find anywhere', says Lena. 'I never went to clubs or smoked hookah pipes or anything like that. When I was 17 I started working at McDonald's while I was studying. Even having a drink with girlfriends was rare for me. I've always been somewhat reserved in that regard.' Like Safya, Lena says that she embraced jihadism and started wearing a full veil only a few months before leaving for Syria, despite the fact that her mother doesn't wear the veil at all. 'My parents weren't good Muslims. When I started following the IS, I realized that my place wasn't in France. Suddenly everything disgusted me. Even my mother, because she didn't pray. I had to remind her to do it, she didn't want to. And she smokes. In my eyes she was a Westerner, she'd go out to the bar with her girlfriends. She had physical contact with men at work. Her job disgusted me. I asked her to stop and she said: "OK, are you going to pay the bills?" She took a trip to Dubai all by herself. I said to her: "You're leaving without your husband, without your *mahram*.[12] You disgust me." I was really hard on her.' She began to wear a jilbab four months before leaving for Syria and the niqab two months before. The same was true for Safya, who began to cover her head and body just six months before leaving for Syria.

From their contact with the group's propaganda, Lena and Safya became convinced that women in the jihadi movement were treated like precious flowers surrounded by a protective community, unlike in the West where they were treated like objects. 'How do people look at women now because of the television reality shows? What is a woman worth in the West? I'm a Muslim woman and in our religion women are honoured and respected. Women give life. We're considered real women under Islam, not like in the West where a woman is treated like a piece of meat. The *kuffars* say things like "your girl is fine" to their friends. Our brothers wouldn't say that.' But once in Syria, as we shall see, she discovered that the opposite was true.

A 'land of humiliation'

Born into a working-class neighbourhood and sensitive to a consumerist culture she does not necessarily have access to, Lena feels that the full veil trumps class relations. 'That's right', she says, 'the more clothing I wear, the more covered I am, the more I feel like I'm equal to the person in front of me. Girls wear the veil out of modesty, it breaks down barriers, we speak from one Muslim woman to another. It's no longer one rich girl in branded jeans talking to another girl who isn't so well-off. We speak as equals. Islam puts us all on the same pedestal. It doesn't matter if you're rich, black, poor or Arab, it's all the same.'

When asked 'Why the IS?' two words come up again and again: 'pride' and 'humiliation'. They consider France 'a land of humiliation', where Muslims are excluded from political, economic and media power, and where the permanent demand to assimilate in the name of the universalizing myth of the French Republic doesn't equate to real possibilities for the social advancement of all citizens. 'I've always felt inferior because I'm a Muslim', says Lena, reiterating her hatred of France. Postcolonial resentment also plays a role: she even begrudges her family for having emigrated from Algeria. 'I realized that I clearly had no place in French society and that my parents were slaves here. I refused to be like them. I'm of Algerian origin, my grandfather died during the [Algerian] war. I don't like to use the word "war", because it wasn't an equal fight. I prefer to say "French genocide". Jihad means fighting to regain the dignity we lost, the dignity they wanted to destroy. You could say that that's what attracted me to it.'

Secularism, propounded since 1905 as a guarantee of religious freedom and the neutrality of the French state, is understood as a tool used against Islam. The two young women, driven by their rejection of France and their conviction that *hijra* is an obligation for every Muslim, saw the proclamation of the caliphate as a dream opportunity. A state where the humiliated followers of 'true Islam' would finally turn the tables on their masters.

'For the first time we had the hope of a country for Muslims. Finally we had a caliphate, we were going to regain our *izza*, our dignity, our pride. After the Holocaust, the Jews wanted their own country and they got it. How many years have the Muslims been waiting? Why do they keep making laws against us? If it's not the veil, it's something else. There's always something that comes out against us. They took away our dignity. I know a lot of Muslims who say: "We're Muslims but we don't practise." It's like they need to apologize for being Muslim. I'm not like that. I'm very proud of being a Muslim. It's the most beautiful thing about me. I love Allah more than my parents, more than anything else. I love the Prophet SAWS[13] even more than my family. We had to regain our honour. *Hijra* is an obligation. I don't feel French, I feel Muslim. I don't need a nationality. I couldn't care less if they took away my passport. My identity is being a Muslim. I don't support the Westerners, they disgust me. I don't want my children to go to a school where they'll learn to respect a person who changes his sex, or why a man loves another man. We can't accept that.'

First comes the embracing of non-violent radicalism

This rhetoric comes straight from the internet, downloadable in PDF format, far from the mosques that both women reject completely. It provides a mental and emotional structure for those who adhere to it. Safya now admits: 'Radicalism stopped scaring me. I was in my bubble; no one could touch me. I felt protected. And I think that all the sisters of *dawla* felt that way.' The movement's propaganda transformed her fears into a feeling of omnipotence. Adhering to the IS, with its extremely marked and standardized group think, had a cathartic effect. Embracing the ideology became a way of overcoming frustrations. 'I considered that power in France belonged only to the unbelievers, whereas it should belong to the Muslims', says Safya. 'We should be the masters, not the other way around. I felt inferior before accepting *dawla*. When I embraced *dawla*, I felt powerful. Better than everyone else. I was like: "Yeah, I'm *dawla*, what's the problem? You've got nothing to say to me, I'm better than you."'

The two young women made their first jihad contacts on the social networks, after having returned to a radical – albeit still non-violent – form of Islam. Safya's mother is a non-practising Muslim; her father is Jewish. She therefore considers that she has converted back to Islam. Her mother is self-employed and her father runs a small construction business. Her return to Islam was guided by her bearded brothers in kamis, who had recently adopted Quietist Salafism. 'In the beginning, yes, they were the ones who influenced me because, before, my brothers weren't anything at all, they went out at night, they smoked. But when they returned to religion, I was so relieved. It even helped bring me closer to the religion myself. I then started to spend time with veiled sisters. They wore the jilbab and everything. They seemed really happy to me, almost carefree, as if they had nice lives. So that's what got me into it. At first I was moderate, but then I became less moderate.'

Before leaving for Syria, she had only been practising Islam for two years. Before joining the Islamic State, she had been expressing jihadist convictions for only six months. How did she make contact with these circles? 'Facebook. That's it', she says. 'I started looking into *dawla* on Facebook a good six months before embracing this *minhaj* [Author's note: a current of Islam] because, before, like most people, I thought they were terrorists who didn't understand Islam at all. But when I started to really look into it, I saw that I had been wrong.' She began to join jihadist groups on the social networks. Lena's adoption of radicalism occurred in an almost identical fashion. Both were induced to leave France after daily exchanges on the internet with a young French woman of the same age who was promoting the Islamic State from Syria.

The total rejection of French societal values went hand in hand with a rational adherence to an idealized life project within the Islamic State. From France, the proclamation of the caliphate created a hope that filled an ideological vacuum, one that allowed its adherents to imagine life beyond the mere satisfaction of material needs. 'Well, yes, that played a role of course. The brothers took pictures of themselves with apartments and houses. It was back when they used to post: "Check out the pools behind us." All the girls thought they'd be living the life of Princess Scheherazade in *A Thousand and One Nights*. Why did all those young girls leave? Because they were thinking: "I'll be with my man, my little bearded prince, we'll have children, we'll have our own house, I'll make him nice meals." If someone had told them: "Everything has been destroyed, you'll sleep in tents, life will be very hard, but come anyway", there would be fewer women and children.' These are young women, sometimes still teenagers, who leave with almost no understanding of the religion. 'When you talk to some of them, you realize that they don't know anything about Islam. You're lucky if they know how to pray. And there were girls who were sick of France just because they couldn't find a job.'

'So good, like a princess'

The very rational idea of leaving to found a family and live under the tutelage of an ideal partner in Syria played an important role for both Safya and Lena. This idyllic image of jihad life is promoted both by the official propaganda of the jihadist groups, and by women active on the internet to incite other women to join them. 'The way they describe their lives over there makes you think that it's perfect. Some of the sisters would say things like: "Life is beautiful over there. You're going to have it so good, like a princess. Everyone is a Muslim." And the more you listen to the videos and the *nashids*, the more you get excited about going.' The young women were also attracted to the image of virility conveyed by the propaganda photos, which responded on one hand to the canons of masculine beauty they sought, while at the same time making use of the Western schemas they rejected. In today's society, according to this worldview, men are no longer really men and women are no longer really women. 'There are no more real men in France, and our brothers don't even defend us. Over there, the men are real. They've exchanged their lives with Allah for us. To regain their dignity as Muslims. So yeah, of course all that played a role.'

These religious and political convictions, delivered in ready-made ideological packages, find willing adherents in post-adolescents who are amenable to any form of radicalism. And yet they are the result of a literalist reading of religious texts, which jihadists refuse to interpret and contextualize, contrary to the overwhelming majority of Muslims. The communitarian, anti-Semitic and anti-France discourses and conspiracy theories have often set the stage for this radicalization, within the context of a marginalization of certain sections of the population and single-parent or dysfunctional family units.

According to what we have learned from our numerous interviews with French jihadists, sexual abuse and a desire for purification may also play a role, though the extent of this phenomenon is impossible to determine. Jihadist circles are not immune to the banality of flirting 2.0 in the age of Tinder. Fundamentalist thought gets lost in a confusion of ethnic origins, self-interest and desires for personal fulfilment and religious redemption. It offers the illusion of belonging to a protective and powerful social group. Even though all of these factors are socially determined, the commitment to jihadism remains nonetheless a rational decision, driven by genuine religious convictions and the hope of reversing social relations and escaping sociological determinants.

Safya and Lena were fully aware of the terrorist nature of the group they were joining before they left. They saw the group's commitment to extreme violence and its exactions as legitimate, in the name of a higher project presented as both revolutionary and universalist, but which ultimately spoke directly to their bruised egos. Their decision was motivated by a transcendental hope for revenge, whether in response to social ills or to family problems – in the same way, and according to the same social dynamics, as the men.

Express weddings and quick divorces

Safya got married over Skype, alone in her room in France, under a full veil and unbeknownst to her family. As a newcomer to the jihadist milieu, which she had only been frequenting online for six months, she was somewhat nonplussed by this manner of forming a religious union. 'Nobody else was there, I was all alone in my room. I really started wondering about the whole thing.' Beyond a few weeks of exchanges over the internet, she had yet to meet her future husband in person. She had only seen his selfies in Syria on Facebook, where he posed as a valiant mujahideen fighter with a Kalashnikov, turban, kamis and trainers, looking like a cross between a neighbourhood rapper and an eighth-century Bedouin.

Medhi and Safya were from different regions in France, but they were about the same age and shared the same social codes. Both grew up in inner cities. Before embracing *minhaj jihadi*, they were both in contact with Salafist Quietists. Both were born in France, came from Maghrebian immigration and grew up in working-class families. Both received a religious education. When they met, Medhi was in Raqqa, the Syrian city that had been the IS's capital since 2014. They were introduced by a 'sister' whom Safya knew from Facebook, in a pro-IS discussion group for women only. Safya, from behind her screen, was a little surprised by the situation. But her future religious husband in Syria reassured her. 'I said: "Wait a minute, I can't do this over Skype, it's too weird." He told me: "No, don't worry, that's how it's done."'

Feelings of love are less important in jihadist unions than religious and political convictions. The encounters never happen by accident. They often come about through classified ads posted on the social networks. In the early 2000s, they were posted on Paltalk, one of the early predecessors of the current social web, and then on Facebook. Today they are found most often on Telegram. Such ads are as poetic and romantic as you might expect in a posting for the sale of a piece of furniture on an auction site: 'Marriage proposal. Salam alaykum, 16-year-old brother seeks an *aqidah* sister for marriage in sha Allah. Only serious proposals please', or '21-year-old sister of African origin looking for a husband. New to the religion. Preferably with a converted brother. She's from the Paris region. Contact me for more information bi iznilah', or 'Salam alaykum, re-convert seeks husband under the age of 27, insha Allah in the north', or '17-year-old man ready to move north because of a family problem! If interested, please contact me in shah Allah.' Virtual unions are tied in this way over the internet between women in France and men in Syria, Iraq or even in French prisons.

'It was ridiculous when I think about it'

That was how Mehdi and Safya met each other. 'For me it wasn't love at first sight, it took time. Of course I wanted to see Mehdi, but it was more for religious reasons that I decided to leave.' Medhi wasn't alone in his apartment in Raqqa for their marriage. The young man, who confessed that he only began to pray after his arrival in Syria, asked 'two brothers' from the IS to act as witnesses. A third Frenchman, a *Sharai*, was also present to act as the religious guarantee for the union. 'He told me the guy was a *Sharai*, somebody who knows sharia law by heart, and then he found two witnesses and we got married.' During the ceremony, Safya had to show her approval but without uttering a word. 'It's done really quickly over Skype. Less than a minute. The woman just says yes. But her voice can't be heard. She just has to nod with her head under her sitar. The *Sharai* said something in Arabic that I didn't understand. Then he asked Medhi if he accepted. He said yes. Then he asked me. I nodded and that was it.'

Safya now casts a critical eye on the experience. 'Maybe I was naive. It was ridiculous when I think about it. I was all alone in my room. It was pretty stupid actually. Nobody gets married like that.' From behind her computer, Safya had no idea of the importance of the man responsible for sealing her online marriage, several thousand kilometres from her student room.

The *Sharai* in question was one of the most dangerous and sought-after jihadists in the Islamic State. Abu Muqatil al-Tunisi, otherwise known as Boubaker el-Hakim, was one of the five most important Frenchmen in the group's hierarchy. The 30-year-old emir already had fifteen years of jihad under his belt, a career in terror that summarized the last fifteen years of the international jihadi movement. In 2003, at the age of 19, this native of the nineteenth *arrondissement* of Paris also belonged to the same Buttes-Chaumont terrorist network[14] as the Kouachi brothers. He was one of the first Frenchmen to fight the Americans in Iraq, whose Baathist regime was then welcoming foreign volunteers with the complicity of the Assad government. In 2004, after his brother was killed in the battle for Fallujah, he was arrested in Syria and sent back to France. Sentenced to seven years in prison, he was released in 2011 just as the Tunisian revolution broke out. Being himself of Tunisian origin, he joined the local jihadist movement Ansar al-Sharia, then in full swing, and settled down near one of its mosques in a middle-class neighbourhood in Tunis.

From 2011 to 2013, he was involved in the trafficking of heavy weapons from Libya to Tunisia. He helped to militarize the Tunisian jihadist movement as it prepared for insurrection. In 2013, he was a member of the commando team that assassinated Chokri Belaïd, an important figure of the Tunisian left, and personally murdered, a few months later, the Tunisian politician Mohamed Brahmi. These two political assassinations failed to derail the democratic transition process and throw the country into chaos. Boubaker el-Hakim then took refuge in the Tunisian jihadist underground movement on Mount Chaambi, on the Algerian border.

He then left Tunisia for Libya. Once there, he participated in the founding of a camp that trained the suicide bombers for the Bardo and Sousse attacks in 2015. The same camp would later serve as an embryo for the Libyan branch of the Islamic State. From Libya, the Frenchman moved to Raqqa in the Islamic State in Syria, where his strong reputation helped to catapult him into the group's upper echelons. 'You could say he had a strong résumé', Safya summarizes.

Safya's tutor

Abu Muqatil also acted as Safya's *mahram*, that is to say her guardian or 'legal representative'. A few weeks after her Skype wedding and her flight to Turkey, Safya met him for the first time in Raqqa, Syria. 'He was really impressive, almost terrifying', she said. 'He was small in stature but super-strong . . . He was probably only a head taller than I was, but he was built like a truck. He must have weighed 110 kilos, but it was all muscle. I was afraid of him. Everybody knew him. Everybody talked about him like he was somebody super-important. He was an example for everyone else. They knew he'd been on some important missions.'

According to several sources within the Islamic State, and as confirmed by Safya, Abu Muqatil, who speaks perfect French and Arabic, is currently a sort of French emir for terrorist attacks. He is one of the most important individuals responsible for the IS's external operations, training combatants to carry out terrorist activities, in particular in France and Tunisia. He is also suspected of being the real mastermind behind the 13 November terrorist attacks in Paris. 'He trained the brothers to attack in France', said Safya, 'he's really high up in the command. He's in the special forces, where they don't accept just anybody. They only take people who are competent and who aren't going to back out. They just need to be in complete agreement with the religion, the *dawla*, and that everybody has to be killed.'

When Safya arrived in Syria, the Islamic State was reviewing its position on Skype weddings. The organization now requires such unions to be reconfirmed at the *marqama*, the Islamic Court in Raqqa. Once in Syria, Safya asked Mehdi to renew their vows in a more formal manner. 'It started to bother me, so I said to Mehdi: "Come on, let's go to the courthouse." All weddings on Skype happen like that. You just have to take someone who knows the religion and have him recite the *fatiha*. After that, you're married. But now things have changed. They don't accept the *dawla* anymore, now you have to go to the *marqama*, the Islamic court. There you go before the *wali* and then you have a real marriage contract.' The young couple went to the *wali* of Raqqa, one of the highest officials of the organization, the Syrian Abu Loqman. Each brought two witnesses. 'Two brothers I'd never met before in my life.' After a few inquiries about their personal background, the *wali* had both of them utter a sentence that Safya, who doesn't speak Arabic, didn't understand. 'He made me say some kind of an oath. I didn't even know what it meant, I just said it.'

Then came the question of the dowry, which is supposed to be determined by the woman. Instead of a dowry, however, Safya asked only for two symbolic dates. 'Because I don't care about money. And the *wali* laughed. He didn't agree. He said no, but I told him yes. He said: "No, you have to ask for money." He explained to me that a lot of the men who marry for free, who don't give anything to the woman, or just two dates, or a Koran they bought for a euro, when they consummate the marriage and things go bad, it's easy to get divorced. Even if they divorce, the guy only has to pay half the dowry. And paying one date is pretty easy. That's why they ask for money, because that way if the husband wants to divorce, he still has to pay the dowry. So the judge said I had to ask for some money, and I asked for 700 dollars. The judge wasn't French, but we had a translator. He said that a woman was worth more than a few dates.'

As a wedding gift, all women in the IS are given an explosive belt and a Kalashnikov, to defend themselves in case of an attack and to avoid kidnappings. 'The first thing they give us when we get married is an explosive belt, so all the women have one', says Lena. 'All women are armed. But you have the right to refuse. I didn't dare touch mine, because I'm clumsy and I was afraid of blowing myself up.'

'A woman has three or four husbands over there on average'

Marriages for the women of the Islamic State can multiply over a short period of time. Firstly because of the very high mortality rate for men. Safya and Lena, who themselves had only one husband during their stay in the IS, agree on this point. 'Yes, it's true, I knew a sister who was on her fourth husband', says Lena. 'I just heard from another sister who married her second husband, even though she had just gotten married to her first husband a few months ago. Her first husband was killed.' Safya adds: 'To be honest, a woman has three or four husbands over there on average. It's shocking when you think about it, because it's a Muslim country. It's crazy. It's too easy to get married over there.' Before remarrying, however, women are required to observe a mandatory waiting period of four months and ten days. According to Lena, 'the *ida* periods are respected. I've never seen the contrary, I've never seen a sister get married earlier than expected.' Safya disagrees. According to her, the viduity period isn't always strictly respected.

In any jihadist group, the question of polygamy also arises very quickly. And it's not always the man who looks for another wife. Lena and Safya confirm that a man's first wife often arranges things for him. 'Yes, all the women do it. They look for another wife for their husband. It's not the husband who goes looking for another wife', Lena explains. 'It's already a big deal that the woman accepts a second, third or fourth wife, so she says to him: "Listen, you're lucky I've accepted this in the first place", so her husband lets her choose. I knew one who was looking for a second wife and who said, "I want the best for my husband. I want her to be more beautiful, more intelligent than I am . . ." That's what she said, anyway. But I don't know what she was really thinking on the inside. I don't know if it was true or not. Life is hard over there, you get tired quickly, so you start to think that it could be helpful to have someone to help around the house. And then there are women who don't necessarily like having their husbands around with them all of the time.'

According to them, the high number of marriages can also be explained by the high number of divorces. 'Yes, it's kind of appalling. For me it's . . . I don't think they respect each other. I knew one woman who had nine husbands, it was disgusting. She was a Moroccan woman, you know, and because I understand a little Moroccan, she told me that she had had nine husbands. But I didn't say "you're disgusting" to her face, of course, but I was thinking it to myself. It was horrible. It's crazy that it's so easy to get divorced in Syria. All you have to do is have a fight, and there you go, you get divorced. Of course, the *wali* tries to fix things, but if a woman wants to divorce, she gets divorced, or if a man wants to divorce, he gets divorced, so it's super-easy. It's not like in France where there are six months of legal proceedings and it's a huge hassle. Over there they divorce because they also know they'll get married again quickly.' Even within the Islamic State, in accordance with sharia law, a woman is entitled to ask for a divorce. Safya has personal experience in this domain. 'Yes. That's what happened to my ex-sister-in-law. She went to the *marqama*, and she told them some crazy stuff. And they listened to her, they gave her a divorce. They even threatened her husband: if he started with the same crap again, he'd go straight to prison. She said he made her do things that were against the religion. She said she had bruises everywhere, but they couldn't check that because she was veiled from head to toe. She kept crying and carrying on. She knew how to make a scene. So she got what she wanted. The girl was nuts. She had psychological problems. She was always starting fights with her husband, and then she wondered why he hit her.'

Safya's brother-in-law wasn't just anyone within the IS. After running a sandwich shop in the Paris area, he became a commando for the Islamic State: a member of one of the small units of hooded men in light-coloured camouflage uniforms charged with executing prisoners in videos. Afterwards, he became the emir of a *katiba* with a French-speaking majority. 'He used to be one of the commandos, but then he wanted to get married. The commandos have to engage themselves for six months at a time. They aren't allowed to marry. They have to stay the whole time in the *katiba*. The commandos are the closest associates to Baghdadi. They're Baghdadi's personal guard. But I don't think they spend all their time protecting him, because they've got other jobs to do. They have no problem executing people. Cutting off heads takes time. Their job is to appear in all the videos and scare people. But decapitating is hard work. Have you seen what they have to do? They leave when their service period is over, because they want to get married, and somebody else takes their place. It's always the same guys in the videos. There are about fifteen commandos in charge of the decapitations. They come from all different nationalities. That's why they're all wearing hoods in the videos, except for one guy. The videos are intended to terrify people. Killing has become commonplace for them, they find it completely normal. My brother-in-law was one of them. He left France on a whim: he used to be a normal guy going to nightclubs, but then one day he flipped out and left for Syria.'

He was just another young Frenchman whose previous life had nothing to do with religious conservatism, much like the vast majority of the men and women who join the jihadi movement.

In the marriage factory

Maqqar: the word alone strikes fear in the hearts of the women of the Islamic State. Almost every woman must pass through this dreaded place at one point during their stay there. The amount of time can vary: Lena endured the experience for a few hours, Safya for many long months. 'When I left France I thought to myself: "They're going to protect me, I'll be important, because we're women and they consider us pearls, as something to be protected. But the reality wasn't at all like that.'

Such women's homes have been set up in every city controlled by the IS. These multi-storey buildings house an average of 100 women under crowded conditions. A life without privacy, cleanliness or logic. A mandatory stop for all women who lose the guardianship of their husbands – for the most part widows, given that the mortality rate for French jihadists is 1 in 5 – but also divorced women and new arrivals from abroad who stay there briefly until a man comes to pick them up. There is only one way to leave the *maqqar*: marriage. But those who have lost their husbands must also observe the mandatory mourning period of four months and ten days.

The period can become unbearable, given the harsh living conditions.

To escape the *maqqar*, some women have preferred attempting suicide or running away. 'It was so horrible, one woman went crazy', remembers Safya. 'She threatened to blow up everything with an explosive belt if they didn't let her out of the *maqqar*. She ended up jumping out the third-floor window and breaking her leg.' Lena also knew this young woman from Europe who had converted to Islam. 'May Allah preserve her, she was so unhappy over there. She wanted to run away too. But they caught up with her at the border. They had to fire shots into the air so she'd get into the car. That scared her. She was messed up psychologically. When she came to the *dawla*, she was in good shape, but she eventually started to lose her mind. She didn't even know how old she was. She really believed in God, her faith was extraordinary. She helped me keep going when . . . when I couldn't take it anymore. And then one day she started to go crazy. I was really upset for her.'

Lena thinks she saw signs that the sister had experienced sexual violence, but she never learned whether it had occurred before or after her arrival in the IS, or both. 'She got married twice, and she was so traumatized by her first husband that she didn't want to talk to me about it. The second one, she told me, would force her to do things she didn't want to do. I think she was referring to intimate things. She never wanted to talk about it when we were alone together in the evening. I used to ask her questions about her life, but she was really scared. She had problems sleeping. There were lots of signs that showed that she'd been either molested or sexually assaulted.'

The purpose of the women's homes is similar to that of the *Lebensborn*, designed by the Nazis to create a 'pure race' by promoting unions between 'Aryan women' and the SS. These marriage factories are at the heart of the Islamic State's strategy to create a new generation of jihadists – fighters who are even more fanatical than the previous ones, since they were born, raised and conditioned under this totalitarian system. In the *maqqar*, everything is done to make life unbearable, so as to encourage the occupants to leave, and therefore to remarry as soon as possible. 'They'll do anything to make us crack and agree to marry someone.'

Oum Adam's whipping boy

The pressure to leave came firstly from the omnipotent authority of the *maqqar*'s matron. Lena describes the woman who ran one of the two *maqqars* in Raqqa, the infamous Moroccan woman Oum Adam, nicknamed 'the black widow of Al Qaeda', as 'domineering, haughty and incredibly smart'. A woman who lived 'in the shadow of her husband. She used to tell us: "You are nothing. My husband was in Afghanistan. We all stand in shadow of our husbands." Even though my husband had given up everything for the Islamic State.'

It was important to maintain good relations with Oum Adam. 'She acted like a baroness, like she was running a mafia. The men almost admired her. She was listened to and respected. They thought she was so wonderful that she just had to ask to have someone punished and it was done.' Lena experienced this firsthand when, still in love with her husband who was killed in battle, she refused to remarry. 'She was always trying to pick fights with me. She did everything she could to make me suffer. I'd get hit and locked up for days. All my things disappeared, I had nothing to wear, I stopped being paid.[15] I thought I was going to die from the cold because I'd lost all my clothes.' Others, after disputing with the mistress of this *madafa*, were imprisoned, or accused of spying or even witchcraft – charges for which the penalty was death.

In this unhealthy environment, without material comfort or privacy, the relationships between women of dozens of different nationalities are described as highly charged and deleterious.

'The worst thing was how the sisters treat each other. They were clearly hurting themselves, they criticized and accused each other . . . It . . . It was very hard and I'm still bothered by it. It bothered me so much because I had put so much hope in the Islamic State, and now, it hurts me to be disappointed. It's a little like my dream was shattered.'

They lived in complete isolation, sleeping together with their children on mattresses on the floor in large common rooms. Television screens broadcast Islamic State videos, in particular those showing children executing prisoners. 'At the *maqqar* there were TVs where the same videos were played over and over, all day. It was almost too much for me. The 14-year-old Kazakh boy shooting a Russian man played constantly at the *maqqar*. I couldn't take it any more. He was such a handsome little boy. So cute. But in the end it was too much.'

Internet access was forbidden, as was leaving the home, other than for group outings organized once or twice a week. Some women found it even harder to bear the aerial bombings when they were locked inside. 'They had panic attacks. They'd start crying and flipping out. They were sure they were going to die.'

The women remained in the building twenty-four hours a day, with nothing to do, in an environment of constant collective suspicion. Lena tells the story of a Belgian woman who decided one day to prepare a meal for the others and who eventually disappeared. 'She cooked for everybody and a girl got sick. She said: "I don't feel very well", and she told her friend, who also said: "I don't feel well either." And a rumour went around that the woman was involved in "witchcraft" and she was denounced by the others. And nothing more was heard from her for a year. We don't know if she was decapitated or not.' The rumour of the decapitation of the young Belgian woman for witchcraft did indeed make its way through the Islamic State, though it was never officially confirmed by the organization.

Slaves captured in Iraq

All household tasks in the *maqqar* were carried out by slaves. Most were Yezidi women[16] captured in Iraq. Lena tells of once being moved by the fate of one of these women. 'I remember once I was taking a shower and I saw a slave cleaning the floor in the bathroom. And she was practically crawling on the floor, cleaning with some kind of mop, a big sponge. I said to her in Arabic: "No, get up, don't do that, I'll clean up." And she looked at me and said: "No, it's got to be me", like she was forced to do it. I'll never forget it.'

The fates of these slaves make it seem like the *maqqar* women were living in a luxury resort. 'There was one slave who used to go crazy every night. She'd drop to the floor and start crying because they'd taken her away from her father and mother. It really killed me inside, because I was over there and I hadn't heard from my father or my mother for almost three months. I tried to imagine what she was going through. She decided to convert to Islam with her little brother, because she'd pretended that he was her son, I think, in order not to be separated from him. She was Oum Adam's slave, but when she got upset or when she cried, she'd get slapped. She was the one who cleaned up the sisters' shit – please excuse my language – she was the slave who cleaned up, and who served the food. She was basically a servant.'

Daily speed-dating

As if they were shopping at the supermarket, men from the Islamic State would visit the *maqqar* every day to choose a wife, or a second wife. The selection process was controlled from beginning to end by the IS, starting with the *mouqabala*,[17] organized like an assembly line. 'It lasts fifteen minutes', says Lena, 'they talk to each other, the man has the right to see the woman's face, but not her hair, so she lifts her sitar. "What's your name? Where are you from? What do you do for a living? What do you do here in the *dawla*? What do you want from your marriage? What are your criteria?" Basic stuff. It's speed-dating. The faster the better. If you like him, you get married, if you don't, wait for the next one.' These expeditious encounters are always conducted under the supervision of the matron of the house. They also explain, in part, the high number of divorces. 'The divorce rate in the *dawla* is really high. The longest marriage lasted two years. One sister told us: "I was with my husband for two years." We were shocked. Because the women in the *maqqar* break down and take the first comer, at the first *mouqabala*. But then they realize that they don't get along with him, or that they don't love him, or that they don't like how he looks, and they ask for a divorce.'

Even during these rounds of speed-dating, despite the strong pressure to marry, the woman's submissiveness is anything but given. Physical appearance remains one of the most important criteria. Both for the man and the woman. Because both have the right to refuse to marry. And, depending on a candidate's ethnicity, not everyone has the same chances. 'Black women look for handsome white mujahideens with beautiful hair, and black *muqatils*, the black fighters, look for beautiful white women with almond eyes. That's how it goes', says Lena. 'There was this black sister from England with me. And one day at the *maqqar*, the woman who ran the *mouqabala* announced that someone with a *kunya in ifrikya* – that is, someone from Africa – was going to participate in the *mouqabala*. And the sister said: "No, no blacks for me." And the woman said to her: "But you're black, aren't you?" She said: "So what? I don't want a black man." A girl from abroad, someone who has emigrated, gets to pick any guy she wants. Whether she wants a white man or a black man. Of course, she'll choose a handsome white guy with long, beautiful hair. It only makes sense.'

Lena remembers the many unsuccessful attempts of a Frenchman of Korean origin. He would knock on the door of the *maqqar* every week, well-groomed and wearing his best shirt, in the hope of seducing a woman. And every week he left the *mouqa-*

bala empty-handed. Why? Because of the racism that still reigns among the members of the IS, says Lena, despite the fact that the group claims to have made it disappear, dissolving distinctions of race and colour into one and the same Umma – the community of all Muslims – in which all are equal. 'Every day he'd go to Oum Adam's *madafa* to say, more or less: "OK, here I am, I'm single." But nobody wanted him because he was Korean. He was Asian, his eyes were too slanted, so no.' According to her, it was also hard for black men to find partners. The same held true for the criteria for men. "There was this English woman of Ethiopian origin. She came in and, before she could even sit down, a German brother of Moroccan origin said to her: "No, I don't want a black woman." They were really cheeky and inconsiderate. There was a lot of racism against blacks. Blacks weren't on the same level as whites or Arabs. Really, the Arabs were the "supreme race".'

'We're fed up, they all want Kim Kardashian'

For the men, the standards of beauty remain determined by the aesthetic codes of television reality shows. 'All the brothers wanted knock-outs. It was obvious. They asked each other: "Hey, doesn't your wife know a knock-out for me?" There were sisters in the *maqqar* who would say: "We're fed up, they all want Kim Kardashian." Physical appearance remained a problem in the Islamic State. In the *maqqar*, sisters were rejected outright by the brothers after the *mouqabala*. They'd say "No, that's not what I want" because they didn't meet their criteria. They wanted shapely figures, long brown hair, brown eyes – the oriental stereotype. But even if a girl didn't meet their standards, the brothers were so frustrated sexually that they'd say yes. Then a month later they'd get divorced, of course. I saw so many girls get rejected for nothing.'

Chechens were considered by the women to be one of the worst nationalities, because they were thought to be equally

brutal in love and in war. Lena can't help laughing when recall-
ing a surreal exchange between a Frenchwoman and a Caucasian
fighter during a *mouqabala* in a *maqqar* in Raqqa. 'He spoke a
little French, and he was saying: "Listen, I've already got a wife
who's on her way here. She's arriving in three weeks"', she says,
imitating his Russian accent. '"You accept, good; you no accept,
not good, you stay at home, me love to make love." She told us
the story, it was horrible.' Lena also remembers a meeting at a
mouqabala between a post-adolescent British woman and a young
Australian convert. The fighter was excited by the recent media
notoriety he had earned in his home country after being seen in
an Islamic State video, earning for himself the nickname 'Ginger
Jihadi' in reference to the famous British executioner 'Jihadi
John'. 'He was a redhead. And right off the bat he said to her: "My
name is Ginger Jihadi." So, after Jihadi John, there was Ginger
Jihadi. Ginger because he was a redhead. It was funny. There
were lots of stories like that.'

Another *mouqabala* ended badly when a jihadist confessed to
owning two slaves and having regular sexual intercourse with
them. 'He was a French brother of Mauritanian origin who came
to a *mouqabala* for a sister, and the sister came back from the
mouqabala saying: "Oh my God, he has two slaves!" She told us
how he treated them, he made them sleep with other brothers.
They passed them around between each other.'

As already described, in the summer of 2014 the IS enslaved
thousands of Yezidi captives from Iraq and authorized its men
to have sexual relations with them. 'The masters slept with their
slaves just to satisfy their desires. But you could tell that the slaves
were sad', explains Lena, 'It was rare that one of them falls in love
with their slave, or that they felt desire for her or wanted to have
children with her. For them, the absolute best was a *muhajira*, a
woman who emigrated from another country.'

It was because of the life in these women's homes in the Islamic
State that Lena decided to flee. 'I didn't want to get married again
just to lose another husband in three months. It's horrible psycho-

logically. People in France have no idea. When you're in France, you follow the Islamic State online from home, and you think you're strong. Allah wants Muslims to be strong and not weak. So we're strong, we can overcome anything. Allah's tribulations are beautiful and I was ready to put up with everything. But it takes its toll, psychologically. You get married, you start having feelings for him, and then he falls in battle. You get married again, you start having feelings for the next man, and then he's killed. And then you give birth, you wait for a year, you get married again, and then that one gets killed. Psychologically, jihad life is hard.'

Lena had fled the male gaze in France, believing that she would discover a purer form of gender relations in Syria. Within the Islamic State, however, she suffered from the same indiscreet looks as she did in France, but with the added torment of physical confinement. It was an experience that was light years away from the idealized vision she had created from behind her computer screen.

PART FIVE
KEVIN AND QUENTIN

The former choirboy from Brittany

Kevin sang in a choir when he was little. 'I was in the Scouts too.' Fifteen years later, in June 2016, he fled the Islamic State where he had spent the last two years of his life, crossing the Turkish border with his four wives and their six children. His name was placed on the UN Security Council's list of international terrorists. What happened in between? How did Kevin the Boy Scout become Kevin the Jihadist, described as a 'big fish' in the French press?

Though he may have gone to Sunday school, Kevin couldn't be described as a prototypical mother's boy from a good family. He speaks slowly, searching even for simple words. His beboured speech is an indication of his chaotic educational background and a low level of schooling. After school, he failed to complete an apprenticeship programme, dropped out of a second one, and then tried to finish a training certificate in maintenance. With no degree or diploma, Kevin is unqualified to work. He lives on welfare and from the occasional odd job, paid under the table. With his beard, his pale complexion, his light brown shoulder-length hair and his small stature, he looks more like a hobbit from the *Lord of the Rings* than a postmodern avatar of Iraqi jihad.

Though we've never met him in person, and have only seen his photos and videos, we've been in touch with him over the telephone for over a year and a half. Kevin was raised by his mother in Brittany. His parents separated shortly after he was born. He never had much contact with his father. 'Our relationship wasn't that great', he says. Individuals from single-parent families with an absent paternal figure are overrepresented in jihadist circles. Their loved ones often say that this ideology provides them with the symbol of the paternal authority they had been lacking.

Converted at the age of 14

Kevin received a Catholic religious education from an early age, which taught him to fear and love God. Or, rather, it instilled in him a belief in monotheism. Like two other jihadists we interviewed who were brought up in a Christian environment, he explains that Catholicism sometimes seemed too complex to understand. Pillars of Roman Catholic dogma such as the Trinity, with its seemingly polytheistic implications, left him perplexed. 'It was too hard to understand. With Islam things are so clear and easy. That really appealed to me.' Islam answered metaphysical questions for the young man. He started to become interested in the religion as a teenager, because, he says, many of his friends were Muslims. He converted at the age of 14 in a mosque belonging to the Tablighi[1] fundamentalist preaching movement. His conversion also coincided with the appearance of his mother's new husband. His new stepfather was a rai singer and a Muslim, though he practised his religion very little. Kevin spent three years with the Tablighi before breaking with them. 'I left them because it's a sect.'

He began to study on the internet in order to gain a deeper understanding of his religion. It was thanks to these studies, he believes, that he discovered 'true Islam'. He subscribed to the Facebook page of a jihadist group in Nantes, France, which eventually led him to reconsider his religious convictions: Forsane

Alizza, the 'Knights of Pride'. Though the group was broken up after the Merah affair in 2012,[2] Kevin was intrigued by the provocative escapades of its leader, Abu Hamza. This 30-year-old Frenchman of Moroccan descent is now doing time in prison – he is known in France in particular for his protests against the law prohibiting the niqab in public spaces, and for having burned a penal code under the windows of a police station in Paris. Kevin was 17 when he joined Forsane Alizza, and met with its members several times in person and participated in their activities. It was his contact with this group that led him to embrace jihadist ideology. 'They introduced me to an *aqida*[3] on the *takfir*,[4] on the *tawaghit*, the nullifiers of Islam,[5] the *shirk*, etc. I'd never heard about such things. I was completely ignorant. They give you verses and *hadiths* which are true, but they twist them around to mislead people.'

He met his wife Salma in these circles. 'I met her through Forsane Alizza, on Facebook.' He also had his first run-ins with the French intelligence services. Shortly after the disbanding of Forsane Alizza and the imprisonment of its leader, his and his wife's assets were frozen by ministerial order. 'When they got picked up by the police, we made calls for donations on the internet for their families, because their accounts had been frozen and they couldn't receive their welfare payments. So they froze our accounts too.'

Departure for Syria

It was at this point that Kevin, then 20 years old, went to Syria with his wife. 'I met a Tunisian man on Facebook. He had a cousin in Syria. He was the one who recommended that I join Jabhat al-Nusra. It would be easier, he said, to join the Sham with my family, and I'd find everything I needed there. I went immediately.' In 2012, they were among the very first French citizens to take the plunge and make a *hijra* to the Levant. Integrating themselves once there, however, turned out to be much more difficult than they had expected. He knocked on the doors of the Front al-Nosra and Al Qaeda, but in vain. He had no *taskia*, no recommendation. 'Anyone who wants to join them, especially a *muhajir*, has to have someone inside the group who knows him.' Without such a contact, Kevin was pushed out and fell in with one of the so-called 'moderate' units of the Free Syrian Army, for lack of a better alternative. He fought in his first battle alongside the Salafist group Ahrar al-Sham. The battlefront proved to be a strange experience for him. 'They were shooting at us with rockets, machine guns, shells. There was carnage everywhere. The guy next to me stood up to shoot and took a bullet to the head. The same thing happened to a second guy, and then the third guy who went to bring the bodies back got shot and killed too.'

He spent several months in these rebel groups before joining the ISIL (now the IS), after he had officially established his presence in Syria in the spring of 2013. 'When they made their first announcement and started saying all those great things, it was like they were throwing flowers at us. They said they wanted to consolidate all the groups to become stronger. I went with more than half of my group to pledge allegiance to the *dawla*. And they accepted everybody, *muhajir* or Syrian. That was good for us too. It was a call for union for all Muslims to impose sharia, everything that the Muslims wanted. And because there were *muhajirun* there, I thought I'd get to meet some French people and that would help me with the Arabs, because I didn't speak the language. I was having a hard time.'

Kevin quickly made his way into the French circles in Raqqa. He got to know the cream of the francophone jihadist movement, including several of the men who would later carry out the 13 November attacks in Paris. This gave him the opportunity to play an enthusiastic role in the propaganda videos the group made to incite others in France to join them. With the help of his wife, he attracted young women in particular to Syria. This is how he found a second and then a third wife – two French women of Senegalese origin. His recruitment activity eventually landed him on the UN Security Council's list of highly sought-after terrorists in September 2014, 'for having concerted to organize, finance, facilitate, prepare or carry out acts or activities for Front al-Nosra'. Though he wasn't actually part of Front al-Nosra, at that time, the international institutions couldn't distinguish between the Syrian branch of Al Qaeda and the Islamic State. When he discovered his and his wife's names on this list, Kevin was surprised: 'I didn't understand. They said I was a recruiter. But I never recruited anyone.' He nevertheless remained very active on Facebook, participating in the first French propaganda videos for the Islamic State in 2014. He also tried to attract a fourth young woman to Syria, this time a minor, but without success. 'We didn't have the same definition of recruitment as they did.' Indeed.

A 'big family' man

While living in Syria, Kevin and his wife Salma used Facebook not only to bring women to Syria, but also to collect money. For those who couldn't leave France, paying someone else's way to Syria or supporting them financially once there were also ways to earn points for paradise. 'People who can't do their *hijra* can be rewarded for helping those who have done their *hijra* and who are in need, like me and my wife. Because I had no money, I started asking for donations over the internet. Little donations, something like 300, 500, 800 or 1,000 euros, every two or three months.'

His efforts to seduce women on Facebook even managed to draw the attention of the anti-terrorism police to his mother. Claiming to have a debt that needed to be repaid, Kevin asked his mother to send money to a 16-year-old girl. In reality, however, he wanted to marry her and the money was to finance her trip to Syria. The school student was stopped along the way, however, in Germany. The investigators had no problem finding out who had provided her with the funds to buy her ticket.

Kevin thrived under polygamy. 'I decided to have four wives because Allah said it was OK, and because the Prophet SAWS had had multiple wives himself. And since the wives help each other out at home, with the housework, raising the children and with the religious duties. And I like having a lot of children. Having several wives makes it easier to have many children.'

Kevin is a 'big family' man. At the age of 24, he already has, with four different women, a total of six children, four of whom were born in Syria, without any legal or administrative proof of their existence. To this list must be added another child, born in France from an earlier relationship. 'It was with my first wife, but we divorced.' His wife Salma helped him to increase the size of their household, through Facebook. Two marriages over the internet were confirmed in the Islamic court as soon as the wives arrived in Syria. His fourth wife, whom he picked up from a *maqqar*, was a French woman who has a daughter from another relationship. Kevin was responsible for bringing her to Syria initially, but she had married a Jordanian man who was later killed in battle, sending her to the women's home.

The purpose of this fourth union, he explains, was to help all of them leave Syria. The fourth young woman wanted to return to France, but couldn't do so without a man. Her family in France offered to help to pay the costs of a smuggler if Kevin would agree to help her by marrying her. In addition, the Islamic State pays a bonus for every new marriage, ranging from 800 to 1,500 dollars for a first marriage, and 800 euros in case of marriage with a widow, which was the case for the young woman.

'The Khawarij sect'

Why did they decide to return to France after living four years in Syria? Kevin explains that he was motivated above all by his fear of being killed. The aerial bombardments had intensified and the IS was retreating on all fronts. 'That's what triggered it for me.' Kevin was also afraid of being executed by the IS. 'I was afraid of the *emni* because, *dawla*, as time goes on and the vice starts to tighten, the more paranoid they become. At the slightest slip, even if you say or do something completely normal, they start to get suspicious. They'll suspect you and then they'll arrest you. They'll say that you're a spy, that you're providing targets to the coalition. And since the coalition is bombing them, you can be executed or be forced to fight to prove your loyalty to them.'

Kevin was also afraid of the fighting. For months, he did everything he could to avoid combat. He went so far as to purposely twist his ankle on his stairs to keep from being sent to the front. After being wounded by shrapnel in a battle, he says that he has been traumatized by combat and violence. 'I'm very scared. It keeps going through my head. I've suffered a lot over here, psychologically. I've seen people crucified, and people get blown up quickly. I'm afraid of stepping on a mine and being killed.'

But even beyond his personal safety, Kevin claims to have broken with the IS from a religious point of view. After reading texts by 'Islamic scholars in Saudi Arabia', he now calls himself a Salafist Quietist and considers the jihadists to be 'a *Khawarij* sect' – those who have been led astray. 'I repudiate them completely. I can't wait to get out of here. For me, jihad as such isn't permitted now according to the rules of Islam. On a religious level, once I'd left the ideology, I finally understood, from my research on the *hadiths* of the Prophet SAWS, what the scholars were saying, and that I had been in complete contradiction with Islam. I can't understand people who carry out terrorist attacks that cause the blood of Muslims to be spilled.'

But leaving the Islamic State, which condemns any form of desertion, wasn't easy. Especially for someone with four wives and six children, some of them very young. Kevin considered his options for a year and a half. He hired a lawyer to take care of the legal procedures with the authorities in France, in order to inform them of their arrival and have his children born in Syria recognized officially. His first attempt to flee landed him in an Islamic State jail. Kevin had contacted a smuggler and given him all his savings in order to cross the border with his family. But his luck was bad, the smuggler was working for the Islamic State. When they reached their agreed meeting point, they were met by armed men wearing hoods – the *emni*. The IS intelligence services took them straight to detention for interrogation. Kevin and his wives barely escaped being sentenced to death for espionage, but, luckily, their stories matched. During the interrogations, they all claimed that they were going to Turkey to get medical attention for one of the women who was suffering from a phlebitis. Their interrogators let them go after two weeks, but continued to have their doubts. The family was now under suspicion – especially since one of his wives had already nearly been executed for sorcery, because of her attacks of epilepsy. They lived in constant fear of being unmasked. They finally managed to flee two months later, with the help of another smuggler.

After crossing the border, Kevin and his wives were arrested and placed in an administrative detention centre. Four months later, in September 2016, the entire family appeared in court in Gaziantep, Turkey. The women and children were expelled and handed over to the French authorities. Kevin was sentenced to a prison sentence in Turkey, before being extradited to France. He now hopes to start his life over again as a good father and earn his high school diploma. 'I've totally changed', he says, 'now I'm a mature and responsible person.' It is now up to a criminal-court jury to decide whether he's telling the truth.

Nice

Quentin fell into jihad as a young boy. He had little choice. His indoctrination took place in the low-income housing estates where he lived in Nice, without raising the slightest suspicion. The preaching of jihad where Quentin grew up was a neighbourly affair, almost banal. The men who undertook it were patient and tireless, and their goal was to produce killers. It was from this bastion of right-wing politics, with its 1,300 video surveillance cameras, that political figures like Éric Ciotti and Christian Estrosi emerged, ardent promoters of the total security state. Nice, renowned for its Mediterranean lifestyle and its mythical Promenade des Anglais, is prized by an electorate of wealthy senior citizens and well-off foreign tourists.

It was in the gentle climes of the Côte d'Azur that, from 2014 on and well before the attack of 14 July 2016 which left 86 dead and 400 wounded, Nice became the most important exporter of French citizens leaving to wage jihad in Syria. In all, more than a hundred men, women and children left Nice between 2013 and the summer of 2016. How might such a paradox be explained? In large part by the presence of one of France's most influential jihad personalities in the city's working-class neighbourhoods until the end of 2013: Omar Diaby.

Omsen, the contraction of 'Omar Senegal'

Quentin was about 11 or 12 when he began attending Omar's 'meetings' in his neighbourhood. He doesn't remember very well when he first started going. 'In the beginning', he explains, 'I used to see him talking to people, but I didn't participate in his debates yet. I didn't go to see him. I didn't even say hello to him. But after a while, since all my friends were going to see him, I started to want to find out what he was saying, out of curiosity.'

At that time, around 2011, Omar Diaby, known as Omsen – the contraction of 'Omar Senegal' – already held great sway among fifty or so young people. He was well known to the intelligence services for attempting to travel to Afghanistan and Yemen with a dozen others. But the group was arrested at the Nice train station on the day of their departure. After being held in police custody, all were let free and placed under police surveillance.

Being on the list of suspected terrorists and wearing an electronic bracelet, however, didn't keep Omar from continuing his preaching activities in Nice and elsewhere. 'He used to show up below my building and visit the young people there, because that's where they hung out. "Salam alaykum" – that kind of a thing. "Why aren't you going to the mosque? What are you doing here? You'd do better to go to the mosque and learn your religion." He'd say to the guys holding a joint: "Stop smoking. It's *harem*, you're going to hell." I remember how he responded when someone said to him: "I can't go to the mosque, I'm going to the beach." Omar told him: "Well you'll get a tan in hell then."'

Omar wasn't making these young men and women feel guilty and pushing them to visit the neighbourhood mosque because it advocated jihad, however. On the contrary. During the official sermons, he would use the mosque's prayer room to teach his own classes, in which he sang the praises of Al Qaeda and emigration to the land of Islam. 'The imam wasn't radical at all, but Omar Diaby was a self-proclaimed imam. He would take his group off to the side in the mosque and, at the end of the prayer, remind them about *fissabililah* jihad. Jihad "on the path of Allah", that's how he called it. Sometimes he'd hold a collective prayer at a football stadium with a dozen or so people. Sometimes he'd hold meetings at his house, where there were young people not only from Nice, but from all over the place. He always spoke of the importance of *hijra*, of emigration, of the *kuffars*, of leaving a country of unbelievers to join a country of believers. When he was asked: "What about Tunisia?" he'd say: "No! It's a country of *kuffars*, because they live under democracy. They're all unbelievers." Before Syria, there was Afghanistan. But there was always one country, according to Omar, that was at war and that wanted to apply the law of Allah. He knew how to make the neighbourhood's youth get excited about the project, because so many of them found him captivating. Like he'd put a spell on them.'

Omar was eloquent, intelligent and manipulative. He promised eternal happiness to those who followed him and hell to those who refused. He targeted adolescents in particular, finding them more easily influenced and amenable to his very personal reading of the religion. 'Some of the older guys, that is, the guys in their twenties and thirties, would say that he was full of shit, but he had an influence on the younger ones.' Omar knew how to be convincing. He seduced. He threatened. He hypnotized. 'He gave us a lot of ultimatums: "Yes, if you don't do that, you're going to hell." It was almost psychotic at times. I don't know, I think it was his charisma.' Quentin considers: 'He had something that satisfied people. People were satisfied with what they heard from Omar. He managed to get them to believe what he was saying. When he spoke about jihad, for example, it seemed like this amazing thing, when in reality it's horrible.'

Within five or six years, Omar formed a small community of faithful in Nice, ready to follow his orders blindly. Like a guru, he had the last word on certain marriages, and many followers would send him money to finance his activities. His constant presence in the neighbourhood made it difficult to escape his prodding. 'Yeah, the young people were ashamed to tell him they didn't want to go to the mosque. Either they'd hide in the buildings to avoid him, or they'd come up with excuses like: "I was going to change my clothes, I'll be right back." Some guys might not have cared the slightest about him, but most of them wouldn't dare say: "No, I don't want to go to the mosque." But most of them weren't that religious to start with.'

The boss

In the lower-income districts of Nice, Omar Diaby was already a well-known figure before he began his relentless jihadist tirades. The tall and sprightly braggart with a gangster past had already earned the respect of the youths in the projects. In the neighbourhoods of Nice, he was the boss. A man both feared and listened to. By the age of 35, Omar already had several jewellery store robberies, an attempted homicide and many years of prison under his belt. While his religious upbringing might not have been rigorous, he was born into a family practising a traditional form of Islam known as Tijaniyah, one of the three most important religious brotherhoods in Senegal.

When we interviewed him for the first time in 2013, he told us that he had had a revelation after leaving prison. He says he saw God and the archangel Gabriel. For this highly narcissistic individual, no doubt suffering from delusions of grandeur, the divine appearance led him to dream of becoming an important emir for Al Qaeda. A kind of Bin Laden on the French Riviera. He told us that when he looked up into the sky, he saw the number 19 appear in the clouds. He took it as his lucky number. He also saw two letters in the clouds: 'HH.' They would later become his trademark in his videos, standing for the 'History of Humanity'.

Omar began to set his sights higher, no longer satisfied with his intense *street dawa* in Nice. The social networks allowed him to reach an audience far beyond the beaches of the Côte d'Azur. He spent his days in front of his computer editing videos for the dozens of episodes of his series *19 HH*, which retraced the true (and secret) history of mankind. His videos were broadcast on his Facebook page, which had several thousand subscribers, and appeared under his pseudonym Omar Omsen. In these interminable artistic montages, he expounded his sermons against a background of images culled from news programmes, Al Qaeda video clips, American films, political speeches and TV series that he downloaded from online video sharing platforms.

In a hotchpotch of conspiracy theory, Muslim eschatology, interpretations of verses and *hadiths* – in which he even found a prophecy of the September 11 attacks – Omar Omsen presented French society as being profoundly corrupt, perverse and hostile to Islam. He insisted, therefore, on the obligation of every Muslim to do his *hijra* and carry out jihad abroad. But where should they go? Was there a place where authentic Islam was practised? Starting in late 2012, his videos began to focus on Syria, described as the most sacred country in Islam, a place where Muslims were being killed in droves. Apocalyptic signs, according to Omar, that the return of the Mahdi[6] and the end of times were at hand.

The message may sound crazy, but its reach was considerable. And not only in Nice, but throughout France. To the point of turning, between 2012 and 2013, Omar Omsen into the most important figure in the francophone jihadosphere. He was contacted over the internet by a certain Abu al-Hassan, who said he was a big fan of his work. The young man from Lyon, 29 years old and a native of the Haute-Savoie region in France, offered his services to help to speed up the video production. His name was Mourad Farès and he would become Omar's right-hand man.

In 2013, the two men helped many dozens of people in France to get involved in jihad. Their Facebook pages created an ideological community which later gave rise to 'physical' meetings throughout 2013, in the lead-up to the first massive departures to Syria. Omar held numerous meetings with his online followers, notably in Lyon and Paris. His goal was to unite all his supporters under the same military brigade, in Syria, under the banner of Al Qaeda.

Mourad Farès

At the same time, Mourad was also travelling throughout France. He met three times with a group in Strasbourg that sent ten people to Syria in batches of two or three, starting in December 2013. They were a group of schoolmates who grew up together, with few educational qualifications. A network of friends from neighbourhoods, football clubs and shisha bars, whose members lived off of odd jobs. Among them, a man named Fued, who would later become one of the three kamikazes in the Bataclan attacks, opening fire on a crowd of people and cold-bloodedly executing young men and women of his age, on the evening of 13 November 2015 in Paris. Before then, the friends with whom he left for Syria were better known for visiting nightclubs than mosques.

It all started with a simple subscription to Mourad's Facebook page. That was how Karim, the kamikaze's brother, got involved in the group. He spoke to us in 2016 over the telephone from prison, where he has been incarcerated since his return from Syria in 2014: 'I was a little naive. I went to Syria with an ideal, after having watched the images of violence, torture and massive bombardments against the Syrian people from my computer screen, warm under my blanket in France. I went to fight the Bashar regime with people who wanted to impose sharia. What attracted me to it? Quite frankly, for me it was the videos produced by Omar Omsen and Mourad, like *Al-Mahdi and the Second Caliphate*. They really captivated me.'

Mourad Farès left for Syria in July 2013. Another French convert from the ISIL, who had been active in the zone since 2012, introduced him into the group after a few exchanges on Facebook. While waiting for Omar Diaby's arrival in October, he began to set up the francophone brigade within the ISIL. The unit quickly grew to almost a hundred fighters. Apart from a few Belgians and two Swiss citizens, almost all were French and came mostly from Nice. His Facebook page acted as a jihadist tourism agency in Syria. Every day, Mourad Farès would pick up new arrivals at the border. And every day he would post audio messages and photos of himself smiling brightly, with his index finger raised and wearing aviator glasses and bearing arms in his 4x4, or sitting majestically astride a horse, calling to mind Osama bin Laden's years in Afghanistan. The reality was much closer to a Three Stooges summer camp, their only theological references being poorly translated by other Frenchmen from the same sociological background as they. Despite these shortcomings, however, Omar and Mourad managed to get people excited about Syria.

And so on

'If I hadn't met Omar', says Quentin, 'I don't think I would have gotten interested in the whole thing. I was touched by what I saw going on in Syria, but I definitely wouldn't have left if I hadn't met Omar Diaby.' The same was probably also true for the other 130 people who left Nice for Syria. All were under Omar's influence, whether directly or indirectly. He pulled the strings that helped to launch, for example, the exponential number of departures in 2013 and 2014. Beyond Nice, dozens also came from other areas of France: from the north of France, from Paris, from Normandy or from the French West Indies. A wide range of minorities were involved as well: two brothers in his group were converts from the Travellers' community, for example.

All left for Syria after watching the videos produced by Omar Diaby and Mourad Farès. The same men and women would then incite their friends and family via the social networks to go to Syria. After hesitating for a year, several of Quentin's friends left before him. Although he knew very little about his religion, he decided to join them in November 2013, motivated most likely by a desire to imitate his friends. He and his older brother, 22 years old, together with a neighbour of Chechen origin, told their parents that they were going out to a nightclub, as usual, but instead took a plane to Istanbul. 'One thing led to the next. Omar left, his brother Moussa joined him, then his family, his two sons, his wives, and then two people from the neighbourhood left to join them. And then it was our turn. That was it.' And so on.

When Quentin arrived in Syria and posted his first selfie with a Kalashnikov on his Facebook page, he was only 16 years old. 'When we left, we thought what we were doing was for a good cause.' He and his brother grew up in an extremely poor environment. The year he left, Quentin was in a vocational training programme and worked in a small store in Nice at weekends. With no criminal record, and never having had problems with the police, he never fell into delinquency, despite his dope habit. His father, born in Tunisia and a practising Muslim, provided him and his brother with a religious education, but also gave them Western names to help them integrate into French society. He is a man with an overwhelming personality, who moves through the streets of Nice on an old moped and lives on welfare. His health is fragile. Their mother, a French woman of the Christian faith, doesn't hold a job either. She suffers from serious health problems and has difficulties speaking. Since Quentin was born, she has been afflicted by a serious illness that isolates her socially.

Both parents, already very vulnerable, were devastated by the departure of their two sons for Syria. Their father remained in constant contact with them via Facebook. He became obsessed with the idea of convincing them to return home. And he eventually succeeded with Quentin, the least indoctrinated of the two. After the sons had spent seven months in Syria, their father borrowed money from relatives to travel to Turkey. He told them to meet him in the southern part of the country. Quentin went to the border town of Atma to see him. He took advantage of the collective morning prayer to escape the notice of his brigade and run away. He walked several kilometres to cross the border and found his father waiting for him on the other side. Back in Nice, he was immediately arrested at the airport by two French intelligence officers. 'I got off the plane, I went through customs, and they told me: "Stop right there, young man." They took me to the airport police station and put me in a cell. I waited for the DGSI to arrive.'

Quentin was detained in the Paris region for one year before being released under judicial supervision. His identity papers were confiscated by the courts. His parents, who found it easier knowing that he was in a prison in France, breathed a sigh of relief. But they were devastated by their second son's categorical refusal to leave the jihadi movement. They were convinced that Quentin's older brother would never return home. He was determined to die in Syria.

In the lion's den

Why did Quentin finally agree to return? He explains that his doubts started once he arrived at the Jabhat al-Nusra training camp, led by an Egyptian who had fought in Afghanistan under Al Qaeda. 'He was an Arab, but there was a French guy who spoke Arabic who translated. It was pretty surreal, suddenly finding myself carrying weapons and being woken up by fake grenades. I started thinking: "Whoa, where am I?" I wasn't really thinking about returning home at that time, but I did start to consider it a little, and I realized that I was in a country at war.' It was a radical change from the tranquillity of Nice for the 16-year-old. The culture shock started the moment he reached the border town of Atma. 'Reality hit me immediately when I got there. It wasn't France any more, it was more hardcore. There were planes and armed men. I saw aerial bombardments two hours after arriving. Right from the beginning, we saw how it was going to be. Once I saw a car bomb in Atma that blew up the entire second floor of a hospital. The car had exploded in the hospital parking lot. The bodies of the people hit by the explosion were torn to pieces.

There were no survivors. They just had to pick up the bodies. I warned some French guys who wanted to come. If they left, I said, they'd better have strong stomachs. I stayed there a long time, seven months, and now I believe there are really only two solutions. Either you don't go back and you go crazy because of everything you've seen and gone through, because seeing dead bodies all day does something to you, most people are really bothered by it. Or you come back having learned something about life. You learn that life is really, really, really important. And that you can lose it at any time. Going there means throwing yourself into the lion's den.'

One month after his arrival in Syria, at the end of his military training period, the *fitna*, or the great discord, began. From the end of 2013 to the beginning of 2014, a fratricidal war broke out between the rebel groups (Free Syrian Army, FSA) and the jihadists of the ISIL, and, as a consequence, between the French jihadists themselves. He still doesn't understand the specific causes behind this internecine and bloody struggle. Quentin simply remembers that when the first shots were fired, he was sitting quietly on a patio in Haritan, enjoying a kebab with the others from Nice. At that point, the brigades of the different factions got along peacefully in this small town on the outskirts of Aleppo. All the foreign fighters crossed paths there. 'We were eating quietly, just chatting, trying to ignore the bombardments, and then, all of a sudden, someone from the IS came up to us and says: "Hey, haven't you heard?" in Arabic. It was a Syrian guy from the IS. And he told us that things were going to get hot with the FSA because the IS had started attacking it.'

'But everybody just passed the blame around. The FSA claimed that the IS had attacked them. We finished our sandwiches because we didn't think things were really going to explode. We just thought that the leaders of the groups would get together, and that there'd be some tension, but we couldn't imagine that it would lead to mortar fire and the armies attacking each other.' A few moments later, however, the unimaginable happened and the city turned into a battlefield, with the Syrian civilians caught in the middle.

'All of a sudden we heard machine gun fire everywhere. The 14.5 mm, large-calibre machine guns mounted on cars started shooting, we saw people running around, panicking, civilians fleeing and everything . . . People started running up with weapons and engaging with us, thinking we belonged to an enemy group. The IS thought we were Jabhat al-Nusra and the FSA thought we were IS.'

Crossfire

But his band of French novices, who still hadn't seen their first combat, belonged to none of these groups. Once they arrived in Syria, Omar and his deputy Mourad decided to break from the ISIL. This was still possible when it was consolidating its power in Syria, but would have been unthinkable a few months later. The small group of 100 or so French citizens found themselves in a tricky spot. A bounty was placed on Omar Omsen's head. A group of French *emni* set out to find him in Haritan and execute him. Omar was forced to go into hiding to save his life, seeking refuge with Jabhat al-Nusra, even though Al Qaeda had been his ideal since he started in the jihadi movement. But compared to the veterans of Afghanistan, former companions of Bin Laden, the erstwhile hold-up man from Nice and his group of post-adolescents with no military experience had some credibility problems.

'Omar wanted to join them, that's what he'd planned. And in the end, he did join them, but his pledge of allegiance was denied. It was all very confusing. Omar didn't give us too many details. But I started to have my doubts at that point, because I heard an Egyptian emir from Jabhat al-Nusra say that the people from Nice would be better back home in France.'

For several days, the group went into hiding – men, women and children – in a building on the outskirts of Aleppo. They were caught in the middle of fighting between rebel groups waging war with each other throughout the city. 'We had to keep people posted at the top and bottom of our building. There were four lookouts at the entrance and four on the roof to prevent snipers from setting up there. Nobody did any shooting – that wasn't the point, because we wanted to avoid being attacked. The only thing we did was to stop anyone carrying weapons when they were in front of the building. We told them that we weren't part of either the IS or the FSA, and that it wasn't our fight. There was so much shooting that it lit up the sky at night. From the roof we could see out like it was daylight. That's when you realize that things were serious. And that you might lose your life. Everything was lit up. There were dead bodies everywhere just below our building. That's when we decided to leave the city, which was hard to do without getting shot. We had to wait for things to calm down a little. We evacuated the families first, in a bus that took them to Idlib. Then we had to wait two or three days to leave ourselves. The problem was that Bashar had gained a lot of ground by taking advantage of the fighting between the Syrian rebels and the IS. Three days later we joined our families. I understood that it wasn't the wonderful place that Omar had made me believe.'

Disputes

The first disputes began the moment the Nice brigade was formed. Omar Diaby left for Senegal to pick up members of his family and returned in early 2014. Once he was back in Syria, Mourad Farès challenged his authority in the group and refused to let him take over as emir. The clash of wills was immediate. Part of the group left. Shortly afterwards, completely isolated and confronted with a much stronger Islamic State that was trying to kill him, Mourad fled to Turkey. With no other option, he finally surrendered to the French authorities in the summer of 2014. He even sent a desperate email to the French intelligence services that must have surprised the investigators: 'I'd like you to listen to what I have to tell you, and then you can decide what to do. You probably find it hard to believe, but I'm on your side.' Since then, he has been sitting in solitary confinement in a prison in France, awaiting prosecution. His name, like that of Omar Diaby, appears in most of the criminal prosecution files for the jihadists who left France between 2013 and 2014.

In the meantime, Omar Omsen's brigade lost even more men. The oldest jihadists, determined to fight, left him for the siren calls of the Islamic State. Only the younger fighters, still fascinated by his personality, stayed by his side. In open conflict with the Jabhat al-Nusra emirs and threatened with execution by the Islamic State, Omar Omsen decided to pretend for nine months that he had been killed in combat. Just the question remained, however, whether he had ever actually fought in battle. 'Omar Diaby never fired a shot', says Quentin, 'and a lot of people accused him of claiming to be an emir even though he obviously didn't have the skills. In a proper army, a man like that would never have been sent to the front. I personally never saw Omar Diaby go to battle. But I don't know whether he fought after I left.'

When he returned from the dead after nine months, his brigade, known as *firkatul ghuraba* or the 'foreigners' brigade', still numbered about forty people, including both men and women. Part of the group was made up of the same teenagers from Nice. They lived in the Idlib region, under the protection of Chinese jihadists of the Turkish Islamic Party, the TIP, from the Uighur separatist area. Omar Diaby would sometimes send some of his youngsters, including his two minor sons, to fight by their side. After 2014, to counter criticism that his group was chronically absent from the front lines, he proudly announced the presumed deaths of six of his French nationals. The first death took place in 2014: a former volunteer firefighter from Grenoble. Then a second in 2015: a man from Hérouville-Saint-Clair, the jihadist breeding ground in Normandy; and one of Omar's cousins from Nice. Then three more in 2016: a young convert, also from Nice; another convert from the Travellers' community; and finally his own brother Moussa. 'Moussa was humble', reads the group's posthumous statement about him.

When we last interviewed Omar Diaby in the summer of 2016, he had been working on a video for several months in homage to the Kouachi brothers, celebrating the *Charlie Hebdo* attacks. He acknowledged having argued with Abu Firas al-Sury, the former spokesman for Jabhat al-Nusra, who has since been 'droned' by the United States. But he said he directly pledged allegiance to Al Qaeda's central organization – something never confirmed by Al Qaeda, however. 'With Allah as my witness', Omar Diaby said angrily, 'those who told you that Abu Firas, may Allah accept him, refused *Bay'ah* [Author's note: allegiance] are liars, even if they number in the hundreds. Abu Firas told us what we should say to take the oath. The oath was: "The *Bay'ah* to Jabhat al-Nusra." And that's where I said no. We wanted to pledge allegiance directly to Al Qaeda. Then he said: "Al Qaeda and Jabhat al-Nusra are the same thing." I insisted, and from there, we swore allegiance directly to Al Qaeda and not to Jabhat al-Nusra. After this *Bay'ah*, ten people left the group to go to the *dawla*. Abu Firas asked me to take all the bachelors to the Idlib region, but I refused. Then they tried to break our *Bay'ah*, but a *char'i* [Author's note: a judge] stated that the *Bay'ah* was still valid.'

'Their blood may be spilled'

Omar was no longer anywhere near as influential as he was in 2014. In jihadist circles, he had been widely discredited. The arrival of the Islamic State videos in 2015, inspired by Hollywood action films, marked the beginning of a propaganda effort that was far more sophisticated than anything put out by other jihadist organizations, and far surpassing Omar's efforts. The IS declared Omar Omsen, his group and even Jabhat al-Nusra to be apostates – that is to say, deeming that 'their blood may be spilled' according to the common formula for those outside of Islam. 'That's proof of indoctrination, because people who would have said before that Omar was *mash'Allah* and everything, once they got to Syria they completely changed their point of view, just because they'd left his group and joined the IS. One day he's a true believer and the next day he's an apostate who has to be killed. It's absurd. You can't help but start wondering when something like that happens. But they've put something in their heads, they've cut them off from real life. And the IS's influence gets stronger and stronger.'

From 2014 on, almost all of the French nationals leaving for Syria did so in order to join the IS. Omar Omsen's recruiting power was greatly diminished. In the summer of 2016, in order to challenge us on this point, his group announced the arrival of a new Frenchman in its ranks. Ironically, this new recruit was one of the two Toulouse minors who had made waves in the French media in early 2014 for being the first jihadists to leave France for Syria.

The two high school students had spent three weeks at Omar Omsen's home before ceding to their parents' pressure and returning home. Two years later, the two teenagers appeared in court, pretending to have repented of their actions. They were condemned to only six months of prison, but the sentence was suspended in June 2016. After duping the magistrates, one month later, one of the two brothers left for Syria.

Return to Nice

In July 2015, we were back in Nice with Quentin, walking down the Promenade des Anglais. We had been in contact with him since his arrival in Syria. We took advantage of his release from prison to conduct lengthy interviews – to understand and to explain what had happened. After his release from prison, the young man didn't take long to return to the habits of a Nice playboy. This 18-year-old with medium-length hair coated with gel wears a T-shirt and sunglasses and speaks with a slight accent from the south of France. A smiling pretty boy who flirts with the girls on the Promenade with some success. The second evening after his release from prison, he spent the night with an Englishwoman in a hotel. 'I feel pretty good today. All that is behind me now.'

He still fosters, however, strong feelings of resentment against two people in particular. The first being, of course, the man who roped him in in the first place. 'I was hoodwinked by Omar Diaby. War isn't *Assassin's Creed*, it's not a game. Considering how he deals with the subject in his videos, I don't think he understands what human life is and that we only live once.' But Quentin also has bitter feelings for the former mayor of Nice, Christian Estrosi, for being too passive about the threat of terrorism. During Estrosi's term, Omar Omsen was able to recruit more than a hundred jihadists in Nice and deeply inculcate them with jihadist ideology. To the point of turning Nice into the French city most affected by the phenomenon today.

'Why did they wait for all of us to leave Nice before investigating, even though Omar Diaby was such a well-known figure? When I left, he was probably on his sixth or seventh season of videos. It had been going on for years, not just a few months, so they should have known what Omar Diaby was up to. He had been arrested on his way to Afghanistan. He knew exactly what he was doing in the Saint-Charles neighbourhood. I'm angry at the mayor of Nice because he was aware of all this and he let it go on.'

Quentin also blames the famous American social network used by jihadists to facilitate and increase the number of departures to Syria. 'Without Facebook there would only be half as many French nationals over there. Even though it wasn't on Facebook that I discovered jihadism, Facebook got me over there. I made my contacts through Facebook. Facebook shares part of the guilt in that regard.'

Today, Quentin still practises his religion, but says that he rejects jihadism. He even claims to support the French bombardments of the Islamic State in Syria and Iraq. While strolling down the Promenade des Anglais, he talks about reintegrating into society and getting a full-time job.

Almost a year to the day after this conversation, on this same spot, a 19-tonne truck drove into the crowd on the evening of 14 July, killing 86 people and wounding nearly 400. The Islamic State claimed credit for the attack. Omar Omsen admitted to knowing the perpetrator of this act of mass killing in Nice, but considered that he had no influence on the radicalization of this Tunisian man.

The drama nevertheless complicated Quentin's situation. After six months working at a Subway fast-food restaurant, he found a part-time job at Burger King. When it came time to turn his temporary job into a permanent contract, his employer asked him for his identity papers. Quentin had a problem. He gave his employer a red card that he had been given by the French authorities in exchange for his confiscated identity papers. He was obliged to provide an explanation and tell his story to the store's manager. The latter decided not to take the risk and refused to renew his contract. Quentin, despondent, spent the next three weeks carousing in the bars of Nice. On three occasions he failed to appear at the police station, as required by his judicial oversight programme. The police visited his family home. He was placed in police custody and brought before a judge. The magistrate referred to the precedent of Adel Kermiche (who had carried out the attack at the church of Saint-Étienne-du-Rouvray, despite wearing an electronic bracelet) and the context of general fear after the terrorist attack in Nice. Quentin was sent back to prison.

PART SIX
THOSE WHO DIDN'T RETURN

Dope, rap, *nashid* and terrorism

Abu Mujahid sits at his computer in an internet café in Mosul, Iraq's second-biggest city, which has been occupied by the Islamic State since June 2014. The summer of 2016 marked the end of the previous euphoria of the jihadi movement. The military pressure on the group has grown more and more difficult to resist. After a series of defeats, their strongholds are falling one by one. With the support of the bombing raids by the international coalition, the Iraqi forces and their allies are at the gates of the city, which is virtually under siege. But this doesn't seem to worry the Frenchman particularly. He has just ordered a melon smoothie on the quiet street corner. We have been conducting interviews with him via WhatsApp for a month now, and his profile photo shows a fearless face with a baseball cap pulled down over his eyes. The black cap bears the white emblem the Islamic State has claimed as its own: the seal of the Prophet. The young man no longer represents the French *département* he comes from, or his local neighbourhood or his crew, but the Islamic State. But his former life has left indelible traces.

'I'm a simple soldier', he says, while also claiming to be an imam. 'But not a professor-type imam', he says. 'I just direct prayers at the mosque. Sometimes I do the *Khutbah*.[1] In France, I was a *takfiri*[2] *khawarij*,[3] hated by Muslims, even by my family, because I supported jihad. Here all the Iraqis know me, and when I arrive in the mosque – you know what? They're all waiting for me, even if I get there twenty minutes late. Everyone stands up when I arrive. I try to do it right before God, humbly.' In Iraq, his allegiance to the IS gave him immediate social status. He is probably more feared than respected by the inhabitants, however. While he thinks he is celebrated, under his jihad garb is still the same immature, bragging and small-time crook – the wannabe gangsta – he says he was back in France, in the huge Parisian estates where he grew up. Towards his native country, this former rapper now converted to jihadism seems to feel both a vindictive hatred and the pent-up frustration of a rejected lover.

An early death

Just 20 years old, his goal in life is to meet an early death. He speaks with the bravado of an IS die-hard, the most fanatical of the faithful, eager to be killed over there or to return to France to commit a terrorist attack. The triumphant phase of IS expansion from 2013 to 2015 is now over, and Abu Mujahid is forced to acknowledge the subsequent setbacks. 'Mosul is soon going to be surrounded like Ramadi, Fallujah, and Manbij[4] have been. That's why I decided to get an explosive belt for my wife', he explains. 'It means she'll be able to fight the enemy, which will be a great victory for her in this world and in the world beyond. Yeah, I know . . . it might sound like a fantasy, but I firmly believe it. I've decided to stay in Mosul with my wife, even if there's a risk of a siege.'

The tide turned in 2016, gradually bringing the situation back to what it was before 2014: an underground war. Since 2012, more than 1 French jihadist in 5 has chosen to return from Syria and Iraq; 1 in 5 has been killed. Almost 700 are still over there.

But the organization continues to present its failures as small victories – propaganda being the art of turning a loss into a win. 'Plenty of people freaked out, they were afraid of dying, they went home. We don't give a damn, the IS doesn't need them. We're losing ground in Iraq and in Syria. But our faith is as strong as ever. You know why? Because it's a test from God. A way of purging the ranks. We're ready to fight to the death. They can do what they did at Fallujah, we couldn't care less. My wife will just walk out and *bang!* blow you to pieces. Killing the enemy is the only thing that matters. Say I'm in a position of weakness. What do I do? Well, I inflict collateral damage on the enemy at the same time that I kill myself.'

Like every jihadist, Abu Mujahid bases his religious arguments on the biography of the Prophet. 'It's like the *hadith* where the Prophet spoke to a companion before battle. The companion asked him: "If I go to into battle now, will I go to paradise?" He answered: "Yes, you will go to paradise." The companion was holding three dates in his hand. He threw away the three dates, charged into the enemy and was killed.'

The IS didn't wait until its position was weakened to launch into all-out terrorism. Before the first coalition air strikes in Iraq in August 2014, the organization had focused uniquely on the construction of its proto-State between Syria and Iraq. After the strikes, however, it moved from a strictly regional strategy to one of global jihad. In September 2014, its official spokesman, the Syrian Abu Mohamed al-Adnani, not only called for fighters to join its territories to help build the caliphate, but for the first time also called for the killing of coalition-member nationals in any manner and wherever possible, in retaliation for the air strikes. Two years later, from May 2016 on, the organization's calls for 'individual jihad' became even louder.

With setbacks on all fronts, and with the progressive closing of the Turkish border, the IS no longer calls on its supporters to come and join it in person. On the contrary, it asks them to launch attacks in their home countries, preferably against civilians, by any means possible. From Syria or Iraq, the organization now calls for its supporters to kill at home.

'They kill us, we kill them'

Like the 'good soldier' he is, Abu Mujahid agrees absolutely with every part of this discourse. His calls for revenge sound like lines from a rap song: 'We're soldiers of the Islamic State, they kill us, we kill them', he barks. 'You kill my wife, I'll kill yours. You kill my child, of course I'm going to kill your children. The coalition guy who's killed who knows how many Muslims in Manbij, he's going to go home, make love to his wife and have his coffee the next morning, no problem. So we don't care either, we kill women, children, dogs, cats, camels! Everything! Destroy it all! Destroy their tourism. Send those countries down the drain. But not just for the sake of killing people. We know why we're doing it, the IS didn't attack France until they came at us with their planes.'

To legitimize the IS's right to apply the law of an eye for an eye in religious terms, Abu Mujahid shows us documents written in French on his smartphone – references from the Koran that support what he says. 'If you want an Islamic justification explaining why the mujahidin can strike the unbelievers in their home countries, well, just read these PDFs and you'll understand. They're based on Koranic verses which are very clear, there's the name of the Surah and the verse: Surah An-Nahl, Verse 126: "And if you punish [an enemy], punish with an equivalent of that with which you were harmed." And then Surah Al-Baqarah, verse 194: "So whoever has assaulted you, then assault him in the same way that he has assaulted you."'

One PDF is entitled 'Clarification on the targeting of women and children'. Another justifies suicide missions: 'How does Islam view missions involving sacrifice, suicide or martyrdom?' One doesn't need to read the document to know the answer. Then he shows us one last text, put together after the Nice attack in which one-third of the eighty-six people killed were Muslim, which justifies the killing of Muslims as collateral damage in the case of an attack carried out in 'a land of disbelievers'. 'For us, there's no more debate about that', Abu Mujahid insists.

Reasons to attack France

But behind these literalist dogmas, downloadable in PDF format, there are other rationales at work. Global jihad is an integral part of the IS and its emulators. Even before the air strikes, every French member of the ISIL we questioned on the subject praised the crimes of Mohamed Merah, and each dreamed of committing the same kind of killings in France. Only the timing wasn't yet right. The coalition's intervention gave them a perfect excuse to kill off French civilians, one which was seized upon by the organization's hierarchy. Abu Mujahid agrees: 'Of course there were reasons to attack France before it joined the coalition.' He describes a political climate that 'enraged even the most moderate Muslims', citing pell-mell the 'pain au chocolat' polemic launched by the French politician Jean-François Copé, the *Charlie Hebdo* caricatures, secularism and, of course, the laws forbidding the wearing of the niqab in public spaces or the veil in French schools. But he also points to French military interventions in Afghanistan and Mali. And he goes back even further, to crimes of colonization: 'We're Moroccans and Algerians, and France came to Algeria and waged war, exterminating us and committing genocide', he says. 'France has killed too. France has cut Algerian throats and cut off Algerian heads. So there's not only the war it's waging against Islam with its current policies, there's also France's history of waging war against Islam. That's why France is one of our main targets.' France is therefore paying not only for its intervention as part of the coalition in Syria and Iraq, and for its current policies deemed hostile to Islam, but also for its colonial past.

During the summer of 2016, Abu Mujahid appeared in an

official IS video broadcast over the internet in tribute to the killers of Magnanville and Orlando. 'Al hamdoulillah, our mujahidin brothers in the United States and in France have responded favourably to the appeal of Adnani [IS spokesman] *hafidu Allah*', he exclaims in his roughneck accent of a Parisian hoodlum; 'Allah orders us to fight the unbelievers to reach the True Life. We trade this *dunya*[5] for the life beyond. Now I've got a message for those who believe in democracy, for the *kaffir*: You Europeans, you Westerners who want to bring secularism to the Arab world, you'd better follow the example of Spain in 2004 when they joined the coalition against Iraq. They were killed in their own country by the mujahidin. So the Spanish went out in the street and called for their criminal government to resign. Now get out on the streets and tell those bastards Barack Obama and François Hollande to resign! Their foreign policy will do nothing but kill you slowly!'

A small-time drug dealer

Back in France, those in his old neighbourhood recognized him in the video immediately. Not without a bit of surprise. They remembered Abu Mujahid from Montreuil, Seine-Saint-Denis, as a small-time drug dealer, hanging out in the tower block stairwells, dreaming of making it big as a rapper. It was his *jahiliya*,[6] typical of a jihadist, as he admits now: 'Sure, I was a rapper', he says, 'I sang at the Montreuil music festival. I even won the Montreuil Mix Festival one year. I had big plans for myself as a rapper, I was all set up.' Before leaving for Syria, he was finishing a technical diploma in high school, and got along rather well in France. 'I sold my dope, I went to school, Hi Dad, Hi Mom. I was doing fine. I had money for my Nikes, my Lacoste. No worries. I was integrated into society. But that was my *jahiliya*. When God started to guide me, it was an act of faith, straight up. It turned my life upside down.' Indeed, from that point on, his life changed dramatically.

Unlike most French jihadists, Abu Mujahid's introduction to jihadism didn't take place on the internet or in prison, but in a neighbourhood mosque. And not just in any neighbourhood, but in Seine-Saint-Denis, the *département* that holds the record for the most jihadists who have left for Syria. Though raised a Muslim, he attended the mosque only sporadically, without taking it very seriously, more as a way to assert his identity. 'Just between you and me, around the tower blocks, you're always hearing "Come on, let's go down the mosque." It's not just a fad, it's something people share.' But whereas he may have discovered jihadism at the mosque, it wasn't because of any angry sermons from an imam delivered from a minbar. On the contrary, almost no Muslim place of worship in France disseminates such ideology.

But jihadists sometimes use the prayer rooms to gather and to encourage other members of the faithful to join them. That's what happened to Abu Mujahid. He was approached one day in his mosque by two brothers, Yassin and Tarek. They asked him if he wanted to take some 'classes', away from the others. Classes quite different from those given by the mosque's own imam. 'They told us: "Come with us, let's sit down at the far end of the mosque, we'll talk with you about *al-wala wal al-bara*,[7] *kufr bi taghut*."[8] As soon as I heard that, *boom!*, I took their sheets of paper, they gave me the names of stuff to learn, they explained all the different things you had to know about Islam, and, once I heard that, once I really understood, I embraced it.'

Hearing the main points of Salafist dogma was a revelation for him. This young rapper and small-time drug dealer, with more ambitions than real prospects in life, was a perfect candidate for radical ideology. In order to take root, such a line of thinking makes use of a background of 'street radicalism', with its splinters of politico-religious consciousness, and the absence of a strong cultural foundation which might equip an individual with the ability to think objectively and contextualize. Moreover, its anti-system hotchpotch is sanctified by being given a religious framework. He used to sing 'Fuck France' or 'Fuck the Police'.

But now the dogma of *al-wala wal al-bara* told him that a Muslim is obliged to 'disavow' all authority not arising out of sharia law, even to the extent of taking arms against it. To refuse this commandment would be a 'nullifier of Islam'.[9]

Where his rap had once exalted the communitarian spirit of the 'khos du ter ter' – his local crew – in defiance of the rest of society, the dogma of loyalty and disavowal encouraged him to sever all ties with unbelievers, and even to fight against them, while simultaneously uniting with Muslims in a spirit of kindness and fraternity. Where he had once rapped against State oppression, the dogma of *kufr bi taghut* taught him that this democratic State was by its very nature a source of unbelief because its sovereignty came from the people, and that he had to oppose it by force. Having rapped against France and its institutions, he now discovered that the religion in which his parents had raised him not only encouraged him to confront his country through words, but also – and above all – through direct action. Everything came together for the young man; he finally began to understand. It was a very powerful experience.

The transformation was immediate. 'It took one week. Just enough time for me to understand how incredible what I was getting into was. Straight away, the classes showed me that it was the truth. I accepted this *aqida*; I studied it for six months to really understand the whole thing, and after that it was jihad. It was really quick.'

'What I called the truth'

After this powerful revelation, he gave up rap and began to study religious texts. 'I locked myself up at home for a whole year, reading one PDF after the other. PDFs like Sheikh al-Maqdisi's "This is our *aqida*". The whole thing went super-fast: in just a few days I embraced what I call the truth, the *Haqq*. I said to myself, "OK, if that's what God has ordered me to do, I have to do it." And you know what? I totally crushed the mosque leaders, the imams of the secular mosques, in our debates. I really gave it to them, in front of everyone. Afterwards they insulted me, saying "you're just young".' Tarek and Yassin's classes were eventually banned in the mosque. But it was already too late.

The two brothers left for Syria at the end of 2014 and were killed a few months later in Deir ez-Zor.

Less than a year into his own personal studies and after obtaining his high school diploma, Abu Mujahid followed them to Syria with his girlfriend, having converted her to his ideology. He also tried to take as many friends and acquaintances with him as he could. 'It's more difficult with the women. They're really screwed up. You really have to explain it to them. I was even giving secret classes at my high school. In my neighbourhood, I used to smoke dope, because before going to Syria I'd started up again. I was *dawa* in my own neighbourhood. And now, when I talk to guys in my hood who smoke shit, they say: "Yeah, nice call on that terrorist attack, it was wild. May Allah bless you." They really want to come out here, but they're not strong enough.'

In just one year, Abu Mujahid went from the metaphorical 'Fuck France' of his rap songs to the more literal 'Blow France Up' of his IS videos – convinced that it is a divine order. 'I've got a weapon, an M16, a Kalach, a Glock', Abu Mujahid says, posing in a jihad video as if in a rap video. Did the anti-France and anti-police discourse of his rap music prepare the ground for his adhesion to jihadism? Not in his opinion. He claims never to have hated his country before embracing this ideology. 'When I was in my *jahiliya*, I didn't hate France. I used to watch French football, I supported the French team, I had loads of girls, I smoked dope, I used to talk to the police, whereas now I think those assholes should be killed. I got on well with everyone. I got into a little trouble, nothing major, but I was following the programme, visiting the youth counsellors like I was supposed to. I got good results in school, I had no problem with France before beginning to follow the *minhaj*. We'd say things like "Fuck France, we don't give a shit about France, let France burn, we're gonna fuck France up good", but I'll tell you the truth, France is where I grew up, and I did everything over there. So I'm French, that's my nationality. I'm Moroccan and Algerian, sure, but I am French. Except that God tells us: "Don't integrate into French society. Fight France and you will reach paradise."'

'But I hold no grudge against Jacquie or Michel'

Today he claims to hate France, but not the French people, while nevertheless calling for their deaths. He says he has long fantasized about his neighbour's wife, in Montreuil, whom he used to watch from his window, but he was outraged when he allowed her to go out wearing a skirt. He claims to see nothing in France but moral decay and decadence. As an example, he mentions the amateur porno actors Jacquie and Michel, whom he continues to follow from Mosul. 'I was shocked when I saw that they opened a Jacquie and Michel TV Shop in Lyon', he says. 'I can sum up French society in two words: libertine and morally corrupting. Opening a porno store that has girls apply to make porn videos. But I hold no grudge against Jacquie or Michel. Why? Because they never got any guidance. For them, when they die it's over. For us, it's not like that.'

Yet another sign of decadence in a society he nonetheless seems to have loved: 'I was doing great in France', he explains. 'On my old Facebook profile, I'd always get at least 400 or 500 likes on my posts. Photos with girls, loads of pals, I used to go to parties with blue-eyed French girls. I'd be the only Arab in the place. I was completely integrated. As for social status, I was doing well. So, I didn't do it for the status.' But it's hard not to hear the opposite when he says 'I'd be the only Arab in the place.'

This story of a former rapper turned jihadist is not unique. Like him, the vast majority of male jihadists we've interviewed (about 100 since 2012) speak of having been big rap fans before turning to jihad. Many were failed rappers or rap fans. And this is not unique to French jihadists. Among the foreign jihadists who have joined the IS, there have been several well-known rappers such as Deso Dogg from Germany, or Emino from Tunisia.

We met the latter in Tunisia in June 2013, in the home studio he had set up in his mother's house in La Manouba, a middle-class suburb of Tunis. Surrounded by bottles of Jack Daniels and ash-trays overflowing with joints from the night before, Emino rapped about his hate for the police and his love of girls, partying, drink and dope. Two years later, he posted a photo of himself in Mosul on Facebook, standing beside a giant IS flag. He went on to trade his bling-bling rap for *nashids* in Arabic, singing the glory of the IS.

From rap to *nashids*

Music is forbidden within the IS. 'You think we listen to Kaaris[10] over here?' asks Abu Mujahid, offended. Nonetheless, music has not completely disappeared. Even though musical instruments (considered illegal in Islam) are regularly burned, vocal music is not forbidden. So, from evening to morning, the jihadists listen to *nashid* – insistent a cappella religious songs, which help to maintain their warlike determination. After his experience with rap, Abu Mujahid hopes to record a *nashid* in French. He talks about it the way he'd talk of a mix tape which might catch the attention of a record company. 'I wrote the *nashid* with a brother and it looks like I'm definitely going to record it because . . . I'm not saying it's just because of a connection, but I know a guy, who knows another guy . . . He's my friend, the head of media. A French guy. We sent him the text, and it looks like they'll accept it. So I'm hoping to record my first *nashid*. I'm really hoping it'll make some buzz. That's what we're doing with the media now. A big video too, but I can't say exactly when. I'm doing my *nashid* and I'm going off to fight.' If he were still back in his *jahiliya*, he might have added 'a big sound, something heavy'.

From rap to *nashid*, everything changes so that everything remains the same. In both cases, the narcissism, the need for recognition and the targets are all the same. Except that what were previously symbolic victims are now physical and very real. The IS's first French *nashid* was recorded by one of the Clain brothers, Jean-Michel, a convert from Toulouse. The members of the Toulouse group were once close to Mohamed Merah, and were often veterans of the first Iraqi jihad of 2003. Such was the case of the Toulouse killer's ex-brother-in-law, Sabri Essid, and of the only Frenchman to occupy a significant religious position within the IS, known as Abu Omar al-Madani (his real name is Thomas). He is a convert whose parents are school teachers, and whose nickname derives from the fact that he studied Islam and Arabic for several years in Madinah in Saudi Arabia.

Each of these men has appeared in official IS videos. The first had his 10-year-old stepson execute a prisoner. The second, wearing a hood, appeared in a video where he burned his passport and called for attacks to be committed in France. After the French *départements* of Seine-Saint-Denis, les Yvelines and les Alpes-Maritimes, Haute-Garonne ranks fourth in terms of the number of departures to Syria. The men from Toulouse have the toughest reputations, even within jihadist circles. Based near Raqqa, this handful of Frenchmen manages the most important francophone element of the official IS propaganda. Its famous media arm Al-Hayat in particular is responsible for selling the IS as an ideal state, and for threatening France via the francophone magazine *Dar al-Islam* – equivalent to (if less substantial than) the anglophone magazine *Dabiq*.

They are also responsible for the daily news bulletins of the Al-Bayan radio station. This audio newscast is read by different voices in turn, and represents a celebratory litany of all of the group's military achievements around the world, without mentioning any of its defeats. It was on this radio station that Fabien Clain read the official communication claiming responsibility for the attacks of 13 November in Paris. Those attacks, incidentally, gave rise to a *nashid* which had echoes of an R 'n' B classic – except that they celebrated the death of 130 civilians killed in Paris.

'A nashid is poetry', explains Abu Mujahid, 'you write it as music with whatever rhythm you want. And afterwards you sing it, but without any instruments. It will encourage more operations in Europe and especially in France, and really get the brothers fired up.'

Rachid Kassim

Getting the brothers 'fired up' in France was the speciality of Abu Mujahid's neighbour in Mosul. Their wives would often have tea together in their apartment. He too was a failed rapper, originally from the city of Roanne in France. Before leaving for Syria, he had released an EP entitled 'I'm a terrorist.' Over the course of six months, this previously unknown individual became one of the main public enemies of the French intelligence services after appearing in an IS video celebrating the death of eighty-six people in the Nice attacks, with the beheading of a prisoner in the public square of Mosul. 'He was my star, he did it', laughs Abu Mujahid. 'It was good, they gave them a prisoner and told them to cut his throat. I couldn't have done it. Yes, I've killed before. I fight to kill, I'll shoot someone in the head maybe, but I couldn't slit a guy's throat.'

His 'star' was none other than Rachid Kassim, who had his hand in all of the attacks of the summer of 2016: from the attack at Magnanville to the murder of the priest at Saint-Étienne-du-Rouvray, and the failed attack with a car filled with gas cylinders, undertaken by three women in the centre of Paris. In fewer than six months, a dozen individuals were arrested in France on the brink of carrying out attacks, and all under his guidance. Some were 15 years old, and half were women. Every day on his private channel on Telegram, he broadcast messages from his internet café in Mosul, with the rhythm of the rapper he used to be, inciting others to kill in France, while providing tips on how to make their mass attacks even more deadly. He also broadcast lists of the names of famous people to assassinate. Among these names were several French rappers who 'misled the youth', according to him. When Booba sang 'I want to be what I should have been', he seemed to hear 'I want to kill what I should have been.'

From the French army to the caliphate

It was just another of the thousands of scenes of daily horror inside the Islamic State. Two hooded giants, armed and dressed in black, led a blindfolded prisoner in an orange jumpsuit to his death. The Syrian man in his twenties had been found guilty of 'insulting Allah' and was sentenced to death by an Islamic court. A crowd of onlookers formed around them. In the middle of the circle, a third hooded man waited alone, patiently, armed with a gigantic sword. At his feet, a wooden log on which he would cut off his victim's head that morning. The person charged with carrying out the beheading was chosen randomly from among the volunteers in the Islamic police. It was a public execution in a small town in northern Syria, largely administered by French and Tunisian jihadists from the Islamic State. The scene took place in front of the state-of-the-art cameras of the IS media brigades and would later be broadcast on the internet by its official propaganda organs. Showing terror is an essential tool for social control, exercised by the organization that governs primarily through fear. The two men who firmly held the prisoner were about the same age as their victim. Both were French nationals and converts to Islam. Formerly outlaws in their country, they now held the monopoly on legitimate violence, the guarantors of the application of their own authority. They had become the masters of the city. Before leaving for Syria, one had been prosecuted in France for sexual assault. The other, a former inner-city drug dealer, had spent a few months in the French army.

The former French soldier turned jihadist never hid the fact that killing made him happy. He loved to kill. And in Syria, he killed a lot. 'There were executions every day', he said. 'It was nothing special.' This was his main task within the organization. He now acts as one of the proto-State's executioners. These murderous impulses, psychopathological in nature, were present in him before jihad. Within the Islamic State, he integrated into the *Shurta*. Unlike the *Hisbah*, the other armed wing of the religious police responsible for enforcing the wearing of the veil, the hours of prayer or the ban on smoking, the *Shurta* is responsible for repressing acts punishable by amputation or death: theft, rape, murder, espionage, witchcraft, adultery, blasphemy or homosexuality. Being part of this unit allowed him to satisfy his desire to kill in the name of a transcendent cause completely.

'The important thing is how you die'

But he had been driven by another ambition since his arrival in Syria in 2012, long before France entered the war against his organization: to return to his home country in order to 'murder as many people as possible', he says, and be killed, because 'everybody's going to die, the important thing is how you die'. Beyond his criminal impulses, however, he was absolutely convinced of the validity of his understanding of Islam and his assurance of earning the favours granted to martyrs in the afterlife by carrying out an attack in France. He had been planning and speaking to us about his attack since 2013, one year before France's intervention as part of the coalition in Syria and Iraq.

'Yes, I've got a list of organizational and human targets', he explained a few months before 13 November 2015; 'organizations, political groups, companies and specific individuals. It's not complicated. I start small, a simple murder, without claiming credit for it. Then I increase the importance of the targets, little by little. And when the goal is reached, we claim credit for everything, providing all the evidence, mocking them. It's like we're saying: we do what we want, wherever we want. When the *khilafa* [caliphate] wants someone dead, it's only a matter of time. Allah is on the side of those who are patient.'

Before his conversion to Islam, and even before he put on a military uniform, this Frenchman, not yet 25, already had blood on his hands. He said he enlisted in the French army not out of patriotism but merely because of the attraction of being paid to carry out legal murder. 'Being allowed to kill was what attracted me to it', he admitted. 'I had no respect for human life before Islam', he continued, 'but now I only have respect for the blood of Muslims'.

Like him, at least a dozen former French soldiers have joined the jihadist ranks in Syria. Not all have done so for the same reasons. Some spent a much longer time in the service, sometimes in elite units. They were careful not to draw attention to themselves. This was the case of Abu Souleymane, a French resident of Moroccan origin from the city of Lunel, who spent two years under the tri-colour flag in the French Foreign Legion, and who participated in multiple foreign operations, especially in Afghanistan. The Islamic State was quick to take advantage of the expertise he acquired fighting for the French army. In 2015, Abu Souleymane set up his own brigade and training camp near the Deir ez-Zor. He later became the emir of one of the main units of the *jaysh khilafah*, the army of the caliphate. This *katiba*, known as 'Tarik ibn Zyad', was mainly made up of Europeans, including many Frenchmen, and took part in fighting throughout Iraq.

Younes the deserter

Another Frenchman had a similar profile. In the jihadosphere, he was known by his pseudonym 'Younes the deserter'.

The nickname fit him well: he says that he integrated into the French army in the hopes of being trained in fighting before deserting and waging jihad. He categorically refused to provide any biographical information about himself. He did, however, accept to be interviewed, as long as the questions focused solely on his time spent in the French army, and, more specifically, among the parachute commandos, an elite unit from which the French special forces often draw their members. When he joined the army at the age of 18, he explained, he knew little about his religion and didn't practise very much. 'At that time, I wanted things to change', he said. 'I looked at the world around me, with its decadence and lack of moral values, and I decided at around the age of 17 to pull myself together and return to my Lord. That was when I joined the army. At the time I had read the chapter about jihad in the *Sahih al-Bukhari*[11] and I had just discovered the merit of the combatants on Allah's path, and the high rank Allah granted to martyrs.'

During the first year of his classes, while going through his military training, he continued his return to Islam and was radicalized even further by the texts he read on the internet, 'because you can find on the internet the books that are banned for sale in France'. Within the army, he joined the parachute commando units. And it was within these units that he said he had a new revelation. 'Praise Allah, who opened my eyes and brought me out of the darkness into the light. I remember exactly the thoughts that crossed my mind as I saw them. I saw the killers of the Taliban, the enemies of Islam. I felt like I'd gone 800 years back in time and landed in the Middle Ages. I really saw crusaders – they had the heads of knights, the only difference was that instead of wearing a white cassock with a red cross, they were dressed in French green and black uniforms with the unit's insignia.'

He added: 'And if that wasn't enough, the building that housed the unit was named after a soldier killed during the Algerian war. I also learned that our commando unit had been disbanded after the war in Algeria for war crimes. It was then renamed and divided into three different units. But the icing on the cake was the book of military songs they gave us. One of them said: "And we will fly the French flag over the lands of Islam." There was a time when I tried to reconcile the army and Islam, but from that moment my disavowal was total. I decided to go and take the side of my Lord and defend my religion.'

From that moment forward, Younes began to isolate himself within his unit. He became more and more determined to desert from the French armed forces and join the enemy camp. But first, he had to be patient. 'Rather than desert, I preferred to keep quiet and stay in the unit to save up money to join the jihadi movement and to receive training in combat that would allow me to serve Allah's cause.' While working in the commando unit, he kept up his religious readings and his daily prayers, hesitating whether to carry out an attack within his unit or to leave it. 'I continued my journey towards Allah and got to know my religion better. I read and reread the Koran every day, as well as the biography of the Prophet.' He took part in a final military action in Chad, but his superiors got wind of his intentions and decided to remove him from service, forbidding him from taking part in foreign operations. They even confiscated his weapons in the end. Younes quit his regiment and left for Syria. 'If you're still wondering why I wage jihad, I'd simply say that I'm one servant of Allah among many, one who knows that his Lord's promise is the truth, and that his threat is the truth. I left behind my father and mother, without the hope of ever seeing them again, and I jumped into battle.'

He always refused to give details of his actual activity within the Islamic State, but he actively participated in battles in Syria and Iraq. He was very critical, however, of the IS's triumphant propaganda, which only announces the group's victories and never mentions its defeats or the number of jihadists who sacrificed their lives in these battles. Nor did he conceal his scorn for the French nationals who hide far behind the front lines by serving in the Islamic police, or the media brigades, or who spend their days flirting with women on the internet and making videos while others wage war to bring them new territories and the spoils of war: 'Equipment, money, furniture, women . . . Kurds, Christians and Yezidies.'

Very active on the front, he was never tempted to take a captive as his slave. When speaking of these women, he did so in a totally dehumanized way, as if describing a household pet. But in the end, for him, a woman was just more trouble than she was worth. He told the story of a Libyan jihadist from his neighbourhood who had too many problems with his own. 'He had bought a *sabbyia* who was 14 or 15 years old. And he never consummated the relationship without the girl's consent. He even gave her gifts, dresses, etc., and she still said no. She simply refused. Until the day she took a grenade and threw it into the house when he was gone. So, when he came home, he gave her a beating, which was completely normal. He must have been too nice to her. She'd gotten her confidence up. And after she finally accepted, she started being nice, naturally. There were women who killed their owners. There was one who committed suicide with her daughter. And some of them are bought with their child for between $1,500 and $12,000. But to tell you the truth, given how the Kurds look, I wouldn't take them even if they were given to me. So I wasn't interested.'

Younes preferred to fight. He sometimes thought of returning to organize an attack in France. 'An eye for an eye', he said. But two years after his arrival, his alleged death in Syria was announced by a close friend in early 2016. 'He fell near Aleppo. His *katiba* tried to take over a wheat processing plant, but the *koffar* hid at the top of the wheat silo. He was trying to pick up a brother from the ground when he was shot. There apparently was an impressive light shining on his face. He was serene. He left with a smile.'

Epilogue

Of all the countries of the West, France is the most threatened, targeted and affected by jihadism. Not only by the Islamic State, but also by Al Qaeda, which remains a very real threat today. From Khaled Kelkal to the Roubaix gang and Mohamed Merah, this phenomenon is anything but new, but two factors have expanded its scope to an unprecedented level. On one hand, there is the proximity of the war in Syria and the possibilities it has offered to foreign volunteers since the summer of 2012, when jihadists first seized parts of Aleppo. At that time, jihadist groups began flooding the video-sharing platforms with images of abuses committed by the Syrian regime against its civilians, with the message 'Come save the Syrian people.' This generated a sincere outpouring of emotion, fed in particular by the inaction of the international community and France's ambiguous foreign policy towards the Syrian rebels. Never before had a jihadi movement been so readily accessible, just at the gates of Europe. On the other hand, there was the massive circulation of extremely sophisticated and appealing jihadist propaganda in French on the social networks. Before these networks, propaganda on the internet was still a relatively underground phenomenon, and reached a smaller public through forums reserved for the initiated. The Ansar al-Haqq forum ('The Partisans of Truth'), for example, played an important role in the translation of jihadist texts that were impossible to find even in the most extremist book stores in France – creating an open access library for the study of jihadism.

What changed was that jihadists started using the internet like everybody else. They came out into the open, so to speak. The public diffusion of their ideology over the internet became a mass phenomenon in 2012: it was then that French citizens began posting photos of themselves carrying weapons on their Facebook pages. These selfies from Syria helped speed up the entire process, turning the French jihadist movement into a kind of television reality show, where 'Five-star jihad' was sold and packaged as a 'LOL' experience. Its participants drew attention to themselves by revealing their inner lives with a narcissism and a quest for celebrity worthy of Andy Warhol, all while pretending to act as the sole defenders of their religion. Their engagement was often a selfish and yet rational decision, motivated by a strictly personal desire for self-fulfilment.

Many of those interviewed said that they decided to leave for banal reasons, such as wanting to trade their boring lives without prospects for the future in France for an exciting existence in Syria. All of the interviewees mentioned feeling frustrated and humiliated in France. For many, coming from a minority popula-tion there made them feel inferior, a sentiment caused by very real problems with discrimination and a lack of effective repre-sentation in French politics and media. A Frenchman who fought in an anglophone brigade for the IS even went so far as to claim that this was why British jihadists hated their country of origin less than the French.

The Islamic State provides these bruised egos with dignity, social status and a faith in spiritual transcendence. The group's propaganda fills the ideological vacuum of postmodernity by selling them a product. At the same time, secularized capitalist societies are no longer capable of arousing hope through political change. The jihadist project is the utopia of an ideal city for all Muslims, which is used to justify all forms of violence done in its name. With jihad, the losers become the lords, and the movement's followers become Islamic superheroes, with the obsessional assurance of reaching heaven in the afterlife. Though their effect is often minimized, the power of real religious beliefs and the myth of the favours granted to martyrs cannot be ignored when determining what triggers lead to violence.

These dynamics go beyond religion, however. The dominated in France are transformed into the masters in Syria. These men and women who are subject to legislation which, they believe, oppresses them become the creators of their own laws in Syria and take over the monopoly on state violence. They play and they kill, live on Facebook, in the defence of 'authentic Islam' and the myth of the Umma.

Starting in 2013, the French began live-tweeting their departures to Syria. In 2016, in France, one of these men used Facebook Live from the doorstep of the home where he had just killed two people, claiming credit for the attack. Thanks to its perfect mastery of the social web, the Islamic State has turned this trend into an industrial powerhouse by inventing viral jihadism. This is a new form of propaganda that makes the previous efforts by Al Qaeda look 'old fashioned', according to the researcher Romain Caillet. The viral popularity and its morbid relativism trivialize extreme violence while reaching broad swathes of youths in what we have called in this book the 'jihadosphere': a digital matrix of collective indoctrination, described by one of the 'returned' as a 'collective trance'.

These tools are also particularly helpful to anyone looking to join the jihadi movement. Would-be jihadists can now use the internet to research their upcoming trip, turning the social networks into virtual travel guides. As early as 2014, terrorist tutorials began circulating in French: how-to guides on committing mass terrorist attacks or targeted assassinations using rudimentary tools – a form of 'Terrorism for Dummies'.

The institutional discourse often reminds us that it is difficult to draw up a typology of jihadist profiles. Nevertheless, certain patterns stand out clearly. If there is one common denominator among all the 'French jihadists', across all generations and time periods, it is their recognition of *jahiliya*, or a period of 'pre-Islamic ignorance'. Before jihad, they describe their lives as devoid of religious piety, often marked by excesses. Their return to a religious and cultural form of Islam is an instinctual and redemptive experience. Jihad for them means both a forgiveness of their sins and vices, and an end to their pent-up frustrations.

Before jihad, some were into music, and many came from rap. They were schoolkids, university students or unemployed men and women living on minimum social benefits. Others were soldiers, taxi drivers, bus drivers, athletes, temps, or worked in factories or in retail stores. More rarely, they were doctors or engineers. Much more frequently, petty criminals. Still others came from happy families. Though it is true that jihadism doesn't only happen to others, as the public authorities now inform us, it doesn't happen to just anybody either. At the moment they break with their *jahiliya*, often in only a few months, a specific set of factors leads them to embrace extremist ideology very quickly.

Socio-economic conditions, perhaps unsurprisingly, are one of the main factors behind this phenomenon. But simply pointing to social determinants neither excuses nor really explains the reality of the situation. Jihadism is not just an ideology of the poor. The problem can't be explained simply in terms of immigration, petty crime and inner cities. This book tells the story of a well-off family of doctors who left for Syria to find their son in the midst of the IS. And there is the tale of a former choirboy from Brittany who returned to France with four wives and six children, after spending four years in Syria. The middle classes, and sometimes even the upper classes of society, can also be affected. But jihadists from well-off families remain exceptions. The large majority of French jihadists come from working-class backgrounds – most of the people interviewed in this book grew up in poor neighbourhoods in France and never let go of their inner-city social codes and behaviours. This would later earn them a poor reputation in Syria, where they were accused of importing a 'gangsta *jahiliya*' from their neighbourhoods back home.

The geography of French jihad supports this observation. Almost all areas of France are affected, of course, but to different degrees. Regional trends stand out, with four *départements* at the head of the list. With well over a hundred departures since 2012, Seine-Saint-Denis is the French *département* most affected by the phenomenon. The official figures must be treated with caution, however, because the surveys carried out by the French Interior Ministry are not always identical with those from the prefectures at a local level, depending on whether women and children are counted. Moreover, a margin of error of 10–15 per cent is generally assumed. But the overall trends are correct. After Saint-Denis comes a bastion of bourgeois conservatism in France: Yvelines. Not, of course, that its capital Versailles has been transformed into a hotbed of jihad activity, but because certain red zones like Mantes or Trappes – the city the most affected by the phenomenon in France, in proportion to its population – have pushed the *département* up to the top. More than 80 people have left Trappes out of a population of 30,000 – the highest ratio in France. Local jihadists have taken to referring to the city as 'Trappistan'. Next on the list are the Alpes-Maritimes and Haute-Garonne *départements*. In absolute numbers (but not in terms of the proportion of its population), Nice has become the city the most affected by jihadism, with more than 100 departures. This is attributable to a high level of extremist preaching in its working-class neighbourhoods, carried out for many years by one charismatic and well-known figure in particular, before his departure for Syria.

Small and medium-sized cities have also constituted fertile recruitment zones, with between 20 and 50 departures from cities with 20,000 to 50,000 inhabitants. Such is the case, for example, in Nîmes, Lunel, Roubaix and Hérouville-Saint-Clair. While the mimetic logic of a 'group of mates' doesn't apply in all cases, it can nevertheless play an important role. Its effects were visible in Strasbourg, in the group of one of the kamikazes who attacked the Bataclan in Paris, or in Lunel, where more than 20 departures were recorded from among the same network of schoolmates and neighbourhood acquaintances. After their departures, the movement slowed to a trickle. One of them told me that one of his brothers, a former hashish dealer and rapper, had been drawn to Syria by his older brother, who wanted to 'put him on the right path'. Just a few weeks before leaving for Syria, he was posing in front of a souped-up BMW wearing gold chains. He started to pray only after his arrival in Syria. Both brothers were killed in Deir ez-Zor a few months after his arrival. Some left for Syria without any particular religious convictions, simply in order to join a neighbourhood friend or a brother, and embraced the murderous ideology only afterwards.

Jihadism finds ready subjects in individuals already exhibiting strong anti-conformist tendencies and a hostility towards public institutions in France. A majority of those interviewed were immersed in the 'fuck France and fuck the police' radicalism expressed in French rap music, and were very familiar with conspiracy theories with anti-Semitic overtones. Petty criminals and prison inmates are particularly susceptible to this ideology: rather than admonishing them to change their criminal lifestyles, jihadism allows them to stay as they are, while providing religious legitimization for their actions. Everything changes, ultimately to remain the same.

The words and behaviours may appear transformed when they Islamicized, but the change is only superficial. Whereas the iconography and social norms of these two worlds appear as polar opposites, in reality they are very close and completely interchangeable. Under jihadism, one no longer represents his neighbourhood, but the *dawla*. Rap is exchanged for *nashids*, and armed robberies and burglaries for *ghanima*. To this is added the possibility of enjoying a hypersexual lifestyle under the cover of polygamy, with stocks of women in the *maqqars* and Yezidi slaves at their disposal.

Criminal behaviour is 'jihadized' by rendering what is illegal under French law compatible with Islam. The criminal is no longer pushed to change his lifestyle, but, on the contrary, receives transcendental blessing for his actions. This explains why the predisposition to religious radicalization is stronger than average not only among petty criminals, but also among prison inmates. Moreover, these two worlds, with their similar socio-economic contexts and compatible social codes and norms, not only encounter one another in prison, but are compelled to a long-term coexistence. These factors turn prison into an ideal breeding ground for jihadism, among a population that is particularly susceptible to its message. The record numbers of terrorist detainees now entering into the French prison system only exacerbate the problem. Care must be taken, however, to avoid hasty overgeneralizations. While petty criminals are disproportionately responsible for terrorist attacks, they are less represented among the French nationals active in Syria. And 70 per cent of terrorist detainees have never spent time in prison before. Even though it is very tempting to explain jihadism in terms of petty crime and juvenile delinquency (and they certainly apply in some cases), other factors are at work.

Before embracing jihadism, many were introduced to Islam by friends or family members, or in highly proselytizing and rigorous, but ultimately non-violent, Muslim mosques, such as those of the Salafists or the Tablighi. Some first became interested in Quietist Salafism, before deciding that they were unable to practise their religion in secular France. They considered the laws in their home country to be a tool used against Islam. They were new to the practice of their religion, and nearly all considered themselves to be converts. They then broke with the Quietist circles, too compromised in their eyes due to their acceptance of secular powers. It should also be noted that almost all of those interviewed received religious educations, in homes that were hostile to jihadism. Their religious upbringing was highly influential, according to them. Many say that, had they not received this education, jihadist ideology might not have resonated in the same way with their early political radicalism.

Moreover, this ideology provides psychological structure to its adherents and helps smooth out problems related to complex and sometimes conflicting identities. Empirically speaking, we can estimate that approximately 70 per cent of those concerned by the phenomenon came from Muslim homes that, though perhaps conservative, nevertheless were hostile to jihadism. The remaining 30 per cent were converts from Christianity and used to go to church regularly. One factor stands out particularly in this group: most come from working-class families and at least half are minorities. Jihadist converts are more often named Kevin than Jean-Eudes. And when they are named Jean-Édouard, Jean-Michel or Willy, they are generally West Indian. The proportion of those raised in Christian homes from sub-Saharan immigration, or from Portuguese households, or, to a lesser extent, from Asian families (Korean or Vietnamese), is very high. France's overseas territories are also well represented among jihad converts. Recruits coming from the Travellers' community have also been noted. For them as well, coming for the most part from working-class sections of society, jihadism provides a protective shield for bruised egos, one that transforms daily humiliations and feelings of social inferiority into a cathartic expression of power, by claiming to erase distinctions of nationality and ethnicity, while at the same time turning them into the sole defenders and guarantors of the 'truth' of Islam.

In addition, the family environment also plays an important role. French institutions often present the families as a solution – but, in many cases, they appear to be part of the problem. Without falling into facile psychological stereotypes, and remembering that large numbers still have both parents, it is nevertheless noteworthy that many of those interviewed for this book say they have a very close relationship with their mothers, in the absence of a father figure. Another recurring pattern is that of children of couples from different ethnic or religious backgrounds. For these children, educated in a predominantly white, republican and universalizing France, their conflicting identities can run counter to the forces of assimilation there. Jihadism offers a barrier against these tendencies, by providing its adherents with a framework to help in the construction of their identities.

Sometimes the family units are completely dysfunctional. For example, one young woman from the south of France, currently living in Syria, converted to jihadism after having been raised by two drug-addict parents. Her mother fell into prostitution and died from an overdose. Another example: a convert from the centre of France whose alcoholic father would beat her and her mother after the latter came home from her factory job. Finally, there was the case of the young French woman who became a prostitute after being sexually abused as a child.

Some speak of sexual abuse within the family unit. Others have been confronted with illnesses or the sudden deaths of family members, or have been abandoned. Such dysfunctional relationships, though they may be imperceptible within the family units themselves, must also be taken into consideration. Jihadism can be a cathartic experience for these individuals, washing away what they perceive as the sufferings or sins inflicted on them by close friends or family members. In this sense, jihadist ideology provides relief and a faith in a paradisiac future, together with a code of conduct that determines all aspects of earthly life and a sense of pride and superiority over non-believers: the feeling of being reborn into a community of the elect.

Of course, these specific cases aren't enough to draw up a clear psychological profile of the typical jihadist, simply because many have never had the slightest traumatic experience and their family and school histories are remarkable only for their banality.

Despite certain extreme cases, not all jihadists are crazy or stupid. Describing jihadism solely in terms of a mental pathology or a form of sectarian indoctrination allows public authorities to ignore the rational decision behind the personal, political and religious engagement that jihadism undeniably represents for the persons concerned. Public institutions and politicians, however, find this reality harder to admit. But the psychopathological aspect cannot be ignored either. Here again, no hard numbers are available, only individual examples. A Frenchman who took pleasure in being able to bring his three children to see a homosexual thrown from the top of a building and then stoned to death in Syria admitted to me that he had undergone psychiatric treatment for schizophrenia during his *jahiliya*. Another man, who was hesitating between returning to France or carrying out a kamikaze attack in Iraq, told me that, before jihad, he had been in a psychiatric hospital multiple times for severe and chronic episodes of depression and several attempted suicides. Still another, who became an executioner for the IS, told me that he enjoyed the act of killing – the sadistic pleasure he took from committing murder was sublimated religiously. Finally, numerous women mentioned suffering from psychological troubles caused by previously suffered sexual or domestic abuse.

Sometimes, sexual repression may be a key to understanding the phenomenon. One man who returned from Syria, currently in prison after spending two years in the Islamic State, confessed to me that he had always been a homosexual, but he was unable to explain whether his sexual orientation might have played a role in his jihadist engagement. Though this scenario isn't unique, the majority of jihadists say that they never experienced particular psychological problems or traumas before jihad.

Until the end of 2016, the French political and legal systems were guilty of a form of gender bias in regard to female jihadists, in which women were considered as victims. Yet these same women consider the wearing of a full veil to be a 'liberating experience' vis-à-vis the male gaze, and they left for Syria voluntarily, demonstrating an ideological determination that equals, or even surpasses, that of the men. They reject with the same violence both the model of society imposed on them by the French Republic, and also the obligations on modern women today: gender equality, which they consider to be against their religion, and the social pressure to succeed in their professional, social and family lives in a society based on competition between individuals. Jihadist ideology, they claim, provides them with the satisfaction of no longer being judged by their physical appearances or by their brand of clothes. They are finally treated as 'equals'.

Their submission is voluntary, even if also socially determined to a certain extent. But their embracing of jihadism arises from the same religious convictions, the same desire for revenge and the same rejection of Western values as we have seen with the men. The reasons behind their departures for Syria, or for their support of terrorist attacks, are identical. In some couples, it is the woman who acts as the motivating force for radicalization, and some are more in favour of terrorist attacks than their spouses.

In their propaganda, French jihadists often highlight the profiles of engineers or doctors in their ranks. While such cases do exist, they remain exceptional. In reality, the general level of education is relatively low. This has no bearing on their level of intelligence, however. In the same way that jihadists are not all clinically insane, not all of them are idiots either, even if it may be tempting and reassuring to believe so. Without specific figures, it becomes hard to say much about the amount of education the French jihadists have received. If I consider only those persons I interviewed for my first book and for this book, some of them completed university studies – in literature, sciences, law or economics – but most stopped at their secondary school diplomas, or after receiving vocational or technical certificates, or dropped out of school completely. The age group of those concerned also helps to explain the phenomenon. Most embraced

jihadism around the age of 20. The generally low level of university and religious education in the Islamic State has even become
the subject of jokes among the jihadists: insults such as 'welfare
baby' or 'special-needs kid' are common in the jihadi movement.

The psychological interpretation of jihad shouldn't lead us
to forget the reality of religious conviction and indoctrination
through religious texts and books written by ideologues. Those
who embrace the movement experience jihad as a religious and
political engagement, supported by the absolute conviction that
they have found the sole authentic interpretation of Islam. This
certitude of practising the purest form of the Prophet's religion
takes place in an ideological echo chamber, making it even more
difficult to challenge. Jihadists don't feel that they've joined a
sect, but instead that they are practising the only true form of
Islam. Their politico-religious interpretation is 'rational', or, in
any case, coherent: jihadists fight democracy because popular
sovereignty usurps God's authority to create laws, putting man
in his place.

This explains why 'deradicalization' efforts aimed at presenting
jihadists with an alternative form of Islam – one that is normative and democratic – while repeatedly maintaining that they
are mistaken in their beliefs, is destined to fail. Jihadists didn't
invent the texts of the Muslim tradition, nor the verses of the
Koran or the hundreds of thousands of *hadiths* they use to justify
their actions in religious terms. But whereas the great majority
of Muslims continue to insist that these texts must be placed in
their seventh-century context, and that they no longer apply to
our contemporary world, jihadists persist in interpreting these
notions of combat in their particular way, and even use them to
disqualify other Muslims and justify their murders.

They apply literal interpretations of these texts, often only
available to them in French translations in PDF documents. They
try to imitate the lives of the Prophet and his companions from
the seventh and eighth centuries, while keeping their Air Max
trainers on their feet and their iPhones in their hands, halfway

Epilogue   243

between capitalist consumerism and the fantasy world of medieval battles of the early days of Islam.

The IS is particularly skilled at creating links between these scriptural texts and contemporary events, with a force that seems impossible to counter. A Frenchman I had met in Paris in 2013 before his departure contacted me in the summer of 2014 from Syria to inform me that he wanted to return to France. He had been wounded in battle and was physically and mentally exhausted. But his mind was changed in August 2014 with the first American air strikes against IS positions. For, in his eyes, the Western intervention was a clear sign that Muslim eschatological prophecies were being fulfilled. When he was in Paris, he said he was going to participate in the construction of a caliphate. He also said that, once this caliphate was proclaimed, according to a *hadith*, a coalition of eighty different countries would come together to destroy it. 'Do you remember the *hadith* about the eighty flags I told you about in Paris before I went to Syria?' he asked excitedly one day in August 2014: 'I told you that there would be a coalition against us after the return of the *Khilafah*! The coalition's intervention against us is proof that the *hadith* was true! It proves that the *hadith* about the eighty flags is authentic, and that the *dawla* is moving forward according to the prophecy! So now all my doubts are gone, I'm not leaving, I want to die here.'

The *hadith* in question has been used by every jihadist group since the birth of contemporary jihad in Afghanistan in the 1980s, in order to spur their volunteers into action. But for him, the coalition's intervention was an indisputable sign from God, proof that the Islamic State's project has divine support.

In fact, the correspondences between prophecies and world events, as established by the group's propaganda teams, provides for many jihadists clear evidence of the Koran's truth. And it is no coincidence that the IS makes extensive use of *hadiths* and Koranic verses in its media productions. The video claiming credit for the terrorist attacks of 13 November was entitled:

'And slay them wherever you find them'. It's an excerpt from the fifth verse of the ninth surah. 'When the sacred months are over slay the idolaters wherever you find them. Arrest them, besiege them, and lie in ambush everywhere for them . . . ' The young people who discover these verses and these *hadiths* on the internet are completely deaf to those who, at the mosque or elsewhere, might try to explain that the meaning of these prophecies must be understood in a symbolic context that is inapplicable to today's world. For those who have come to the texts on their own, however, or through jihadist propaganda, the figurative and modernizing interpretation is an 'innovation' – an anathema because it distorts and slants the meaning they believe to be the original one.

For them, Muslims who deny their literal interpretations of the texts are guilty of blaspheming their religion, in so far as they reject part of the texts in order to 'please the unbelievers'. In the absence of clergy, however – even if a spiritual authority exists in Saudi Arabia for the Quietist Salafists – no one seems sufficiently credible to challenge their ultra-sectarian reading of Islam. French media, however, by refusing to accept the reality of a link between the texts of the Muslim tradition and jihadism, prefer to hide behind a rhetoric claiming that terrorism and Islam have nothing to do with one another. At the same time, influential Muslim leaders remain mired in conspiracy theories, refusing to consider jihadism as anything but a Western or Zionist invention.

This allows, for example, one of the 'returned' in this book to consider himself to have repented of his engagement, while continuing to view this form of Islam as the only authentic one. He has joined the ranks of the 'ex-Muslims' as they call themselves, by denying his religion as a whole. Several others claim to have abandoned jihadism in favour of Quietist Salafism. Finally, a majority of them, and especially those who have spent time in prison, express disappointment with their experience, but without repenting of their actions. They remain loyal, and profoundly attached, to the jihadi movement. Two women who have returned from the Islamic State say they would like to return there. One of them even says she hopes to see new terrorist attacks in France.

Since the spring of 2016, the Islamic State has been losing ground on all fronts, and has lost its outposts along the Turkish border. It can no longer welcome massive numbers of new recruits from abroad. Now, in France, the number of departures risks being overtaken by the number of returning jihadists. The public authorities, overwhelmed by the inflow, are trying to figure out how to deal with this potentially very dangerous population. Whereas Al Qaeda never disappeared completely, the Islamic State is beginning to decline – in both military and propagandistic terms – but continues to exist in a different form. And its message remains. Its videos are fewer, and, in France, its supporters have become much more discreet, as a result of the increasing number of prison sentences for inciting terrorism. They no longer dare reveal their true identities on the social networks. The euphoric period is now over for them.

This gradual return to the underground, however, is not necessarily good news for France. The IS's global terrorist strategy has shifted to align itself with that which is practised by Al Qaeda. Whereas its spokesman in May 2016 incited others to come to the areas under its control, in his final message before being 'droned' by the United States, the group no longer calls on its supporters to carry out their *hijra*, but now orders them to remain where they are so as to kill as many civilians as possible by whatever means at their disposal. The threat is three-fold: there are the returning individuals who have received military training and who have been tasked with carrying out terrorist attacks. There are also the 'returned' who are disappointed by their experience but who have not repented of their acts and remain capable of carrying out attacks individually. And, finally, there are the group's supporters who have stayed in France and who have embraced the terrorist discourse. According to some of the 'returned', these individuals are sometimes even more fanatical than those who have left for

Syria. This threat, which will remain in place for decades, can be summarized using an Islamic State slogan, coined after their loss of the city of Manbij in Syria: 'We may have lost a battle, but we've won a generation that knows its enemy.'

Notes

Part One   Bilel

1 His first name has been changed.

2 The Syrian branch of Al Qaeda, active since the first terrorist attack it claimed as its own in late 2011. The unit was first sent from Iraq by the Islamic State of Iraq (the current IS). When, in 2013 in Syria, the IS's territory and military strength grew, they separated from the Jabhat al-Nusra. Its emir, the Syrian Abu Mohamed Al-Jolani, is now willing to join forces with other rebel groups, including non-jihadists, to fight the Syrian regime and the IS.

3 The term means 'emigration' in spoken Arabic. In the Muslim imagination, the word refers to the Hijra period of the seventh century, when the Prophet Mohamed had to leave Mecca for Medina. For jihadists, it represents an emigration from the land of Islam and those who practise *hijra* are known as *muhajirun* (literally 'those who have emigrated'), as opposed to locals, known as *ansar*.

4 In Syria, a *fitna* refers to the division between rebel groups: those pro-Al Qaeda and those close to the Islamic State.

At first dogmatic in nature, this *fitna* began in the spring of 2013 and took a clear military turn in early 2014, with executions and armed battles between the different groups.

5 Islamic law, based on Muslim holy scriptures and legal schools, whose interpretation is more or less rigorous or literal, depending on the religious current to which those who apply it belong. This question was one of the main methodological points of disagreement between the Syrian branch of Al Qaeda and the Islamic State in Syria. For Jabhat al-Nusra, the priority was and remains the fall of Bashar al-Assad's regime, with the application of sharia law being considered as the end goal, but only after the taking of Damascus; for the IS, however, from 2013 the priority has been the strict application of sharia law in the conquered territories, without waiting for the fall of Damascus.

6 *Dawla*, meaning 'State' in Arabic, is the name used by the members of the Islamic State and its partisans to refer to the organization.

7 An *emni* is a member of the secret services of the IS, in charge of information-gathering within the group and counter-espionage.

8 The term *bayah* refers to an oath of allegiance. The oath takes place orally, in public, and is made to the IS caliphate, considered as 'the emir of the believers'.

9 The *zakat* is one of the five mandatory pillars of Islam. It refers to almsgiving: everyone must give 2.5 per cent of his property and annual income. Within the territory that it controls, the IS looks after the collection of this levy and its redistribution.

10 The equivalent of a prefect in Arabic, the *wali* is the most important person in the IS's regional administrative hierarchy.

11 Her first name has been changed.

12 The jihadists themselves sometimes accuse each other of extremism. *Ghulat takfir* is an expression used only by jihad-

ists, and means literally 'the exaggerators of *takfir*', or 'those who excessively accuse other Muslims of disbelief'.

13 For more than a year, the IS pushed the other rebel groups out of Deir ez-Zor in eastern Syria, and now faces only the regime in this strategic and oil-rich city. Several thousand Syrian soldiers and civilians are still surrounded by the IS in the area around the airport and a part of the city centre they still control. Cut off from the world, with no ground access to the outside, this pro-Bashar pocket of resistance only receives supplies by night from Damascus, by helicopter and by air. The airport is a vital strategic point for both sides, and the theatre of a fierce and deadly battle.

Part Two   Yassin

1 For security reasons, his first name has been changed and the area in France where he lives will not be mentioned.

2 A small town of 25,000 inhabitants in the Hérault region in France. Around 20 people have left this town to wage jihad in Syria. Half of them have been killed there.

3 For four months, the Kurdish city of Kobanî was the theatre of one of the costliest battles for the Islamic State, which had engaged all of its forces there. Symbolically, the coalition bombarded the city massively in order to break the jihadists' momentum following their victory. The strategy was successful, and the IS was defeated there in January 2015, from which time the group has steadily lost ground on all fronts.

4 Full veil that covers the eyes, with gloves to cover the hands.

5 The Islamic State announced his death on 30 August 2016, presumably killed by an American drone attack.

6 The qamis or kamis, meaning 'shirt' in Arabic, is a masculine religious garment now worn in France by individuals belonging to different currents of Salafism and jihadism, but not exclusively (members of the Tablighi Jamaat, or other conservative Muslims, also wear it, in particular on Fridays). Considered in these circles as conforming to the Sunna, it

has largely replaced the djellaba of yore, less in fashion now. It consists of a broad tunic and short pants that stop at the ankles.

7 [Translator's note] Nagui Fam, a popular television and radio host in France.

8 The same civil servant who negotiated Bilel's entry into Turkey [see part one, 'Bilel'].

9 The General Directorate for Internal Security was established in 2014. It took over the functions of the Central Directorate of Internal Intelligence (DCRI), created in 2008, which was itself the result of the merger of the General Intelligence (RG) and the Directorate of Territorial Surveillance (DST).

10 One of the strengths of jihadist propaganda is its ability to describe itself in terms of Muslim eschatology, and the return of the Mahdi (the expected Messiah), the Antichrist and Jesus to Damascus before the End of Days. For the jihadists, there are numerous signs of this apocalypse visible today, especially in Western society, which has fallen prey to the end of ideologies and to liberalism. According to them, the End of Days will take place in Syria. In its media productions, the Islamic State (but also Jabhat al-Nusra) often correlates this prophecy with events occurring in recent history and in particular with each of its actions, in order to present itself as the only truly Muslim group.

Part Three   Zubeir

1 'S' files (for 'State security') are assigned by the French intelligence services to anyone they consider jihadists, hooligans or extreme right- or left-wing radicals. The system allows the authorities to track discreetly the movements of an individual, without setting up a proper tail. When the police check the ID of someone with an 'S file' in the street or at a border crossing, a special code tells the official what to do: check the identity of the persons accompanying him, notify a

specific police service, etc. Some 20,000 people have 'S files' in France, unbeknownst to the large majority of them.

2 For security reasons, his first name and some place names have been changed.

3 Not one of the thirty or so French citizens returning from Syria or Iraq who were interviewed for this book, nor the dozens of jihadists interviewed in the region since 2013, claim ever to have seen a Captagon pill circulating within the IS. On the other hand, most admit to having occasionally taken Tramadol – a painkiller distributed to wounded combatants, known as 'the poor man's cocaine' – for recreational purposes. Some French nationals have also been sent to prison by the IS for using the drug without being wounded. Captagon is an amphetamine easily found in the area, manufactured in Lebanon. In its propaganda, the IS regularly announces the destruction of large amounts of seized stocks, with supporting photographs.

4 *Four Lions* is a 2010 British comedy by Chris Morris that tells the story of the disastrous trip of five friends – two of whom have been through a training camp in Pakistan – who want to commit a terrorist attack in Britain.

5 The two pillars of Sunni Islam are the Koran and the Sunnah, from which it derives its name. Sunnah is a legislative, theological and political source of Sunnism. It could be translated as 'divine rule': it is the sum of thousands of *hadiths* which recount the life, words, deeds and exhortations of the Prophet Mohamed, transmitted orally by his companions after his death, and later published by medieval imams.

6 The Centre for the Prevention of Sectarian Abuses related to Islam (Le Centre de prévention des dérives sectaires liées à l'islam) is a controversial association backed by the company Bouzar Expertises, directed by the anthropologist Dounia Bouzar and her daughter, Lylia Bouzar. At the end of 2014, the French Interior Ministry entrusted this centre with the principal deradicalization programme for young

people – almost exclusively women – who are tempted by jihadism, or who are returning to France from Syria or Iraq. According to the French newspaper *Le Journal du dimanche*, the CPDSI received nearly 1 million euros in public subsidies, but its methods have been criticized as opaque and its results contested. Several members of the French parliament, including Senator Nathalie Goulet, have called for an independent evaluation of its results and operation. To date, no such evaluation has been conducted. In early 2016, its director announced that its public mandate would not be renewed but that it would pursue its activities in the private sector.

7 Salafism is typically understood as being divided into two branches: Quietism, which makes up the majority of the faithful; and jihadism, a minority in France. These two currents share a doctrinal framework and common ideologues, such as the thirteenth-century theologian Ibn Taymiyyah or the eighteenth-century preacher Muhammad ibn Abd al-Wahhab (who gave his name to the Saudi doctrine of Wahhabism). This fundamentalist dogma aspires to return to the purity of the first centuries of Islam, that of the *salaf salih*, or the 'pious predecessors'. Many refuse to follow the rite of one of the four Sunni jurisprudential schools, often regarded as a human religious innovation distorting original Islam. Quietists and jihadists live in an antagonistic relationship, each accusing the other of not being true Salafis, or of being *Khawarij* – that is, deviant unbelievers. One of their principal disagreements concerns armed jihad. Quietists have developed a theory supporting submission to temporal authority, even to the French Republic, whose values they nonetheless reject as a whole. In this sense, Quietists are non-violent, unlike jihadists, who go so far as to consider armed struggle as a religious obligation, in order to impose the law of God. However, many jihadist Salafists have gone through a period of Quietism before breaking with it.

8 The *shahada*, the first of the five pillars of Islam, is the Muslim profession of faith: 'There is no god but God and Mohamed is his messenger.'

9 The Tablighi Jamaat is a fundamentalist and missionary movement founded in 1920 in India, and introduced in France as early as the 1960s. This highly proselytizing current of Islam presents itself as being apolitical and peaceful. Its members take it as their mission to contact non-believers with the clear intention of 're-Islamicizing' society, particularly in lower-income neighbourhoods. Even if they don't openly call for jihad in France, the mosques held by the Tablighi movement, which follow a literalist reading of the sacred texts, are sometimes frequented by Salafist Quietists and jihadists.

10 On 21 September 2013, the Somali jihadist group Al-Shabaab carried out an attack on the Westgate shopping centre in Nairobi, killing 68 people and wounding more than 200. The Kenyan army took three days to secure the area.

11 In Muslim terminology, a *dalil* is a religious 'proof'. Without a priesthood, in order to settle the debates within the Muslim community, believers often ask those who disagree with them to 'show a *dalil*' in order to demonstrate the orthopraxy of this or that fact, act or practice in daily life. The jihadists, with their scrupulous literalism, are therefore careful to accompany each of their actions with a *dalil*, so as to legitimize their acts in terms of Islam. A *dalil* is a surah or a verse from the Koran, or a *hadith*, the word of a companion explained by a sheikh.

12 See the article by Scott Atran on the website of the American review *Aeon*, where he develops his thesis on the 'revolutionary dynamic of the IS'. Available in French on the website of *L'Obs* (behind a paywall).

13 The concept of a 'jihadosphere' was first used in the book *Les Français jihadistes* (*The French Jihadists*, Les Arènes, March 2014), written by the author of this book. It refers to a highly

codified and parallel world where everyone knows one another, and where jihadists capitalize on the digital isolation of social networks to proselytize to others. The jihadosphere allows them to circumvent the traditional media, which they consider dishonest. Networks of ideological affinities, separated geographically, initially constituted themselves online before structuring themselves physically, whether in the form of religious marital unions or departures for Syria or plans for attacks in France. The emergence of the jihadosphere began in France in 2012, when the first selfies of French nationals holding weapons in Syria were posted on their Facebook profiles. From then on, the terrorist organizations abroad and their supporters in France could exchange with each other freely, on a daily basis, even in prison. The promotion of terrorism took on a 'viral' dimension and brought jihadists out of the isolated internet forums of 1990–2000, allowing them to influence and radicalize a broader population that was younger, more naive and non-Arabic-speaking. From 2012 to 2014, the francophone jihadosphere was mainly active on mainstream platforms such as Facebook and YouTube. But as their accounts were shut down on Facebook and then on Twitter, and as the first criminal convictions for promoting jihadism were made, the form of the jihadosphere changed. It remains active across the social web today, but broadcasts its most aggressive content and exchanges on the Russian messaging service Telegram, to which intelligence services have very limited access.

14 Al Qaeda in the Arabian Peninsula is the Yemeni branch of Osama bin Laden's organization, founded in Saudi Arabia in 2009, when Yemeni and Saudi factions united. The AQAP claimed responsibility for the *Charlie Hebdo* terrorist attack of 7 January 2015. The organization is also present in Yemen under the name Ansar al-Sharia. Its favourite international targets are the Saudi monarchy, the United States and France.

15 The *houris* are the seventy-two virgins promised to martyrs when they reach the *firdaws*, the highest circle of paradise. Among the other benefits to martyrs are the ability to intercede on behalf of seventy people to help them enter paradise, by cleansing them of their sins, as well as the possibility of being transformed into a green bird to fly around the throne of Allah.

16 Untranslatable in French, the word comes from Moroccan Arabic (*darija*). It is used before talking about something that could be shocking. It means something like 'with all due respect' or 'without wishing to offend'.

17 *Minhaj salafi*: Salafist Quietism.

18 *Ghanima* means 'booty'. Jihadists have a rather liberal understanding of this notion. According to the interpretations of several sheikhs, almost all consider that the 'property of the disbelievers is licit' during wartime. In other words, it is permissible to steal such property, because the act is no longer considered theft if the purpose is to finance jihad. This is also true of robberies or consumer credit scams, even if there is still debate around the practice of taking out loans. Credit, based on speculating on time, is forbidden in Islam, because time belongs only to God. As a result, the Bahraini sheikh Abu Sufyan al-Sulami, one of the most influential religious leaders in the Islamic State, finally decided to discourage the use of this type of scam, even to finance their cause.

19 'Dawlat al Islam Baqiyah wa Tatamaddad' is the war cry and slogan of the supporters of the Islamic State. Meaning 'The IS remains and expands', it was popularized in the summer of 2013, when Al Qaeda's highest leader told Al-Baghdadi's fighters to leave Syria and return to Iraq. The IS's military retreats, starting in 2015, have undermined the significance of the slogan.

20 Literally, the word means 'the age of ignorance' in Arabic. In the Muslim tradition, it refers to the pre-Islamic and polytheistic period before the arrival of Islam in Arabia in

the seventh century. Jihadists often use this term to refer to their personal lives before Islam. Their *jahiliya* is, in most cases, relatively recent and far removed from any form of piety.

21 Telegram is a popular Russian messaging application used by jihadists to communicate directly with other individuals, including by means of secret and encrypted chats, and to participate in discussion groups. It was by infiltrating this messaging service that the French security forces were recently able to make several arrests from among the Telegram contacts of the French jihadist Rachid Kassim.

22 For Jabhat al-Nusra, see part one, n. 2.

23 Untranslateable in English, the word 'takbir' is a rallying cry for a group of Muslims, who are supposed to respond together: 'Allah Akbar!'

24 See also n. 27 below.

25 An outgrowth of its Iraqi-Syrian mother cell. Its first embryo appeared in the spring of 2014, after one of its most famous brigades in Syria, the Al-Batar brigade, led by Libyans (and through which several French and Belgian fighters passed, including Abdelhamid Abaaoud, the coordinator of the 13 November attacks), was ordered to disband, and instructions were given for its members to return to Libya. It moved to the city of Derna, in the east, the historic bastion of Libyan jihad. The unit pledged allegiance to the IS and became its official representative in the country in November 2014.

26 '*Shirk*' in Islam refers to any association of God with a deity. More broadly, it can be understood as any sign of polytheism. Anything that is worshipped other than God is a sign of *shirk*. Jihadists often repeat that 'democracy is a form of *shirk*'. Any system of government, considered as 'the religion of the West', is considered a form of idolatry based on a sovereignty of the people, and not divine, and, as such, polytheistic. The concept of the Catholic Trinity, for example, is considered a major *shirk*, in the same way as the Sufi current

is seen as particularly 'guilty' of *shirk* because of its practice of worshipping saints in its mausoleums. That's why the jihadists destroy them systematically in the territories under their control.

27 This French acronym, standing for 'personne radicalisée par l'islamisme' ('person radicalized by Islamism'), is used informally within the French penal system, but is not an official term. Prisoners incarcerated for common criminal offences and radicalized in prison are called 'DSCR', for 'détenus droit commun susceptibles de radicalisation' ('common law prisoners likely to be radicalized'). Those imprisoned for terrorist acts are also referred to as 'Islamic terrorists', or 'terrorist detainees', in everyday prison parlance.

28 Prison integration and probation counsellors (CPIP), who work for the Reintegration and Probation Prison Service (SPIP). This government department, attached to the French Ministry of Justice, is tasked with monitoring the persons entrusted to it by judicial authorities, and supporting their reintegration into society.

29 The killer at the Hyper Cacher store in Paris in January 2015, who had several prison stays, during which he became close to Djamel Beghal, a radical Islamist.

30 Originally, the *anashid* (*nashid* in the singular) were an ancient form of Muslim poetry. Now they are used by the Islamic State as *a capella* war songs.

31 In the Muslim tradition, *taghut* refers to idols: everything that is 'worshipped', other than God. For jihadists, the term refers to any state authority or enemy, 'idolatrous' by nature, because they arise from an authority other than that of God.

32 'The Supporters of Sharia' is a jihadist organization founded in Tunisia in 2011, four months after the fall of Ben Ali, by former Al Qaeda veterans from Afghanistan, who had just been released from prison and had been directly involved in the assassination of Commander Massoud on 9 September

2001. In 2013, the movement controlled more than 10 per cent of the mosques in Tunisia and was finally classified as a terrorist organization after the murderous attack on the American Embassy in Tunis in 2012 and two political assassinations in 2013.

33 This 30-year-old Syrian man is the emir of the former Jabhat al-Nusra, which was active in Syria from 2012 on. This rebel group, originally part of the Islamic State of Iraq (the current IS), broke with the latter in the spring of 2013 to become the official branch of Al Qaeda in Syria. On 28 July 2016, Abu Mohamed al-Jolani showed himself in public for the first time ever, in a video that announced he was breaking with the Al Qaeda leadership and creating 'Jabhat Fath al-Sham', which would henceforth no longer be affiliated with 'any outside entity'.

34 This book of more than 600 pages was written by the Indian Sheikh Safiur Rahman Mubarakpuri in the second half of the twentieth century. It is a favourite among jihadists and conservative Muslims in general.

35 Prayer according to the Koran.

36 The *dunya* (*Hayat al-dunya*) refers to the earthly and materialistic life of this world. Tempting by nature, the *dunya* appeals to human passions in order to divert man from his religious imperatives. Jihadists therefore call on others to become *ghuraba*, or strangers to this world, and to seek only the 'real life', that of the beyond, through death. Hence the expression, which is repeated as a mantra: 'We love death just as you love life.'

37 [Translator's note:] An elite French police unit that intervenes in critical or violent situations, including hostage recovery and prison riots.

Part Four The Women

1 For security reasons, her first name and some place names have been changed.

2 [Translator's note:] French acronym for the Direction générale de la Sécurité intérieure, the intelligence gathering agency in France, responsible for counter-espionage, counter-terrorism and the surveillance of potentially threatening groups and organizations.

3 'We were perhaps a little too scrupulous in the beginning, when we thought that the women were just leaving to be with their husbands.' Read the interview with the Paris public prosecutor François Molins, which appeared in *Le Monde* on 2 September 2016.

4 *Salil Sawarim*: 'Clashing of Swords' in English – from a series of videos broadcast by the propaganda teams of the Islamic State. The fourth instalment, released with teasers like an American blockbuster on the social networks, takes up the same cinematographic codes common to the genre. But it isn't fiction. It's a string of more than one hour of targeted murders in Iraq, of prisoners humiliated before being executed, and of ambushes with explosive devices. All scripted and shot with multiple camera angles, slow motion, sophisticated sound effects, with jihadist songs playing in the background. The goal is twofold: to terrorize and to recruit. As the central element of psychological warfare, the advertising of savagery aims to demoralize the enemy while creating the illusion that the IS is a military superpower. *Salil Sawarim 4* was broadcast a few days before the offensive against Mosul in June 2014. Many experts believe that this video helps to explain why the Iraqi army fled as soon as the jihadists entered the city. The staging of terror also has to make the group's followers believe that the group is invincible, despite its numerical inferiority, because it is supported by divine providence and has its role in Muslim prophecies.

5 *Tawhid*: the term refers to the uniqueness of Allah, and jihadists insist in particular on this fundamental foundation of the Muslim religion, at the heart of their profession of faith and affirming monotheism. Jihadists use this notion to

disqualify other Muslims, because violating *tawid* by associating another deity with God means leaving Islam. For jihadists, the mere acceptance of democracy means calling into question *tawid*, just like refusing to leave the company of, or fight against, non-Muslims. Such actions imply the refusal to apply the dogmas of the *kufr bi taghut* – the rejection of idolatry (all that is worshipped outside of God) – and the *al-wala wal al-bara* – loyalty (to Muslims) and disavowal (of non-Muslims).

6 For security reasons, her first name and some place names have been changed.

7 The jilbab is a full-length veil that wraps around the face while leaving it uncovered, unlike the niqab, which allows only the eyes to be seen, and the sitar that hides them completely. It is the most covering veil allowed by French law.

8 The attack against *Charlie Hebdo* (which killed twelve people and wounded eleven) was claimed on 14 January by Al Qaeda in the Arabian Peninsula. Amedy Coulibaly, the hostage-taker at the Hyper Cacher grocery store (who killed four people), claimed allegiance to the Islamic State.

9 In order to support their use of suicide bombers in theological terms, the jihadists refer to a *hadith* that tells the story of a companion of the Prophet who had thrown himself in the midst of the enemy line during a battle. An *inghimasi* intends to kill himself in the attack, but, unlike a *shahid* (martyrdom) operation, death is not certain. Such an attack entails rushing towards the enemy with a gun, rather than in a vehicle filled with explosives 'to kill and be killed'. The *inghimasi* may exceptionally come back alive from this attack.

10 This expression, which refers to a suicide attack, was popularized by jihadists in Syria and Iraq. According to the researcher Romain Caillet, it comes from the word meaning 'button' in dialectal Arabic, referring to the button used to blow oneself up in a *dogma*. The expression is now used by all jihadists, and has even given rise to a *nashid* (a jihadist

song) celebrating suicide attacks, and whose refrain is none other than 'dogma, dogma, dogma, wallah I can't wait for paradise'.

11 [Translator's note:] A 24-hour news channel in France.

12 A woman's legal representative or guardian, literally a man who is forbidden from marrying her: her father, grandfather, uncle or brother. In the absence of a *mahram* from the family, an emir may act as a *mahram* in his place. A *mahram* must be present for a woman to marry. According to a literal interpretation of Islam, a woman is not allowed to travel without her *mahram*.

13 Whenever a Muslim mentions the name of the Prophet, he is supposed to add the formula '*salla Allah alaihi wa salam*', which means 'peace be upon him', hence the acronym SAWS or PBUH in English.

14 This jihadist cell, dismantled by the police in 2005 in a mosque on the Rue de Tangier in the nineteenth *arrondissement* of Paris, was founded by a 19-year-old man linked to the Algerian GSPC (ancestor of AQIM), Farid Benyettou. This group, known as the Buttes-Chaumont, sent fighters to Al Qaeda in Yemen and Iraq as early as 2003. Its members included the Kouachi brothers, perpetrators of the *Charlie Hebdo* attacks, as well as Boubaker el-Hakim.

15 In theory, widows are supposed to receive their husband's wages.

16 This Kurdish community was conquered by the IS during the capture of Sinjar, Iraq, in August 2014. The jihadists, considering this population to be devil worshippers (*ibliss*) because of their beliefs that go back more than four millennia, decided to kill most of the male prisoners and reduce the women and children to slavery. The institution of slavery was formalized by the IS in its magazine *Dabiq* in October 2014 in these terms: 'After the Yezidi women and children were captured, they were divided between the IS fighters who helped take Sinjar in accordance with sharia law. This

large-scale enslavement of polytheist families is a first since the abandonment of sharia law' – understood as having occurred in medieval times. According to its interpretation of verse 50 of surah 33 of the Koran, the IS authorizes forced sexual relations with these women, qualified as 'captives', or *sabyya* in Arabic. They are sold on the market at prices ranging between $1,000 and $15,000, depending on their age, attractiveness and the number of their children.

17 Literally 'encounter' in Arabic. In a marital setting, it refers to a pre-marriage meeting, according to the Islamic conventions practised in conservative Muslim circles.

Part Five   Kevin and Quentin

1 See part three, n. 9.

2 [Translator's note:] Mohammed Merah, a 23-year-old petty criminal of Algerian descent, carried out a series of shootings around the cities of Toulouse and Montauban, targeting first French soldiers and then a Jewish teacher and school children. He killed a total of seven people and wounded five, four seriously. He was killed by police after a thirty-hour siege at his family's apartment.

3 *Aqida*: 'dogma' in Arabic. Jihadists often call each other 'brothers or sisters of the *aqida*', meaning of the correct faith.

4 See part one, n. 12, and part 6, n. 2, for additional information.

5 Nullifiers of Islam: these are the 'nullifying acts of Islam' that are considered instant apostasy. According to Ibn Abdelwahab, one of the main historical sources for Salafism, there are ten main nullifiers: associating any other being with God (the *shirk*), putting an intermediary between oneself and God during prayer (worship of saints), not excommunicating idolaters, believing in another religion, hating one of the Prophet's practices, mocking religion, practising witchcraft, allying with unbelievers against Muslims, exempting

someone from following the rules of Islam, or abandoning Islam.

6 See part two, n. 10.

Part Six Those Who Didn't Return

1 The *Khutbah* is the sermon the imam gives to the faithful during Friday prayers.

2 *Takfiri*: the term is used as an insult. The Egyptian security forces are credited with having invented it in the 1980s to designate jihadists. *Takfiri* is derived from the word *takfir*, i.e. to turn into an 'unbeliever' – that is, to excommunicate other Muslims whose religious practice they consider deviant. Within the context of Syrian jihad, this is an accusation with serious consequences, as it is equivalent to calling for the death of the person who is to be *takfir*. Despite their tendency to excommunicate all Muslims who resist them, the jihadists reject this term, especially since *takfir* accusations are regularly made within their own group. In the IS, dozens or even hundreds of people have been executed for this reason. In such cases, the jihadists speak of *ghulat takfir* [see part one, n. 12], literally 'exaggerators' or 'extremists' – a euphemism for those who 'exaggerate in *takfir*'. In Nigeria, the leader of Boko Haram, Aboubakar Shekau, was distanced from the leadership of the African branch of the IS when accused of being a *ghulat*.

3 *Khawarij*: plural of *Kharijite*. Historically, the *Khawarij* – 'the dogs of hell' according to a *hadith* – are considered by the Sunnis to be one of the first heresies of Islam, occurring in the first century [see part three, n. 7]. The term is now controversially used to designate extremists who have strayed from Islam. According to many Muslim anti-jihadists, the Salafists in particular, all of the *khawarij*'s characteristics currently apply to the Islamic State.

4 In the summer of 2016, the cities of Fallujah in Iraq and Manbij in Syria were recaptured from the IS by local forces,

supported by the international coalition's air-raids. In these two cities, the IS suffered very heavy losses. During the siege of Manbij, coalition bombs killed a record number of civilians, a fact repeatedly cited in IS propaganda.

5   See part three, n. 36.

6   See part three, n. 20.

7   *Al-wala wal al-bara* – 'loyalty and disavowal' in English – is one of the essential tenets of Salafism and jihadism [see also part four, n. 5]. According to the researcher Romain Caillet, it can even be considered unique to Salafism. Theorized for the first time by a grandson of Mohamed Ibn Abdelwahab in the nineteenth century, it directs believers respectful of monotheism to unite with Muslims and to 'disavow' non-Muslims. Applied with more or less rigour, expression of the *al-wala wal al-bara* can range from a rejection in daily life of non-Muslims to the use of force to combat them. The *al-wala wal al-bara*, therefore, prohibits any collaboration with democracy, which by its nature is a source of non-belief, depending as it does on popular rather than divine sovereignty.

8   *Taghut, tawaghit.* The word literally means 'idol'. By extension, the jihadists take it to mean 'tyrant disbeliever' – that is, someone who does not apply sharia, or who applies other legislation. The term refers to any form of 'associate' authority, in the sense of associating another divinity with God, and becoming by that fact an idol. The jihadists' injunction, therefore, is not only to reject, but also to combat, the *taghut* wherever it is to be found. Democracy by its very nature is *taghut*, relying as it does on popular, non-divine sovereignty. The *kufr bi Taghut* – rejection of unbelief – is one of the pillars of the Salafist dogma [see also part three, n. 31].

9   See part five, n. 5.

10 Kaaris is a successful French rapper from Sevran. While he describes himself as a practising Muslim, he made a name for himself with quasi-pornographic lyrics celebrating delinquency, drinking parties and sex.

11 Sahih al-Bukhari and Sahih Muslim are two medieval imams
    whose collections of *hadiths* are unanimously accepted by
    almost all Muslims, and are considered the most authentic.
    They both contain several thousand *hadiths*. The *hadiths*
    are classified according to their authenticity, according to
    a chain of evaluation of their transmission since the time of
    the Prophet.